THE

The Illegals

The Double Lives of the Cold War's Most Secret Agents

Nigel West

CORONET BOOKS
Hodder and Stoughton

First published in Great Britain in 1993 by
Hodder and Stoughton
a division of Hodder Headline PLC

A John Curtis Book

Coronet edition 1994

10 9 8 7 6 5 4 3 2 1

British Library Cataloguing in Publication Data

West, Nigel
Illegals: Double Lives of the Cold War's
Most Secret Agents
I. Title
327.12092

ISBN 0-340-61764-0

Printed and bound in Great Britain by
Cox and Wyman Ltd, Reading, Berks.

Photoset by Rowland Phototypesetting Ltd, Bury St Edmunds, Suffolk.

Hodder and Stoughton Ltd
A Division of Hodder Headline PLC
338 Euston Road, London NW1 3BH

Contents

	Acknowledgments	vii
	Illustrations	ix
	Charts	xi
	Abbreviations	xiii
	Foreword by Vladimir Kuzichkin	xv
	Introduction	1
1	*Conspiratsia:* The Pre-War Networks	13
2	*Der Rote Kapelle*	41
3	Sorge's Contacts	69
4	The Swiss Networks	91
5	Atomic Secrets	111
6	Squad 34 v. the Line N Illegal Support Officers	141
7	The Illegals from Germany	177
8	LAST ACT and SHAH	201
9	Double Agents and Dangles	229
10	The End of the Cold War	253
	Postscript	279
	Source Notes	285
	Select Bibliography	297
	Index	301

Acknowledgments

The author gratefully acknowledges the help of:

John Costello; Oleg Gordievsky; Larry McWilliams; Hayden Peake; Lise-Lotte Sokolova; Paul Tompkins; Oleg Tsarev; John Vassall; Cleveland Cram; Vladimir Kuzichkin; Tom Bower; Barrie Penrose; Fiona Ratiu; Bill Branigan; Bill Hood; Jurgen Kuczynski; Ursula Kuczynski; Len Beurton; Joe Evans; Dr Alfred Laurence; Evelyn Fisher; Scotland Yard's Black Museum; and numerous other former British, American and Soviet intelligence personnel.

Illustrations

Ernest Weiss, the organiser of a GRU network in Britain, who survived undetected throughout the war.

Zalamon Litvin, the key illegal who operated in California between 1938 and 1945 (© *Tom Bower*).

The New Zealand passports issued in the names of Peter and Helen Kroger by Paddy Costello in Paris to Morris and Lona Cohen (*courtesy of the Black Museum, New Scotland Yard*).

Gordon Lonsdale's Canadian passport (*courtesy of the Black Museum, New Scotland Yard*).

Konon Molody, alias Gordon Lonsdale, entertaining friends from his London University course.

An enlargement of a microdot message addressed to Konon Molody's wife and found among the espionage paraphernalia recovered from the Krogers' home.

The death notice published in the *Los Angeles Times* of Emil Goldfus, the identity adopted by William Fisher, the illegal *rezident* who called himself Rudolph Abel.

A portrait of Colonel Abel by Sheldon Fink.

The shortwave radio transmitter and high-speed magnetic tape-recorder which was seized from the Krogers and was recognised as standard issue to KGB illegals (*UPI*).

Konon Molody and Rudolph Abel reunited at KGB headquarters (© *Tom Bower*).

Yuri Loginov, pictured in his flat in Johannesburg shortly before his arrest, and his Canadian birth certificate in the name of Edmundas Trinka.

The front cover of Alexander Orlov's KGB file, as photographed in the KGB's archives, Moscow.

Alexandre Sokolov at his trial in 1963.

Dmitri F. Polyakov, the senior GRU officer who was executed in March 1988 after his exposure as an American source for the past twenty-five years (© *David Wise*).

Vassilli Dozhdalev, the Line N specialist who supervised Konon Molody from the London Embassy *rezidentura*, worked as George Blake's case officer and later was appointed head of Directorate S's training branch, where he still works (© *Tom Bower*).

A rare picture of Vadim A. Kirpichenko, formerly the long-serving head of Directorate S, taken in Moscow in 1992 (*Russell Warren Howe*).

Erwin van Haarlem in a snap taken in the Kremlin when he travelled to Moscow in support of refuseniks (*Dr Laurence Carmi*).

Charts

1	Trepper's group at the time of the arrest of Makarov and Danilov (December 1941)	49
2	Schulze-Boysen's network	53
3	Von Scheliha's network	55
4	Harnack's network	58
5	Effremov's network	64
6	Robinson's network	65
7	Rado's network	96–7
8	The Canadian network	118
9	The KGB Reorganisation in 1973	260–1

Abbreviations

AFSA	US Armed Forces Security Agency
ARCOS	All-Russian Co-operative Society
ASIO	Australian Security Intelligence Organisation
BfV	Federal German Security Service
BND	Federal German Intelligence Service
CAZAB	Canadian, New Zealand, Australian, British and American Counter-intelligence Exchange
CIA	Central Intelligence Agency
CIDA	Canadian International Development Agency
CPGB	Communist Party of Great Britain
CPUSA	Communist Party of the United States of America
DCI	Director of Central Intelligence
DGSE	Direction Générale de Sécurité Extérieure
DIA	Defence Intelligence Agency
DST	Direction de la Surveillance du Territoire
FBI	Federal Bureau of Investigation
FCD	First Chief Directorate of the KGB
G-2	US Military Intelligence
GCHQ	Government Communications Headquarters
GPU	Soviet Intelligence Service
GRU	Soviet Military Intelligence Service
HVA	East German Intelligence Service

KDP	German Communist Party
KGB	Soviet Intelligence Service
KOS	Yugoslav Security Service
MI5	British Security Service
MSS	Chinese Ministry of State Security
NATO	North Atlantic Treaty Organisation
NKVD	Soviet Intelligence Service
NSA	National Security Agency
NTS	Union of Ukrainian Nationalists
OGPU	Soviet Political Intelligence Service
OKW	Wehrmacht High Command
OSS	Office of Strategic Services
PNG	*Persona Non Grata*
RCMP	Royal Canadian Mounted Police
RFIS	Russian Foreign Intelligence Service
RHSA	Reich Security Agency
SD	Sicherheitsdienst
SIDE	Argentine Security Service
SIS	Secret Intelligence Service
SVR	Russian Foreign Intelligence Service
UB	Polish Intelligence Service

Foreword

by Major Vladimir Kuzichkin

Directorate S, First Chief Directorate of the KGB

For many years Soviet 'illegals' have been surrounded by an aura of mystery, omnipotence and even admiration. Until recently the media in the West has exaggerated the achievements of the illegals run by the KGB and GRU. Allegedly they had succeeded in penetrating many top-secret targets and had run hundreds of agents. However, if we examine specific cases we find that the illegals achieved rather less than has often been claimed for them. So how did the mythology develop?

After 1917 the Soviets depended heavily upon illegals, and there were practical reasons for this. Most of the leading countries of the world had refused to recognise the Bolshevik regime and, therefore, diplomatic links were very limited. Thus, to prepare for the proletarian revolution they envisaged, the Bolsheviks were wholly reliant upon illegals. The Bolsheviks, of course, were well versed in illegal operations because their party had been outlawed in Tsarist Russia since its creation in the nineteenth century. The Bolsheviks were virtually illegals in their own country and routinely worked under false identities. The traditions of *conspiratsia* were so strong that even after they had seized power in the coup of October 1917, their leaders retained their underground pseudonyms. Thus, Ulyanov remained as Lenin, Dzhugashvili as Stalin, Bronstein as Trotsky, etc.

Obsessed with the idea of a forthcoming world revolution,

the Bolsheviks relied on illegal methods while pursuing their aims in the West. In this endeavour they were assisted by local Communist Parties and members of the Comintern who considered Moscow their political and ideological home. Many of the illegals of that era were members of foreign Communist Parties and were selected by the Soviets for intelligence work because it was easier for them to operate in their own familiar environment.

This was the golden age of Soviet illegal intelligence. The West's security services were weak and had consistently underestimated the threat of Communism, thereby allowing illegals access to the most secret information. The best example of this is perhaps Richard Sorge, the former German Communist who became a Soviet illegal. He worked under cover as a Nazi journalist in China and then Japan, where he managed to be appointed press attaché at the German Embassy in Tokyo. He obtained advance warning of the German plans to attack the Soviet Union in June 1941, but when he was arrested by the Japanese he confessed to being an illegal, an admission that made him a traitor in the eyes of Moscow. Long after his execution he received wide publicity in the West, and this interest prompted the Soviet authorities to declare him a hero as part of a policy to promote Soviet intelligence successes. Sorge's portrait even appeared on a Soviet postage stamp.

In fact, Stalin had ignored the warning from Sorge, as well as others he had received from illegal networks which had risked everything to alert Moscow. Consumed by paranoia about imagined treachery, Stalin brought the golden age of illegals to an abrupt and bloody conclusion. From 1937 he exterminated those he perceived as his opponents and rivals. Millions perished in the gulags and among the victims were hundreds of loyal illegals, who, on the basis of the very slightest suspicion, were recalled to Moscow and liquidated.

During the Cold War, conditions for illegals improved dramatically. Under the influence of a pervasive xenophobia, and with only rare exceptions, the KGB avoided the use of foreign nationals as illegals. They were chosen only from Soviet citizens, and this limitation proved to be lengthy, expensive and ineffective. It was difficult for illegals, accustomed to life behind the Iron Curtain, to integrate smoothly into Western lifestyles. Their cover stories were often so weak that they were unable themselves to penetrate any targets which were protected by even basic security. The effectiveness of the illegals declined, as did the value of their information. Failure became routine, although the Western media interpreted events differently and presented Moscow Centre as the architect of many successes. Yet from Moscow, the perspective was quite the opposite.

The best example of this was the case of Rudolph Abel, who was caught in the United States. He refused to cooperate and was sentenced to a long prison sentence. Though the evidence from Abel's arrest showed otherwise, the Americans persuaded themselves that Abel's silence was a manifestation of his professionalism, and maybe proof of the existence of an undiscovered network of illegals. When this idea was picked up by the media, Abel became a celebrity. However, the truth was that Abel had nothing to tell the Americans for there was no network. According to Abel's KGB case officer, to whom I spoke, he had simply been 'living in New York, doing nothing of importance and painting his pictures'. From the KGB's viewpoint, Abel had been a failure. He would have been regarded as a disgrace if the KGB had not decided to use his case for its own purpose, the promotion of its omnipotence. Western publicity saved Abel from obscurity and ensured that his picture was placed in the KGB's famous Memory Room.

By the mid-1970s most of the KGB's information originated from the legal *rezidenturas* working from inside Soviet diplomatic missions. A debate initiated within the KGB dismissed the illegals as ineffective and contemplated abolishing them completely. Finally, it was decided that the illegals had a future, if only for emergency support. During this period the illegals deployed abroad concentrated on the development of their own covers and only occasionally sent reports to the Centre, which had invariably been gleaned from open sources. Drunkenness was not uncommon and defections became more frequent. This situation was compounded by an order from the Party leadership, during detente, to the KGB to avoid international scandal. For the KGB, detente became a period of stagnation, but neither the KGB nor the illegals complained. Who wanted to risk their life for a corrupt and universally despised regime?

The war in Afghanistan changed the position dramatically. Illegals from across the globe were withdrawn and redeployed to Afghanistan to conduct clandestine operations against the local mujaheddin.

Gorbachev's *perestroika* rocked the Soviet Union out of stagnation. The irreversible process of collapse started and total destruction occurred in August 1991. The Party *nomenklatura* remained faithful to their corrupt traditions and in the last moments of their power used their obedient servants, the illegals, to transfer billions in stolen hard currency to secret bank accounts in the West. The operation was conducted so professionally that the new democratic Russian authorities have been unable to trace the money.

An extraordinary mythology, enhanced by the KGB's deliberate disinformation, has been constructed around the illegals and what they are supposed to have accomplished. For the first time, this book reveals the Soviet illegals in their true colours.

Introduction

An illegal's role is demanding, dangerous, and sometimes lethal.
William R. Corson and Robert T. Crowley in *The New KGB*[1]

The importance of intelligence should not be underestimated. It is what politicians base their decisions upon, and what historians later rely on to chart their mistakes. Knowledge is power, and timely intelligence can prevent bloodshed. If the United States had possessed a Central Intelligence Agency (CIA) in December 1941, running well-informed sources in Tokyo, Imperial Japanese aggression might have been deterred. Similarly, if General Galtieri's intentions could have been read with any accuracy, the campaign in the South Atlantic in 1982 might have been avoided. If any of the coalition allies had recruited a worthwhile agent in Baghdad, perhaps one close to Saddam Hussein, the dictator might have been dissuaded from moving against Kuwait. Certainly there is good evidence to show that reliable intelligence can be exploited to save lives. The Iraqis opted against occupying the Gulf states in 1966 when British troops were despatched to the region in a swift response to a timely tip. The Argentines also abandoned a plan to land troops on the Falklands in 1977 after news was deliberately leaked in Buenos Aires that a pair of nuclear-powered hunter-killer submarines had been deployed in the area. Certainly the history of the Second World War would have been quite different if Britain had not possessed the invaluable signals intelligence source code-named ULTRA; and if the US navy had not had access prior to the battle of Midway to the cryptographic material circulated as MAGIC. Could the strategic deception campaign which misled the enemy about the timing and location of the D-Day landings in June 1944 have been accomplished without the participation of MI5's famed double agents? In each case, a highly secret intelligence operation effectively changed the course of history.

Apart from signals intelligence and the so-called technical sources that range from the interception of communications and other electronic emissions, and the monitoring of listening devices, either remotely through satellites or sophisticated equipment planted near sensitive military installations, there is the all-important human source. No overhead surveillance system can read a despot's mind, and the apparatus that can resist shrewd manipulation by a resourceful opponent has yet to be invented. One man's ingeniously placed telephone tap, perhaps inserted into a target embassy or hidden in a tunnel dug beneath East Berlin, is another's conduit of misinformation for deception purposes. Only by careful analysis over a lengthy period, with the benefit of comparison with other components in the complex mosaic of intelligence, can the authenticity of a single source be ascertained. One of the lesser known conclusions of the Franks Committee Report[2] into the origins of the Falklands War, contained in the unpublished classified appendix, was trenchant criticism of the Joint Intelligence Committee's ill-judged preference for a categoric assurance from the Government Communications Headquarters (GCHQ) that, by maintaining a watch on the signals traffic of a particular Argentine commando unit, then stationed atop the Andes overlooking the Chilean frontier, a clear ten days' notice could be given of any planned assault on Port Stanley. The justification for this apparently impressive capability, which was misinterpreted as an unqualified guarantee, lay in the fact that this particular battalion, which consisted of regular troops who had been trained at the US Special Forces School at Fort Bragg, just outside Fayetteville, North Carolina, was universally acknowledged as the only branch of the Argentine forces suitable for deployment in an amphibious role. In the event, however, it never moved from its base, and the unexpected invasion of the Falklands was executed by ill-prepared conscripts and opposed by a mere handful of surprised British Royal Marines, who, vastly outnumbered, promptly surrendered. Nearly a decade earlier the Israelis had made much the same mistake and had placed inordinate faith in their technical expertise, thus allowing the country to be taken entirely unawares at the outbreak of the Yom Kippur War.

Throughout history strategic and tactical surprise has given the vital edge in battle to the side taking the initiative.[3] North Korea's attack on the south, the Tet Offensive in Vietnam, the installation of ballistic missiles in Cuba, even the construction of the Berlin Wall, are all examples of unanticipated actions that were each to have profound consequences. However, there are also occasions when the individual agent can make, or could have made, the difference. If more weight had been given to the Abwehr questionnaire relating to Pearl Harbor, entrusted to the wartime double agent Dusko Popov,[4] the appropriate precautions might have been taken to prevent the Japanese raid. If Stalin had accepted warnings from Richard Sorge that Hitler intended to betray the Molotov–Ribbentrop Pact and to launch a blitzkrieg against the Soviet Union, the Red Army might have been able to take the necessary counter-measures. This last lesson was learned by the Soviets at a heavy cost to the motherland, the *Rodina*, and it has also left the Soviet intelligence structure with an exaggerated and characteristic bias towards what is known as *razvedka*, the secret intelligence from agents.

Universally, the collection of intelligence is divided into two quite distinct sources: those that are deemed to be 'open', and consist of the legitimately accessible published data that can be studied, be it in the form of articles appearing in small-circulation academic journals or newspaper reports of parliamentary proceedings, and the more sensitive, secret sources. Within the latter category are the closely guarded technical skills manifested by such organisations as GCHQ and its American counterpart, the National Security Agency (NSA), and the *sub rosa* information that comes from indi vidual agents.

Even, or particularly, in the age of reliance on high technol ogy, the human source has an essential place. To find the young Shah, who, to the CIA's dismay, disappeared to Italy in the midst of the Agency's 1953 coup in Iran, the Secret Intelligence Service (SIS) relied upon his Swiss tutor, a close confidant from the King's childhood and a long-time SIS asset; to betray the entire military structure of the Communist guer rillas in Malaya, the local Special Branch leant on its star mole, Lai Teck, who happened to be the Party's duplicitous General-Secretary;[5] to identify the Viet Cong cadres in the delta hamlets, in what was probably the most successful American intelligence operation of the war, the CIA deployed the highly effective, euphemistically named 'Provincial Reconnaissance Units', which were manned exclusively by disillusioned defectors led by Agency paramilitaries.[6] Indeed, it could easily be argued that, *without exception*, behind every post-war counter-intelligence success was not some well- oiled counter-espionage machine, relentlessly following up obscure clues, but rather a single human source, who, for his own very mixed motives, was willing to reveal his country's most prized secrets. Such conclusions, of course, can only now be reached with confidence, as the secret archives of the Cold War finally are opened and made available to patient researchers, but there has always been a suspicion that no technical source could equal the best human source. At the very least, this was the view which had long prevailed in Moscow.

For every disaffected intelligence officer who switches sides, there is the necessary meal-ticket of betrayals, which, at one time, would have ensured his decoration with the Order of the Red Banner or an honorary Commander of the British Empire. In the United States the equivalent award is a secure future under a new identity in Florida. Now that the KGB's much-feared long arm of retribution has been eliminated, and the contents of previously classified personal dossiers are released for public consumption, such conclusions can be made and be justified with documentary evidence.

These all-important human sources are managed in target or third countries by a 'legal' apparatus, usually based on diplomatic premises and thereby protected by international convention. The local collection effort is directed by a *rezident*, who operates under Foreign Ministry cover and whose exact counterpart is the SIS station commander and the CIA chief of station, who will also routinely acquire diplomatic status to conceal their true roles. In terms of tradecraft there is minimal difference between these three professionals, who, of course, will always be known to the host country's security authorities. However, the same cannot be said for the illegals, whose membership may range from a suitably briefed journalist sent on a specific, short-term mission by SIS or the CIA, to the altogether more expensive variety, the long-term, deep-cover Soviet spy who adopts his or her chosen role as a lifestyle. These are regarded with envious respect by their Western opponents as the very acme of intelligence collection, and by their nature they emerge only rarely into the light of public scrutiny. Nor have Soviet illegals been despatched, as might have been expected, simply to those countries such as South Africa where the lack of diplomatic links with Moscow has precluded the installation of a legal *rezidentura*. Indeed, the two main Soviet intelligence organisations, the GRU and the KGB, prefer to duplicate their collection efforts by developing an illegal structure in isolation from the legal *rezident* whose activities may well be circumscribed by hostile surveillance. Thus the Kremlin's perceived preference for *razvedka* may manifest itself by the installation of an illegal *rezident*, perhaps the ostensibly innocent proprietor of a television repair shop, whose identity will be unknown to the legal *rezident* at the local embassy and who will head an entirely separate *rezidentura*. As a security precaution, such parallel systems offer protection against penetration, so that the elimination of one spy ring will not necessarily lead to the discovery of another. Equally, there is an opportunity to set one network to double-check the credentials of the other.

By definition the illegal, although no doubt carefully concealed behind an almost impenetrable cover, is especially vulnerable to arrest. He has no diplomatic immunity and, at the very least, faces the certainty of a lengthy prison sentence if he is apprehended. The concept of an illegal, someone sent to live an entirely false life in a foreign country with bogus documentation, is almost completely alien to Western intelligence agencies, especially in peacetime. Certainly they employ intelligence personnel under diplomatic cover, and both the British and the Americans have a long history of persuading commercial organisations to provide their officers with what is termed in Washington DC as 'non-official cover'. At the CIA's headquarters in Langley, Virginia, an entire branch is dedicated to cultivating useful contacts in the private sector that can provide the Clandestine Service (now termed the Directorate of Operations) with plausible pretexts for its officers to penetrate target countries. When the need arises, the CIA will run its own companies for the same purpose and these are known within the US intelligence fraternity as 'proprietaries'. For many years the CIA station in Manhattan has been concealed behind what appears to be a legitimate trading enterprise. The CIA has also found it useful to run retail outlets and the preparations for the Bay of Pigs invasion of Cuba were made behind Zenith Technical Enterprises Inc., a business selling electrical goods which employed a staff of 300 on the south campus of the University of Miami.[7] The CIA's proprietaries even included air-charter companies. Indeed, in its heyday Air America, one of the CIA's most successful commercial undertakings, was ranked by turnover, fleet size and personnel as the third largest air-charter company in the world. In reality, Air America was a wholly owned subsidiary of the CIA, employing CIA personnel and fulfilling the CIA's covert transport requirements across the globe.[8] Following disclosure of some of its abuses, the CIA is now prohibited by law from employing journalists as agents, or running news agencies as fronts. Nor is this some dim memory of the distant past. During the Tower Commission hearings into the Iran-Contra scandal in late 1986, evidence was given that several Caribbean airlines and companies registered in the Cayman Islands, including the Santa Lucia Corporation, were really CIA fronts. Similarly, in England, the revelation that intelligence personnel in Northern Ireland had sometimes been issued with press accreditation led to a public undertaking from the Government, in the form of a ministerial statement, that the practice would cease because of the potential danger to legitimate newsmen.

The borderline between journalism and intelligence-gathering is a fine one. When Yu Zenshan, the former head of the Foreign Bureau of China's Ministry of State Security (MSS), defected to the CIA in 1985, he confirmed, as had long been suspected, that the New China News Agency was virtually an internal department of the MSS. Similarly, French foreign correspondents routinely report to the Direction Générale de Sécurité Extérieure (DGSE), while the TASS news agency has with justification always been regarded as a branch of the Soviet military intelligence service, the GRU (and, to a lesser extent, the KGB). Several senior members of the British media establishment enjoy strong intelligence connections and at one time a news agency based in Cyprus provided a convenient and plausible cover for an SIS network that operated across the Middle East. Anthony Cavendish, a former SIS officer who subsequently took up a career as a foreign correspondent with United Press International, recalled in his controversial memoirs, *Inside Intelligence*, that in the post-war era several Fleet Street newspapers, including the Kemsley conglomerate which owned the *Daily* and *Sunday Telegraph*, willingly gave cover to full-time SIS personnel.[9] However, neither the American CIA nor its French or British counterparts have made anything like the same commitment to the development of the illegal as that invested by the Soviets.

Perhaps it is because of the wealth of opportunities offered by the business community to Western agencies that only one routinely resorts to the use of deep-cover illegals. Only the Israelis boast a history of despatching long-term agents to target Arab countries where they have no diplomatic representation, the best-known examples being Wolfgang Lotz,[10] who posed as a former Nazi to work in Cairo and study the then embryonic Egyptian missile programme, and Eli Cohen, [11] who succeeded in penetrating the highest echelons of the Syrian Government before his arrest at his apartment in Damascus in 1964. Of course, it is only those cases that end in exposure which are likely to receive publicity, Mossad being understandably anxious to avoid drawing attention to its reliance on illegals for fear of inadvertently compromising those assets still active in the field. As well as exploiting its journalists, the Soviets also took advantage of their state-controlled international trading organisations, and the United Nations, to plant intelligence professionals in the West. Often these personnel fulfilled the role of 'illegal support officers', whose sole task was to distance themselves from the 'legal' *rezidentura* and, thereby, avoid falling under the hostile scrutiny of the host security apparatus, and to maintain secure contact with spies operating under even deeper cover.

The ideological commitment made by any agent willing to sacrifice what might be termed a normal existence for a life of continuous duplicity, fraught with danger, cannot be underestimated. Alexander Orlov, one of the few Soviet illegals to write about his craft, has listed the qualifications essential for success:

(1) He had to have previous experience in intelligence and counter-intelligence.
(2) He had to acquire a working knowledge of the language of the country of his proposed assignment and to master the language of the country of which he would represent himself to be a citizen.
(3) Inasmuch as the officer was obliged to conceal his real past, he had to contrive and prepare a new and sound life story which would withstand at least superficial investigation.
(4) He had to acquire a legitimate occupation or business which would justify in the eyes of the authorities his protracted sojourn in their country. [12]

Certainly some agents cannot take the strain and, like the Finnish-born Reino Hayhanen, succumb to alcohol. Others lose their determination and either drop from sight, failing to respond to signals from their controllers, or take on the hazardous role of double agent by volunteering their services to the opposition. Those agents who declare a desire to remain in the West to their controllers are invariably summoned home to face an uncertain future in a limbo where they are trusted only to participate occasionally in training programmes. According to a few who have completed their missions, and returned home in triumph, life was never quite the same again, for in the eyes of their suspicious colleagues, their experience in the West had left them contaminated, particularly if they had been detected. For Rudolph Abel and Konon Molody, who both acquired notoriety as illegals, their post-assignment existence in Moscow was one of frustration, resentment and suspicion.

There can be little doubt that before and during the Cold War the Soviets proved the past masters of the illegal technique, going to extraordinary lengths to acquire suitable documentation for their agents and devoting considerable resources to the support of their illegal networks. As we shall see in the pages that follow, the Soviets also exercised great judgment and discrimination when selecting their illegals. This is recognised by Charles Elwell, now a retired senior counter-intelligence officer, who interrogated Molody and spent much of his career studying the phenomena from within the counter-espionage branch of the British Security Service:

In selecting people for the dangerous and difficult job of an illegal intelligence officer, the Russian Intelligence Service would have to look for a rare combination of qualities. An illegal intelligence officer would require courage in the face of the continual risk of exposure and severe punishment, endurance to withstand long periods of loneliness and isolation from family, friends and colleagues, the capacity not only to live a cover story convincingly but to live one which would be useful in Western Europe or the USA, an ability to dominate and command the respect and confidence of his agents, a knowledge of the matters on which he is directed to obtain intelligence, and enough technical competence to enable him to operate the complicated communications system upon which the success of his mission, and perhaps his life, would depend. But quite apart from, and above all, these qualities, the Russian Intelligence Service must be absolutely confident in the loyalty of an illegal officer, whose opportunities for defection and betrayal are much greater than those of his comrades who work under supervision and within the framework of a Soviet official organisation, either at home or abroad.[13]

Elwell's opinion is shared by other counter-intelligence professionals. Robert Crowley, a veteran CIA officer with an encyclopaedic knowledge of Soviet operations and the author of an unclassified study of the KGB, has characterised the illegals:

The illegals lived in constant fear because their status denied them the comfort of fraternal contact with like-minded souls. For the most part, they operated in hostile environments with no protection except their wits. The possibility of betrayal, compromise, or accidental arrest was and is a constant, palpable threat. Their lives were completely structured, with direction coming from a single authority. The operational objectives of many of their activities were never fully disclosed to them, making their concept of the unknown infinite in its bounds.[14]

In past years Western intelligence personnel understandably have been reticent to comment publicly on the subject of illegals, partly to avoid divulging any information that might be of help to the opposition, but mainly because they were reluctant to admit the vulnerability of the democracies to hostile penetration by agents separated from the more conventional (and more easily detected) networks run from diplomatic premises. Accordingly, whenever some fanciful assertion was made about illegal methodology, the relevant security agencies maintained a discreet silence. This allowed a number of myths to develop and go uncorrected, the most extravagant being the invention by the Czech writer Joseph Heissler, who called himself J. Bernard Hutton, of a special academy for illegals located at Bykovo, outside Moscow. In 1961, Hutton alleged in *School for Spies* that an entire American community had been constructed deep in the pine forests to acclimatise candidates for illegal operations and prepare them for Western lifestyles. The proposition gained much acceptance, even among professional analysts, who swallowed the claim that the site even included a roller-skating rink which had been built in 1940 after an unlucky and ill-equipped spy had been injured at such a venue in the United

States. The story was a hoax, but nevertheless received wide circulation.[15]

The purpose of this book is to sweep away the mythology and use the expertise of those who previously have been obliged to maintain their silence to describe an extraordinary phenomenon that became a hallmark of Soviet intelligence operations and shows no sign of having been abandoned.

1 · *Conspiratsia:*
The Pre-War Networks

Soviet illegal operations are based on one of the most
casually accepted privileges of life in an open society – the
free movement of individuals from one country to another.
William Hood in *Mole*[1]

The phenomenon of the Soviet illegal first came to the notice
of a Western security agency in 1927 when MI5 investigated
a tip from an insurance underwriter that a young man named
Wilfred Macartney had approached him for information
regarding shipments of weapons destined for the Baltic.
Macartney was placed under surveillance and in due course
was offered a relatively innocuous document, with the
'restricted' classification, in an operation known as a 'barium
meal' to see where he passed it on to. At that time the British
authorities had gained more expertise in monitoring Soviet
espionage than any other Western agency. Through the successful interception and decryption of Russian wireless traffic
in 1924, the Metropolitan Police Special Branch had exposed
the official Soviet Trade Delegation in London as a front for
subversion, and it was generally assumed that, in the absence
of any Soviet diplomatic representation in London, Macartney's planted classified paper would end up with an intermediary in one of the Soviet international trading organisations.
In May 1927, when the police and MI5 were satisfied that
Macartney had handed on the secret material to his Soviet

contact, a raid was mounted on the All Russian Co-operative Society (ARCOS). This was the commercial agency established in London following the Anglo-Soviet trade treaty of 1921, but in the intervening period the Government had expressed concern that ARCOS had developed close links with British Communists and had engaged in seditious agitation. Although the item in question was not recovered during the raid, detectives searched the building for a period of three days and found a mass of other incriminating evidence, enough to prompt similar operations which were conducted by MI5's counterparts in Berlin, New York and Buenos Aires.[2] In France a very similar investigation had been under way for some time, which in many respects had paralleled the way MI5 had handled Macartney.

In October 1925, a mechanic at the Versailles Arsenal named Singre, who happened to be secretary of the local branch of the Communist Party, had been approached for classified information concerning the production of gunpowder and military vehicles. Singre, who was able to distinguish between legitimate trade-union matters and espionage, promptly told the police, who arranged for some suitable material to be handed over by Singre to a man identified as Pierre Provost, a locksmith; he in turn passed them on to another leading Communist, Jean Cremet. The subsequent investigation revealed an extensive network headed by Cremet. The crucial link had been established when Stephan Grodnicki, one of Cremet's lieutenants, was caught on 9 April 1927 meeting an artist who called himself Abraham Bernstein. Both men were arrested and 'Bernstein's' true name turned out to be Colonel Uzdansk-Yelenski, a man who previously had been expelled from Warsaw for his suspected involvement in espionage, and had himself replaced two Soviet officials, Ivan I. Maslennikov and Boris M. Fradkine, who had been expelled from Paris in March 1925. Of particular interest to the French police was the fact that Uzdansk-Yelenski's wife worked in the Soviet Embassy. Cremet and his mistress, Louise Clarac, took refuge in the Soviet Embassy in Paris and then fled to Moscow, but eight members of the ring were charged with espionage in April

1927 and convicted at a trial that served to alert the West to the existence of Soviet espionage on a grand scale. Some of the most incriminating evidence came from a retired quartermaster of the marines named Roussel, who produced a questionnaire that had been handed to him by Louise Clarac as a guide for the kind of information the Soviets were anxious to acquire:

1. Information concerning the armour and protection of new tanks under trial or under construction, particularly the new C2 heavy tank, the Type C light tank and the Vickers medium tank. Details of tanks used in the last war are already known.
(a) We are interested in the following: 1. Power and weight; 2. The engine; 3. The power system; 4. The weapons; 5. The armour; 6. The thickness of the side and top armour; 7. The speed and capability of negotiating steep gradients; Fuel capacity and duration.
2. Identify the twenty-two regiments of light assault tanks and the total number of tanks (three hundred); State if they are deficient in any way, and what they consist of. Find out if the medium tanks have integral weapons, and with what tanks are the heavy assault battalions equipped.
3. Procure all information concerning the tanks and their combat support vehicles.
4. What refuelling and resupply vehicles are there, and what information do you have about them? What is the range of the artillery pieces?
Identify first:
1. What parts of the guns require replacement?
2. Find out the construction data and strategy of the artillery: (a) The caterpillar tractor system; (b) The power and the engine; (c) The factories where the tractors are built; (d) The speeds on and off road.
Identify everything regarding the construction and the trial results of the Schneider tractor with the Kegresse strip and the St Chamond caterpillar tracks.
Identify secondly:
1. Which factories build tanks and armoured vehicles.
2. Other data concerning tanks and their observation and communications equipment, their propulsion system, and their anti-gas precautions, etc.
3. What is the capability of the tanks to tackle obstacles; of disguising their exhaust; of noise reduction, etc.?

4. What is the state of readiness of the tanks and their trained crews? The status of the tank crews and those of the armoured vehicles.[3]

It was evidence of this kind that established the complicity of the French Communist Party in Soviet espionage, and provided eloquent proof of the way in which the Soviet diplomatic mission had involved itself in gathering what was unmistakably intelligence of a military significance. A study of the material confiscated from ARCOS in London, conducted by Nigel Watson of MI5, also demonstrated that the Soviet intelligence organs relied on their Government's foreign trade companies to support their illicit activities. Suspicion that the equivalent organisation in Germany, known as the *Handelsvertretung* and located in Berlin's Lindenstrasse, had been involved in espionage had hardened following scrutiny of a list of addresses seized from Anton Miller, one of the ARCOS employees detained during the police raid. MI5 had arranged for copies of the suspect addresses to be circulated to the appropriate authorities abroad, and more evidence had been acquired when Polish, Turkish, Austrian, Swiss and Chinese security agencies uncovered local spy rings. In the United States the Federal Bureau of Investigation (FBI) was alerted to a network run by Jacob Moness, whose daughter Pauline, a student studying chemical engineering at Ghent University, was also to become an agent. His New York address, that of the Moness Chemical Company at 426 Broome Street, had been on Miller's list and it too was raided on 16 May 1927 by detectives who found it unoccupied.[4] A search of the empty premises revealed documents suggesting that the Moness family was involved in espionage and that Jacob's wife, Rachel Garsov, and their daughter Pauline had fled to Paris some two months earlier, in March, apparently in fear of having been compromised by the arrest of another Soviet agent, Ethel Chiles.

Jacob Moness had been born in Libau, Latvia, and had subsequently lived briefly in England and Germany before emigrating to the United States. His sudden disappearance from New York had been prompted by the conviction in

London on 2 May 1927 of Ethel Chiles. In fact, by that date
Ethel Chiles had been in custody for nearly six weeks, but she
had stubbornly refused to help her Special Branch interrogators establish her true identity. She had been arrested in Dover
on 15 March, having disembarked from the Calais cross-
channel ferry with a British passport identifying her as Chiles,
but an alert Special Branch officer had recognised her as Kathe
Gussfeldt, alias Edith Blaser, a German who was already well
known to his colleagues. She had previously been in England in
February 1924, ostensibly to attend the International Workers
Relief Committee (IWRC) meeting in Manchester, and three
months later she had visited Glasgow for a similar political
event. However, on the latter occasion she had switched
clothes with a travelling companion in a railway carriage and
thereby had successfully evaded police surveillance. Later in
the year, in October, she had entered Britain for a third time
and had been granted an extension to her visa so that she could
attend another IWRC conference. Upon her departure it had
been noted that she was carrying a false German passport and
an order was issued barring her from re-entry.

   The Metropolitan Police Special Branch had maintained a
rather incomplete record of Gussfeldt's subsequent movements and had spotted her in Paris in September 1925, and
on a voyage to Quebec from Cherbourg later the same year.
She was then seen in Brussels, where she attended a meeting
organised by the League against Imperialism. Immediately
following her arrest in Dover Gussfeldt had been escorted to
Victoria Station, where she was met by Inspector Charles
Frost, who collected her suitcase from the left-luggage office.
When searched, it was found to contain a mass of incriminating material, much of it written in secret ink.[5]

   The only link that could be established between Gussfeldt
and Moness was handwriting found on a questionnaire recovered from an unlit stove at the Broome Street office. Evidently Moness had been tasked to acquire certain US military
publications by Gussfeldt, and this had been enough to ensure
her deportation to Germany, but only after she had served
a sentence of two months' imprisonment. Because of incriminating entries found in her diary, she became the subject of

a lengthy investigation conducted in London by Captain Hugh Miller of MI5. Her notes, written in a secret ink of the type used by the Germans during the Great War, showed that she had been in contact with the French spy, Jean Cremet, and an American espionage suspect named Robert Switz, of whom more will be heard shortly. She was also found to be carrying a photograph of herself with Willi Munsenberg, the prominent German Communist and founder of the Communist Youth League. There were also a series of poems which, when analysed, suggested that, after her arrival in Canada in September 1925, she had visited New York the following month. Thereafter, little was known of her movements until her arrest in Dover, when she declared herself to be a steno-typist and interpreter who intended to travel to Holland, Germany, France, Switzerland and Belgium for her health. She also claimed that on another visit she had translated a report of a British trade-union delegation to Russia.

When the police traced the origin of Gussfeldt's British passport, they discovered that it had been issued on 1 March 1927, following an application made in London a few days earlier. The referee who had authenticated the applicant was a physician, Dr Gerald Gateley of Bow. He had apparently certified that she had been born at Garston in Liverpool and was presently residing in Rendlesham Road, Clapton, a poor district in London's East End. When challenged, the doctor had denied any knowledge of 'Ethel Chiles'.

In parallel to the investigations conducted in London, attention was also focused on Amtorg, the Soviet commercial agency that was believed to accommodate a Soviet intelligence apparatus among its 500 employees at its headquarters at 261 Fifth Avenue. Amtorg, the Russian abbreviation for *Amerikanskaia Torgovoia*, had started trading in 1924, but the US authorities noted that only a select group of trusted staff were allowed into two specially protected floors of the building where the Soviet political intelligence service, the OGPU, and the GRU were believed to be concentrated.

Moness and his family were investigated by the American authorities although, controversially, they were never charged with any offence. J. Edgar Hoover, head of the FBI, testified before Congress on 9 June 1930 that 'since 1924 to date there has been no investigation conducted by the Department of Justice of communistic activities'.[6] This assertion is unbelievable, considering that in 1929 a Soviet defector, who called himself Georges Agabekov, had revealed that the OGPU's first *rezident* in the United States had been a man named Tschatzky and that, 'as there is no Soviet diplomatic representative in America, Tschatzky was known in America as a collaborator of Amtorg'.[7]

As a direct consequence of the ARCOS raid Soviet front companies, local Communist Parties and diplomatic missions came under intensive surveillance from the respective host security agencies. Combined with the embarrassment experienced by the Kremlin when it found itself publicly linked to espionage, the Soviets opted to concentrate on the expedient of developing the 'illegal' apparatus, the agent operating alone who had no ostensible connection with the Soviet Government and could, therefore, allow the Kremlin plausibly to deny any direct involvement in espionage. As a further refinement, these illegal networks were to be supervised by specially selected intelligence officers who would conform to what became known as *conspiratsia*, the tradecraft and strict code of secrecy used to conceal the identities and origins of the illegals despatched from Moscow to build new networks in the West and isolate the official Soviet organs of government from embarrassment and complicity in espionage.

Soon after the ARCOS raid the British Special Branch arrested its first Soviet illegal, a German student named Georg Hansen, who had been caught red-handed while keeping a rendezvous with Wilfred Macartney. Hansen and Macartney were sentenced to ten years' imprisonment for their involvement in espionage, and although Macartney continued to live in England after his release and was later to become a political commissar in the International Brigade fighting in Spain during the Civil War, Hansen simply disappeared after his deportation to Germany. Who was he, and why was he spying in England? Under interrogation Hansen had stuck to his cover story and pretended to have acted as an innocent intermediary between Macartney and an unknown stranger, whom he was unable to identify. Thus, although the British authorities had caught Macartney and Hansen, they were unable to uncover the remainder of what was actually a very extensive network. As we shall see, more than a decade later MI5 was to learn that several other agents, all in contact with Macartney, had escaped undetected. If the Soviet intelligence chiefs had harboured any doubts about the wisdom of isolating their official structures from their intelligence operations, Hansen's silence must have proved encouraging. However, although Hansen had proved unco-operative, the same could not be said of Georges Agabekov, an Armenian who had been sent under commercial cover to Constantinople in October 1929 to run a Soviet company selling typewriters and bicycles.

Within a year of his arrival in Turkey, Agabekov had acquired a private tutor to teach him English, and Isabel Streater had fallen in love with him.[8] Equally smitten, he confided his secret mission to her and in October 1929 they eloped to France, where Agabekov opened negotiations to sell his memoirs. Once established in Paris, Agabekov sought the help of the British SIS to secure Isabel's hand in marriage, in the face of intense opposition from her family. Eventually, Agabekov did wed Isabel and they went to live in Brussels on the proceeds of his exposé, *OGPU: The Russian Secret Terror*, in which he described his experiences as the head of the OGPU's Eastern Section. Agabekov's remarkable book was the first authentic inside story from a Soviet defector and he detailed the close relationship between the Ministry of Commerce in Moscow, *Narkomintorg*, and the OGPU:

I have spoken before of the necessity of camouflage for OGPU residents. There are instances of commercial missions furnishing such, but obviously it is far less satisfactory than that furnished by diplomatic missions, since employees of the Ministry of Commerce do not enjoy diplomatic immunity. And Moscow, remembering certain experiences, has grown cautious of imperilling commercial missions by such 'questionable' associates.[9]

Despite Agabekov's first-hand knowledge of the OGPU's internal structure and personnel, he was largely ignored in the West. He was expelled from France in August 1930 and denied a visa to enter Britain, despite his offer to help the authorities identify a Soviet source in the Foreign Office who was allegedly haemorrhaging secrets to Moscow.

The intercepted reports of the British Ambassador to America has been to us a splendid source of information concerning the activities of the American Government. I remark in passing that the Foreign Section has in its hands copies of the reports of almost all the British foreign representatives – ambassadors to the Powers and high commissioners in countries under British mandate. I have from time to time glanced at these reports. Indeed, Moscow owes deepest gratitude to the British diplomats. Their accumulated reports, neatly filed and indexed, take up a vast amount of shelf-room. [10]

This tip was virtually ignored by the British authorities, who seemed unmoved when the author repeated in his book the charges he had been voicing privately to SIS for months in the hope of being allowed to come to London with Isabel. However, if Whitehall was unwilling to listen, Agabekov's former masters were enraged and made at least two attempts to silence him.

Agabekov's damaging disclosures about Amtorg's links with the OGPU were to be confirmed not just by the FBI but by former members of Amtorg's staff, including Basil W. Delgass, a vice-president of the organisation who, upon his retirement in July 1930, stated publicly that defence information 'has been gathered by Amtorg's agents and transmitted to Russia', [11] and repeated the claims before a Congressional committee chaired by Hamilton Fish. There was other evidence connecting Amtorg to espionage, including an affidavit submitted by Mikhail Hendler, described as a former Amtorg official and an OGPU agent. Coinciding with Delgass's testimony was the arrest of a senior Amtorg official, Vladimir Asaturov, on charges of smuggling Swiss watch movements into the United States. When searched by American officials, Asaturov was found to be carrying a quantity of the baptismal and birth certificates then needed to accompany US passport applications. Similarly, several of his colleagues had been identified as senior OGPU officers, including Feodor Ziavkin, formerly an OGPU chief in a Soviet town.

The proof of Amtorg's direct complicity in espionage presented itself when the FBI was informed that William Disch, a designer working on classified naval contracts in the Arma Engineering Corporation, had reported an approach for information from Solomon Kantor, a former colleague who was a well-known Communist as well as a talented draughtsman. Disch duly entrapped Kantor, who in turn led the investigators to his controller, Moishe Stern, who routinely took Disch's documents and photographed them in the Amtorg building. Surveillance on Stern revealed his connection with another mysterious figure, Robert Gordon Switz, who was to become a key figure in the expanding Soviet network of illegals.[12]

Robert Switz had been born in New Jersey to wealthy parents of Russian origin and had been educated in France. He was a Communist idealist and, after his recruitment, had been trained in Moscow. In 1931, he was back in New York, working for Stern by running a source in the US army. His contact was Robert Osman, a former activist in the Young Communist League, who had been posted to Panama with the rank of corporal. His parents had also been Russian immigrants, and he supplied Switz with copies of documents he routinely typed while on administrative duties as an office clerk. Osman was compromised when his mail-drop in New York failed, and a package full of incriminating papers was returned by the Post Office to the army in Panama and traced to Osman. In August 1933, Osman was sentenced to twenty years' hard labour, but his conviction was overturned and a new trial ordered when the eminent lawyer, Louis Waldman, took up his case.[13] Osman's second trial led to his acquittal when Waldman demonstrated that the accused could not have mailed the package to the mail-drop in New York. He showed that far from being an active Communist agent, his client had been the unwitting dupe of Frema Karry, his Russian girlfriend, who had disappeared at the time of Osman's arrest.

Waldman also learned that Osman's principal contact was

a man known to him as 'Harry Duryea', but when, coincidentally, a photograph of Switz appeared in *Time* magazine on
26 March 1934, following his arrest, Osman recognised Switz
as Duryea. In fact, Switz had fled to Paris as soon as Osman
had been taken into military custody and had resumed his
activities there, this time running a network of sources in the
French army and in the War Ministry, assisted by his recently
acquired American wife, Marjorie Tilley. Both were arrested
in December 1933 and, after months of interrogation, they
confessed to having participated in a Soviet espionage ring.
Furthermore, under interrogation they implicated dozens of
others, including Lydia Stahl, a veteran Soviet intelligence
officer. The confessions of Robert and Marjorie Switz earned
them their release in 1935, but they had also implicated more
than two hundred people, including several with access to
the French Ministry of War's research into chemical and germ
warfare. Six of those who were caught in the first wave of
arrests also incriminated others in return for lighter sentences, and the French Deuxième Bureau was more than
satisfied when only ten suspects were convicted *in absentia*,
having evaded capture. The Stern–Stahl–Switz Group, as it
came to be known in Western security circles, was to prove
a mortal blow to the OGPU's foreign intelligence apparatus,
particularly in the United States, where Stern was obliged to
make a swift departure for Moscow, via Canada.

The arrest of Lydia Stahl was a particularly impressive
coup for the French for she had been one of the founders of
the Soviet illegal network in the United States. Born in
Rostov in 1885, her husband had been a member of the
nobility who had lost his estates in the Crimea during the
revolution. The family had emigrated to New York, where
Lydia's husband had started a new career as a stockbroker
and she had studied medicine. But, after the death of her
only son in 1918, she had returned alone to Paris, where her
interest in photography and her American passport made
her an attractive target for Soviet recruitment. After taking
a course in law, Stahl had returned to New York, where she
worked with Stern until 1932, when she re-established herself in Paris and liaised with the Switzes after Osman's arrest

had prompted their hasty exit. In March 1934, Stahl, who declined to co-operate with the French authorities, received a four-year prison term; upon her release, she resumed her activities in the United States. One of those closely associated with Stahl in both the United States and France was Alfred Tilton, a Latvian who appears to have been the GRU's illegal *rezident* in New York, operating under a commercial front, that of a shipping office in Manhattan. Tilton developed a network of couriers based on Communist seamen and later handed control of his organisation to Nicholas Dozenberg, of whom more will be heard later.

It was mounting evidence of a close link between the Comintern, the international wing of the Soviet Union's Communist Party, pledged to worldwide revolution, and the Soviet intelligence-gathering apparatus that prompted MI5 to develop its penetration operation by placing a girl agent close to Percy Glading, a leading member of the British Communist Party (CPGB), who had worked at the Woolwich Arsenal until his dismissal for militancy. After three years of voluntary work for the Friends of the Soviet Union, helping to edit the organisation's paper, *War*, Olga Gray was entrusted with carrying Comintern funds to India.[14] As well as being the CPGB's National Organiser, Glading was also a key Soviet agent, being controlled by an illegal who lived in north London and was known to Glading as 'Mr Stephens'. According to Olga's reports to MI5, Glading and Stephens had kept in touch with the Woolwich Arsenal and were operating a network of informants among the workforce. On one occasion, when Stephens had been absent abroad, his place had been taken by a man calling himself 'Peters'.

Although much is now known about Glading, Stephens and Peters were exceptionally mysterious individuals and both occupy a special place in intelligence folklore because, although MI5 had managed, undetected, to place an informant right inside a suspected spy ring that had extracted secrets from Woolwich Arsenal, it was never able to catch either Stephens or Peters. Sworn testimony at the Old Bailey from Olga Gray ensured that the footsoldiers of the operation were arrested in January 1938 and convicted in court, but their controllers had simply vanished, never to be seen again. Stephens and his wife had left London on 6 November, ostensibly having been called back to Moscow because their daughter had been taken ill. During the trial of the ringleader, Percy Glading, and his colleagues, the prosecution mentioned the mysterious role played by the absentee couple named Stephens, but, once again, the use of an illegal had allowed the Soviet authorities to distance themselves from an embarrassing incident that might otherwise have caused a serious diplomatic rift. Glading, the principal spy who had played a key part in recruiting his former workmates at the Arsenal, had held a senior position in the CPGB and thereby had unintentionally discredited and undermined the Party. It was only after Glading's release from prison, and his expulsion from the CPGB, that he re-established his Soviet links and went to live in Moscow, where he died.

Although MI5 failed to catch Stephens, it did learn a great deal about Soviet illegal tradecraft and the complexity of Russian espionage, which evidently, since the ARCOS raid, had acquired a new dimension. At a time when British intelligence personnel gathered information under the semi-transparent guise of British Passport Control Officers, operating under rather flimsy consular cover provided (reluctantly) by the Foreign Office, their Soviet counterparts were investing in *conspiratsia*. To MI5's tiny handful of investigators, with only limited resources and less experience of such Machiavellian manœuvres, there was no alternative to a dogged pursuit of Stephens, which was conducted entirely in secret on both sides of the Atlantic. It was to reveal a labyrinthine construction of false names and bogus marriages, all apparently intended to support a mission undertaken by a single individual.

Surveillance on 'Mr Stephens' before his flight had led MI5 to a flat at 31 Forset House, an apartment block in the Edgware Road, north London, which he shared with Mary, his wife. A neighbour recalled that their marriage had been a stormy one, and that the couple had spoken to each other in French. Enquiries with the building's owner revealed that 'Stephens' was known to him as William Brandes, a businessman who spoke English with an American accent, who had claimed to be of Romanian origin, but said that he had become a naturalised Canadian citizen.[15] As proof, he had held a Canadian passport, number 22247, issued on 2 October 1936. When Brandes had first introduced himself to his landlord, he had mentioned having crossed into the United States from Canada and, somewhat archly, having worked without a permit in New York City, where he had lived at 34 East 32nd Street. Indeed, his landlord produced a letter written by an American businessman, Walter Charak, on the letterheading of his company, the Charak Furniture Company of 444 Madison Avenue, New York, a document which Brandes had used to establish his credentials as a trustworthy tenant who had been engaged to scout for antiques in England at a handsome salary of $300 a month. MI5 also discovered that Brandes had posed as an agent of the Phantome Red Cosmetics Company, also of New York, and, according to British immigration records, had first entered the country in January 1937, equipped with a large number of samples of Phantome face powder. Significantly, when 'Stephens' had hurriedly left the country in November 1937, he had made a special request of his landlord: in the event that a sub-tenant could be found to take on the remaining few months of the lease, could he refund his rent to Walter Charak.

An investigation was launched in New York and Canada which shed further light on Brandes's antecedents. A check was made on his Canadian passport, and his application was found to have been supported by an authentic naturalisation certificate and a Montreal lawyer named Abe Mitchell. The official Canadian records revealed that early in September 1936 Brandes had been issued in Montreal with certificate number 2297OE Series 'E', by stating under oath that he was the son of Schulem Brandes of Montreal, who had himself become a naturalised Canadian on 9 October 1913. At this stage the story becomes complicated, for William Brandes was certainly not Schulem's son. Schulem, who was then eighty years old and, since September 1936, had been a resident of the Montreal Old Persons Sheltering Home, confirmed when interviewed that he had no son. He explained hat, soon after entering the Home, he had been approached by Aaron Marcovitch, of the Hebrew Sick Benefit Association, who had borrowed his naturalisation certificate, number 10164, which he had been granted in 1913. It was this legitimate document which had been presented by William Brandes to support his own application, together with recommendations from Marcovitch and a Montreal Member of Parliament named Webber. According to the latter, he had been approached by Marcovitch on 22 September with a plausible tale: Brandes was a Hebrew teacher at a local school and, having recently married, was anxious to go on his honeymoon. Would the MP intervene with the authorities and expedite the groom's passport application? This was the kind of request that MPs received routinely from constituents unused to dealing with government bureaucracy, and Webber had accepted the story at face value. Impressed by Brandes's other two sponsors, Marcovitch and Mitchell, Webber had arranged for the passport to be released immediately, without the usual police checks. This trail of paperwork led the investigators to the city's records of marriages.

According to the civic records kept by Montreal, Brandes had been married on 9 September 1936 to Mary Stern by the Reverend J. Aspler. However, although a marriage certificate had been issued after the ceremony, when interviewed the rabbi could not remember the couple, and no trace could be found of the two witnesses, or of Mary's parents, identified as Michael and Leah Stern, also of Montreal.

Prompted by MI5, the Royal Canadian Mounted Police (RCMP) began to build a case for prosecuting Marcovitch for fraud. The FBI made a discreet visit to 444 Madison Avenue and learned that the owner of the furniture business cited by Brandes to his landlord in London, one Walter Charak, had been born in Russia and that his company, registered in Massachusetts in 1919, was a thriving concern. A check on the Phantome Red Cosmetics Company showed that, despite the impressive title, it was 'a one-man lipstick agency' run from a single room at 33 Fifth Avenue by Philip Sweetosh, an American of Russian descent who had

previously traded in textiles in Philadelphia. When inter
viewed, both Charak and Sweetosh described Brandes as a
stranger who had offered to work in Europe as a salesman
on commission. There the American end of the trail seemed
to peter out, but meanwhile in Canada the RCMP had
uncovered an extraordinary web of false identities associated
with Brandes and his wife.

Interrogation of Marcovitch had led the RCMP to Armand
Labis, who had made the introductions for Brandes to acquire
his false documentation. A background check on Labis
revealed that in February 1936 he himself had obtained a
passport, number 3921, by using a false birth certificate in
the name of Abraham Feldman. Then, the following
December, and calling himself 'Armand Labis Feldman', he
had married a woman named Marcia Brett. She had anglicised
her maiden name from Marza Brajt, and their marriage had
been conducted by Rabbi Aspler in Montreal, coincidentally
the very same clergyman who had married Brandes. A few
days after the ceremony Feldman had applied for his Canadian
naturalisation papers, which had been granted, and the couple
had then left for the United States.

Although the RCMP failed to find Feldman for many years,
they did trace his father, Marcu Labis, who was then still
living in Montreal. He explained that his son Armand had
been born in Paris but had been brought to Canada when still
only a few months old. He had run away from home aged
eleven, and had only recently returned in order to acquire a
passport with the aid of his father's entirely legitimate naturalisation certificate. No trace could be found of Armand or
Marcia, but cheques written on his savings account in Montreal, which had previously received large deposits, were
drawn on a New York bank, which suggested that the couple
had moved to that city. Nothing more was heard of Brandes,
and it was not for some years that evidence emerged that
suggested that he, along with his wife and many other illegals,
had been liquidated. As for Feldman, who died recently in
Canada, he was later to feature in a case of industrial espionage in the United States and was to be pursued with equal
vigour by both the RCMP and the Soviets.

The Brandeses, together with the rest of the Soviet illegal apparatus in Europe, had been recalled to Moscow in a purge that was to eliminate an estimated twenty thousand Soviet intelligence officers, an entire generation of experienced personnel, the old Chekists. A manifestation of Stalin's paranoia about Trotskyite counter-revolutionaries, the bloodbath decimated the Soviet intelligence structure and filled the survivors with a fear of the dread signal from Moscow requiring an immediate return 'for urgent consultations'. Invariably, this summons amounted to a death sentence, executed by Stalin's intelligence chief, Nikolai I. Yezhov, who gave his name to the purge which became known as the *Yezhovschina*. Ironically, Yezhov himself was not to escape and he fell prey to 'liquidation' by assassins from his own euphemistically titled 'Administration of Special Tasks' in 1939, following what purported to be a trial.

The *Yezhovschina* was conducted in great secrecy, but as rumours of the purges circulated among the European networks a few of those selected for the firing squad in the cellars of the Lubyanka under Dzerzhinsky Square opted to defect. The first dramatic insight into the Soviet illegal apparatus was given by just such a defector, Walter Krivitsky. Born Samuel Ginsberg in Galicia, Krivitsky had operated as the Soviet military intelligence service's illegal *rezident* in Holland in the guise of an antiquarian bookseller. When, in late 1937, he had learned that he was to be liquidated, he had defected, staying in Paris under the ineffective protection of the French Sûreté, to whom he gave enough information to fill eighty volumes, until he took his valuable knowledge to America and then to Canada.[16] However, for two months after his arrival in New York the authorities were reluctant to take him seriously, and one of his most significant revelations, regarding the existence of a Soviet spy in London, did not reach the British Government until early September 1939, when Isaac Don Levine, a Russian-born journalist collaborating on a book and a series of articles with Krivitsky, sought an interview with Lord Lothian, the British Ambassador in Washington DC. Levine disclosed enough of Krivitsky's information for MI5 to identify Captain John King, an important

Soviet source working in the Communications Department of the Foreign Office, and arrest him on Wednesday, 27 September. King was convicted in October 1939, but no public announcement was made regarding his subsequent trial until after the war. Under interrogation he identified his recruiter as Ernest Oldham, a disaffected former Foreign Office colleague who had resigned his post in September 1932 and had been found dead, gassed in his London home, a year later.[17] The exposure of King, who served a long prison sentence, served to highlight the claims made by Georges Agabekov, whose offer a decade earlier to assist the British authorities had been ignored.

Krivitsky was also to alert the West to the existence of an extensive network of illegals in Europe and to give a first-hand account of the purge under way in Moscow. Although Krivitsky was directly responsible for leading MI5 to King, and was to be the target of several assassination attempts, not all his claims were taken seriously. It was only after his mysterious death in a Washington hotel in February 1941, and the testimony of Hede Massing in 1948, that the scale of the Soviet illegal structure, and the trauma it had experienced at Yezhov's hands, was even begun to be belatedly understood.

Among those to return to certain death was Krivitsky's friend Theodore Maly, a key illegal controller who called himself Paul Hardt and had operated in Britain. Indeed, according to evidence taken decades later from Anthony Blunt, Maly had helped to recruit and run Kim Philby. Of Hungarian origin, Maly had taken holy orders as a priest and, until his capture by the Tsar's forces, had served in an Austrian cavalry regiment. In captivity he had become a committed Bolshevik, a conversion that was later to seal his fate. The Soviet defector who used the name Alexander Orlov recalled that he 'could with equal ease pass for a Hungarian, Austrian, German or Swiss'. He was 'a six-footer with a strong, manly face and large, almost childlike, blue eyes'.[18] Until the age of twenty he had studied at a seminary in Tiflis. In Paris, while on his way back to the Soviet Union, he had learned the terrible fate of three other doomed NKVD comrades, Steinbruck,

Sily and Bodesko, all, like himself, Hungarians who had joined the cause as captives in the First World War and had been summoned to headquarters. Upon his return to Moscow in July 1937, Maly was pleasantly surprised to be assigned a desk job, but in November he disappeared, the presumption being that he had been shot as a Trotskyite, together with numerous other victims of the *Yezhovschina*. His younger brother was a pianist with an international reputation, but even though Theodore had reportedly once attended one of his concerts in London, he had deliberately avoided making contact with him for fear of compromising his illegal cover. Blunt, who never met Maly, was later to confirm Philby's admiration for the charismatic ex-priest, who willingly responded to his recall to Moscow even though he had guessed what was likely to be in store for him. Maly's involvement in espionage in England, initially indicated by his use of the alias 'Peters' while temporarily handling the Woolwich Arsenal spy ring in tandem with Willy Brandes, was later to be confirmed by John King, who confessed in 1939 that he had supplied copies of secret telegrams to a man answering Maly's description between early 1936 and his sudden departure the following year.

Further information about Maly and the Soviet purge came to light from two unexpected sources, both defectors from the Soviet cause. One, Leiba Lazarevich Feldbin, known as General Alexander M. Orlov, fled to Canada in July 1938 and used his clandestine skills to build a new life for himself, his wife and his daughter, Vera, in the United States, where he was eventually to surface in 1953. The other valued insider who defected was Elisabeth Poretsky, the widow of Ignace Reiss, a Soviet illegal and Krivitsky's friend, who had chosen to take refuge in Switzerland rather than obey orders and return to Moscow to face execution for the crime of having supported Trotsky. Reiss had known Krivitsky since their childhood and came from the same small town in Galicia, at the edge of the Austro-Hungarian Empire. Acting on a tip from Krivitsky, Reiss had gone into hiding, but had been tracked down to Lausanne and shot in September 1937, but not before he had confided details of his activities to his wife, herself a well-trained illegal, who had only herself escaped being poisoned because her intended assassin, her friend Gertrude Schildbach, had at the last moment lost her nerve and snatched back a box of chocolates laced with strychnine. Reiss had been initiated into the Comintern in Vienna, where he was 'centred in the Soviet Embassy. In later years such open contact with Soviet diplomatic officials would have been unthinkable, but at the time there had not yet been police raids on Soviet trade missions and similar bodies so no precautions seemed necessary.'[19] On his first mission abroad, to Poland, he had been arrested and imprisoned on a charge of Communist subversion, but had escaped after eighteen months and had then been assigned to Holland, where, according to his widow, he was given 'a much more important assignment; he was to direct operations aimed at obtaining information in Great Britain. The headquarters were not to be in England but in the Netherlands.'[20] Reiss and his wife stayed in Holland, working with the Dutch artist and accomplished illegal, Henri Pieck, for '1928 and part of 1929' before leaving for Moscow. Three years later Reiss was back in the West, operating in Berlin and then Paris, whence he had been obliged to flee in 1937.

During the terror, neither wives nor children were exempt and the entire Reiss family had been sentenced to death. Elisabeth knew only too well what was likely to happen and was quite aware that another murder squad would have been despatched from Moscow to complete the 'executive assignment'. In July 1931, Georg Semmelmann, a former OGPU agent who had worked in Germany under *Handelsvertretung* cover, was shot in broad daylight in Vienna after he had threatened his old employers. He had been fired by the OGPU for having married a German regarded by Moscow as a security risk, and had compounded the error by publicly demanding his job back and hinting at sensational disclosures. Semmelmann's murder was an unmistakable warning to others tempted to break the code of *conspiratsia*, and the lesson had not been lost on Elisabeth. She promptly went into hiding with friends in Holland, moving to America from Lisbon in 1940, and was later to write a bitter denunciation of Stalin, *Our Own People*, and of her husband's murderers. She was also to co-operate with the FBI and MI5, helping them to solve some of the more baffling puzzles of the illegal *conspiratsia*, including some of the assignments undertaken by her husband who had spent twenty years as an illegal, operating in Berlin, Vienna and Paris. Her sketches of personalities among the cosmopolitan illegals were also exceptionally useful, for they tended to corroborate much of what Krivitsky had disclosed. For example, Elisabeth had known Maly well and had remembered him as 'in his forties, a handsome, tall Hungarian with blue eyes and the charming smile of the naturally shy'. Significantly for MI5, she confirmed that he had been 'sent to London and then to Moscow' to recruit agents and run a Soviet spy ring. As Orlov later explained, 'even during Stalin's blood purges in which several dozens of Soviet intelligence chiefs and underground *rezidents* perished, the holocaust did not touch the informants, who merely acquired new chiefs after the old ones had been liquidated'.[21]

In addition to condemning what he perceived to be Stalin's real political objectives, and revealing the truth behind the disappearance of so many old Chekists from their usual haunts, Krivitsky also identified a Latvian immigrant named Nicholas Dozenberg as the Soviet military intelligence chief in the United States. Until 1927, Dozenberg had been an ardent Communist, but thereafter he had cut his overt links with the Party and had apparently operated as a spy. In 1929, he had been recalled to Moscow and then had been sent on a mission to Romania, where he had created a front company, the American-Romanian Film Corporation, which was eventually to own a small cinema in New York specialising in foreign films. This company was also to be the vehicle for a scheme to flood the American economy with counterfeit dollar bills, but the plot had collapsed early in 1934 when some of the minor participants had been arrested by the Chicago police while passing the forgeries. A skilled cameraman, Dozenberg had represented Bell & Howell in Bucharest and had owned, through intermediaries, a camera business called Josef Bartok. When the counterfeiting operation failed, Dozenberg

fled to Romania and later turned up in Germany and Tients-
ien, China. At the end of May 1939, Dozenberg was spotted
in England en route by ship from Leningrad to New York,
carrying a Greek passport identifying him as Nicholas Dallant.
Krivitsky believed that Dozenberg 'had been swept away in
the great purge',[22] but in fact he had slipped back into New
York where he was arrested on a charge of obtaining his
American passport by fraud and sentenced to a year's imprisonment. Dozenberg always refused to co-operate with the
American authorities or to incriminate anyone else, although
he was believed to have become disenchanted with the Party
during his last visit to Moscow. Dozenberg's place, according
to Krivitsky, had been taken by Colonel Boris Bykov, who
was posted to Washington in 1936 as the Soviet Military
Attaché.[23]

Evidence that the Soviets valued American travel documents, and that Stalin's purges were taking a heavy toll within
the Russian intelligence community, took several forms. In
December 1937, for example, there were press reports from
Moscow of the disappearance of Donald L. Robinson, who
had been taken ill with pneumonia while staying at the
National Hotel. His wife, Ruth Robinson, had vanished the
day after making her complaint and the State Department
started to make enquiries. It transpired that the passports
held by the Robinsons had been granted the previous year,
in April 1936, and were supported by birth certificates that
had been issued originally to a couple who had died thirty
years earlier.[24] When *Izvestia* reported the disappearance of
the Robinsons, they were described as having been associated with Trotskyites, and the Communist press in the United
States printed much the same kind of hostile story.

The technique employed by the Robinsons to obtain American passports was used by numerous other Soviet agents,
and there was some evidence to suggest that the Robinsons
were actually Adolph and Ruth Rubens. In January 1938,
the State Department sought MI5's help in clearing up the
mystery over their identities and disclosed that the handwriting on the passport application for Ruth Robinson matched
that of Adolph Rubens's wife, Ruth Boerger. He was thought

to have been of Russian origin, spoke Russian, German and French fluently, and, according to the records, had applied for his first passport by claiming to be the son of a naturalised Russian named Rudewitz. Having adopted the identity of Donald Robinson, he had married his wife in New York in 1936 and had then described himself as a book publisher at the Galleon Press of 361 Fourth Avenue, New York. Coincidentally, this was also the address of International Publishers, the US's largest distributor of Communist literature. When Mrs Rubens's family was traced, her membership of the Party was confirmed. Furthermore her sister, Constance Boerger, identified a man named Leon Minster as having introduced Ruth to her future husband, Adolph Rubens. Minster was himself a well-known Soviet agent, as was his brother Robert, who had been active as an illicit radio operator in China in 1934. In yet another link to Soviet espionage, Robert Minster had married Emma Kantor, whose father Solomon had worked as a draughtsman in the Arma Engineering Corporation and had been implicated in the William Disch case.

Another curiosity about the passport application made by Ruth Rubens was that the photograph attached to it bore a strong resemblance to Pauline Moness, the daughter of Jacob Moness, who had disappeared from New York soon after the ARCOS raid in 1927. She had been expelled from Belgium back in 1932 and had last been heard of in Moscow in May 1934. A check of immigration records for Mr and Mrs Rubens showed that in April 1936 they had travelled to Paris via Cherbourg and, during the next two months, had visited Stockholm, Copenhagen, Amsterdam, Madrid, Stockholm again and Vienna before arriving in London on 2 July 1936. A day or so later they sailed on the *Empress of Britain* back to New York. In October the following year, they had made a single journey straight to Italy, where they reported the loss of their luggage, and then went to Paris, where they checked in at the Hotel Scribe on 2 November, not to be sighted again until the incident in Moscow later the next month. In New York, the photos used on the fake Robinson passports were found to have been taken in a small studio on Fifth Avenue run by Ossip Garber, who was arrested in March 1938 and subsequently convicted of passport fraud and sentenced to two years' imprisonment. He was a member of the Communist Party of the United States (CPUSA) branch in the Bronx, along with Arthur Sharfin, who was convicted on the same charge. However, that was not the limit of the links between the Party and the false passports. It was later discovered that after they had been issued, the Robinson passports had been delivered to a Communist front organisation, the Drama Travel League, headed by Helen Ravitch. She in turn was married to a Doctor Bernstein, who happened to be the physician of William Z. Foster, the CPUSA's future General-Secretary.

The peregrinations across Europe of the Robinsons strongly suggested that they were Soviet agents and that they had fallen victim to Stalin's purge, then in full swing. In the West little was understood about what was happening in Moscow for, although there were a few clues to be discerned, such as the sudden recall and disappearance of Vitovt Putna, the Soviet Air and Military Attaché in London in 1936, it was not until January 1937 that Moscow made an official announcement. The communiqué stated that dozens of senior apparatchiks had confessed to participating in a vast espionage plot, variously described as having been inspired by Trotsky or the Germans. However, once Krivitsky had revealed the scale of the purge within the Soviet intelligence apparatus, a total of 350,000 political arrests in the first five months of 1937, more evidence emerged, although some was to be delayed for a few more years. Hede Massing, a Vienna-born Communist and naturalised American who was recalled to Moscow in 1937 and subsequently broke with the Party, was one of the very few to return to the West after her interrogation at the hands of the NKVD.[25] She moved to a farm in Bucks County, New York, and was twice contacted by the Soviets, who let her know that they were keeping an eye on her and her husband Paul, who was also a GRU agent. She eventually volunteered a statement to the FBI in late 1946 and testified against another Soviet agent, Alger Hiss, two years later. In a similar case of disillusionment, Elizabeth

Bentley approached the FBI in August 1945 and described her clandestine career as a Soviet agent which had begun in 1938, three years after she had joined the CPUSA. The cases of both Hede Massing and Elizabeth Bentley will be described in chapter 3.

Another link between Soviet espionage and Amtorg was established in December 1938, five years after formal diplomatic relations had been established between the United States and the Soviet Union, when Mikhail Gorin was arrested in California on a charge of espionage. Secret documents had been found in the pocket of a suit he had absentmindedly sent to be cleaned, which had implicated Gorin's source, Hafis Salich, a Moscow-born US naval intelligence officer with family in the USSR. Salich had been persuaded to copy dozens of classified assessments of Japanese naval strength prepared by the Office of Naval Intelligence, a topic the Soviets were anxious to learn more about. Gorin had originally worked for Amtorg in New York and had subsequently transferred to Intourist's office in Los Angeles. Gorin and Salich received terms of six and four years' imprisonment, respectively, but in March 1941 Gorin was deported to Moscow.

In a similar episode another Amtorg employee, Gaik B. Ovakimian, was arrested in May 1941. Officially listed as an engineer, Ovakimian had been the *rezident* for the OGPU (and latterly the NKVD) in the United States since 1934, when he succeeded Valentin Markin, who had died after a brawl in a 52nd Street night-club in New York. Since his arrival in 1932, Ovakimian had controlled numerous illegal networks and had been linked to a ring headed by Armand Feldman which stole industrial secrets, but he was too shrewd a professional to be directly implicated by any of his agents. The 164-page report prepared by the FBI characterised him as a well-educated cosmopolitan who inspired loyalty in his subordinates, and who had been sufficiently politically adept to evade the purges that had decimated the OGPU and NKVD during his decade in the West. Ovakimian was eventually charged with a breach of the US registration of agents legislation, and his claim to diplomatic immunity was

initially rejected. However, pressure was applied to the State
Department and a deal was negotiated to allow Ovakimian to
return to Moscow in exchange for the release of six Americans held in Soviet jails.[26]

Post-war testimony from Elizabeth Bentley supported the
FBI's view, which had been reinforced by the GRU defector
Ismail Akhmedov, that Ovakimian had been a key NKVD
officer responsible for organising several overlapping networks in the United States. Born in August 1898, according
to his Soviet travel papers, he and his wife Vera and their
daughter Engina had led an extraordinary double life, constantly under threat of discovery. The fact that he had
remained in the field for so long, and had survived his covert
career, is a credit to his professionalism, even if he was
eventually to be duped by Feldman. Ovakimian was never
seen again in the West and was probably yet another victim
of Stalin's paranoia, but Feldman's disappearance was
prompted by a quite different motive. The RCMP Security
Service investigators eventually tracked him down to an old
people's home in Vancouver, where he submitted to a lengthy
interrogation. He died, peacefully, in 1989, having spent most
of Ovakimian's funds, a fugitive to the end, convinced that
he was in constant danger of discovery by his successors. In
his statement Feldman admitted having set up several front
companies for the Comintern and alleged that he had also
run a particularly useful source inside the US Department of
Justice. This man was never prosecuted, but Feldman
claimed to have used him routinely to check the names of
various Soviet agents, including his own, against the FBI's
records. When to his dismay he learned that he had acquired
an FBI file, Feldman had fled to Canada, but before his departure he cleaned out all the bank accounts he had been given
access to. He successfully eluded the FBI's surveillance
teams and went to ground across the border.

Ovakimian was to be the last NKVD *rezident* to be an
illegal. His replacement was Vassilli Zubilin, whose wife
Elizaveta was also a senior NKVD officer. Together they
had operated as illegals in America throughout most of the
1930s, but in January 1942 he was posted to the Soviet

Embassy in Washington with the rank of third secretary. By the time he was recalled to Moscow, in August 1944, he had been promoted to the rank of second secretary and had supervised an extensive spy ring that had penetrated to the heart of the Allied atomic weapons programme.

Canada had become such a centre of pre-war Soviet espionage that in later years the RCMP undertook a long-term study of the techniques adopted by the Soviets to manipulate Canada's passports. Codenamed WEST WIND, the RCMP learned that the practice known to the *cognoscenti* as 'tombstoning', the use of birth details taken from the deceased to acquire legitimate travel papers, had been perfected by Soviet illegal support officers. It was also realised that Haileybury, a small town in northern Ontario on the western shore of Lake Timiskaming, had become a favourite with Soviet personnel because two devastating fires, in 1906 and 1922, had destroyed all the local records, making it virtually impossible to verify the details of individuals purporting to be Canadian citizens from the district. Once the RCMP discovered the loophole and that dozens of passports had been issued, counter-intelligence officers around the world were alerted to watch for the estimated forty illegals identified by RCMP officers who had cross-referenced passport applications with names purporting to have come from the area of Haileybury. For a small town of just 4,000 inhabitants it certainly appeared to have acquired more than its fair share of foreign travellers – and Soviet agents.

2 · Der Rote Kapelle

I belong to a generation that has been sacrificed by history.
Leopold Trepper in *The Great Game*[1]

While the American networks were moving from the control
of illegals to that of the Embassy in Washington DC and the
Consulate-General in New York, the opposite was happening
in Europe. Stalin could not have anticipated the Nazi blitzkrieg
which swept through Europe in 1940, but the Soviet reliance
on illegals, run in isolation from the diplomatic missions, certainly worked to his advantage. Manipulating the ease with
which Canadian passports could be obtained, and exploiting
Belgium's traditional tolerance to foreign espionage conducted against third parties, Soviet illegals gathered in Brussels
to concentrate operations in the remainder of Western
Europe. The key figure in the development of what was to
become a vast military intelligence spy ring was a Pole who
carried a Canadian passport, number 43761, in the name of
Adam Mikler and issued in Ottawa on 12 July 1937. Mikler
gave his address to the Belgian authorities as 131 rue
St Louis, Quebec, and took up residence with his wife and
son in Brussels at 198 Avenue Richard Neyberg. However,
although Mikler's passport was authentic, a check revealed
that it had originally been granted to Michael Dzumaga,
formerly of Winnipeg, who had reported his travel papers
lost during the Spanish Civil War when he had fought on the

Republican side in the Mackenzie Papineau Battalion. The address in the rue St Louis did not exist. Mikler's wife's passport, number 45584, was discovered to have been issued in August 1937 to Agnes Syme, *née* Lockie, who had once had close links with the Communist Party in Holland. In fact, Mikler's true name was Leopold Trepper and his son had not been born in Vancouver, as stated on his wife's passport, but in Moscow. He was an experienced GRU officer, trained by General Orlov, and had lived in France and Palestine before his assignment to build a network in Western Europe. When the German counter-espionage authorities came to unravel the extraordinary complexities of Trepper's organisation, they called him 'the big chief' and dubbed his network '*Der Rote Kapelle*', or Red Chapel, but it also became known as the Red Orchestra and the Red Choir.

Aged twenty-seven, Trepper had first arrived in Belgium in 1931 carrying a Polish passport in his true name and, after studying political science at the Free University of Brussels, had subsequently travelled to the Soviet Union. His return in March 1939, ostensibly from Quebec, marked the foundation of a major GRU network of illegals, which he had planned from Paris where he was residing in December 1936. Like previous rings, it was to be based on a commercial front and the chosen enterprise was the Excellent Raincoat Company, a subsidiary of the Roi du Caoutchouc, a well-established business whose general manager, Léon Grossvogel, was also a former Comintern agent as well as Trepper's acquaintance from Palestine, where they had both lived in the late 1920s. A French Jew of Polish extraction, Grossvogel had worked for the garment manufacturer since 1926, as had his sister Sarah, who was married to one of the directors, Louis Kapelowitz. The new venture was intended to export its well-established and popular product to Scandinavia, with the English market as another objective. Apart from Grossvogel's involvement, the firm was entirely respectable, having Jules Jaspar, formerly the Belgian Consul in Indochina, whose brother had been Prime Minister of Belgium, on the board. Grossvogel's Communist sympathies and his chequered past (he had been cited in a divorce action and had been imprisoned briefly on an assault charge) were known to the company's directors and they had welcomed with relief his decision to initiate an export-orientated subsidiary. Trepper, posing as the wealthy Canadian businessman Mikler, supplied Grossvogel with the necessary capital to open foreign branches in Stockholm and Copenhagen as a preliminary to operating in London, a city he visited several times in 1937 and 1938. Proof of at least one of Grossvogel's trips to Britain was provided by his marriage certificate. In May 1938, he had married Jeanne Pesant at the Holborn Registry Office in London, and on this occasion he may have been accompanied by Trepper.

Trepper's interest in England has been pieced together from several different sources, one of which was Ernest D. Weiss, a key figure in what became known as the British branch of the *Rote Kapelle*. Born in Breslau in 1902, Weiss had been recruited into the GRU by a former university contemporary and had agreed to travel to England on a long-term mission.[2] He arrived on 11 May 1932 and was supervised by an illegal support officer codenamed HARRY I, who arranged for him to meet two seamen who subsequently acted as his couriers. This mysterious controller has never been identified, but it is believed that he went to the United States for a brief visit in December 1932, but had returned in time to introduce Weiss to Robert Switz in September 1933 in Kensington Gardens. Two months later Switz and his wife Marjorie were arrested in Paris and, according to Weiss, who supported himself by playing the piano, this was the first moment that he realised that he was involved in Soviet espionage. Whether true or not, Weiss was clearly undeterred by the newspaper reports from France of Switz's arrest, for late in 1935 he went to Enge in Switzerland to meet his new controller, HARRY II. This meeting resulted in Weiss handling British secrets stolen by two Soviet agents, an Air Ministry official named Major Wilfred Vernon and an Irishman, Frederick Meredith. Both were overt CPGB members working at the Royal Aircraft Establishment at Farnborough, who had visited Russia in a group of eight tourists in May 1932. Weiss, who had by now adopted the identity of 'Walter Lock', ran Vernon and Meredith until August 1937, when, during his absence on holiday, Vernon's home was ransacked by burglars. In the subsequent police investigation, Vernon was found to have accumulated a quantity of classified documents, and this led to his prosecution and dismissal in October on a charge of unauthorised possession of government papers. However, the authorities never realised that the relatively trivial offence of which Vernon was convicted was infinitely preferable to him than espionage, which would have been more appropriate. Significantly, Vernon had confided in his defence counsel, Denis Pritt KC MP, but the latter had deliberately suppressed the information. When Meredith later disclosed this to MI5, its suspicions of Pritt, already renowned as a Soviet apologist, heightened considerably.

Soon after the Vernon case Weiss was assigned a new controller, a man he knew as ANDRE but who was later identified as a GRU illegal named Henri Robinson. Born in 1897 in Germany, his father a Russian Jew, Robinson studied in Geneva during the First World War and became closely associated with the Communist Youth International. In 1936, he was working alongside the Soviet Military Attaché in Paris before being placed in charge of all the French and English networks the following year, but there is some evidence that he lost Moscow's confidence during the purges. Upon the outbreak of war he was ordered to subordinate his activities to Trepper, and reluctantly he obeyed. There was no love lost between the two men, and their mutual hostility was later to be exploited by the Germans.

Weiss's cover was so good that when he was called up for military service in England, he went undetected and was granted a commission. After the war he worked as a concert pianist and his first encounter with MI5 occurred when he was interviewed by Jim Skardon at the end of a recital he had given in the Albert Hall. He co-operated fully with the Security Service and was never prosecuted. He died in 1982 without disclosing to any of his friends his secret role as a GRU agent.

One curiosity about the Soviet concentration of effort on

England at this time is the number of illegals deployed there to run a relative handful of known sources. As well as Trepper, Robinson and HARRYS I and II had been active, as had Theodore Maly and the Brandeses. In addition, another Soviet illegal, General Waldemar Ozols, is known to have visited Britain between 1934 and 1939, and yet another GRU officer, Henri Pieck, had run the Foreign Office spy, Captain John King, so there would appear to have been a distinct imbalance between the number of illegals operating in London and the very few agents now known to have worked for them. This implies that there were rather more Soviet sources in London than has been discovered hitherto. When one considers that two important Soviet agents, Donald Maclean and Kim Philby, spent much of this period abroad, it can only be concluded that there were others in the same mould to occupy the illegal talent apparently based in the capital.

According to testimony given to MI5 by Weiss, his circuit had been quite small. He had received scientific information from a German refugee named Hans Lubszynski, a former Telefunken radio engineer who had come to England in 1934. Lubszynski was in turn in contact with an unwitting source, a physicist from Berlin named Dr Heinz Kallmann, then working as a researcher pioneering television technology for EMI. However, Kallmann had moved to the United States in February 1939, thus reducing Lubszynski's usefulness. Weiss's other contacts included André Labarthe, a scientist who had worked for the French Ministry of Air until 1938; Professor Marcel Prenant of the Sorbonne, who was a leading French biologist and prominent Communist; and Jacques Soustelle, another academic who was to rise high in de Gaulle's intelligence service.

Whatever the reason for the disproportionate accumulation of illegals in London, where Anton V. Schuster was the NKVD *rezident* at the Embassy under second secretary cover, and Simon D. Kremer, secretary to the Military Attaché, headed the GRU's office, the GRU was intent upon expanding its range of contacts inside the British Isles. In March 1939, Trepper was assigned another Soviet intelligence officer to assist with communications. Lieutenant

Mikhail Makarov, who had fought in the Spanish Civil War
as a pilot, had travelled to Brussels on a circuitous route via
Stockholm, Copenhagen and Paris, where he had adopted
the identity of a Uruguayan named Carlos Alamo. Reputedly
the nephew of the Soviet Foreign Minister, Vyacheslav Molotov, Makarov had been born in Leningrad and had first
entered Belgium in January 1934, aged thirty-one, while in
transit to America. Once established in Belgium Makarov
was posted to Ostend by Trepper, where he took over the
management of the local branch of the Excellent Raincoat
Company which had previously been run by Léon Grossvogel's wife, Jeanne. Makarov was to use the company as a
cover for his true role, that of wireless operator offering
technical training courses to Trepper's recruits.

One of Trepper's first students was Viktor Guryevitch,
another veteran of the Spanish Civil War, who had been born
in St Petersburg in 1911 but travelled on a Uruguayan passport, issued in New York in April 1936, in the name of Vincente Sierra from Montevideo. Prior to his arrival in Ghent
in July 1939, where he had kept a rendezvous with Trepper,
Guryevitch had spent two years in France, based in Marseilles, and had operated briefly in Germany, probably as a
courier. Once in Belgium, he enrolled as a student of languages at Brussels University and, later that summer, made
a trip to Switzerland to introduce himself to the GRU's local
network. However, in addition to taking a course in commerce, he was taught cipher procedures by Trepper and
acquired a wealthy mistress, Margarete Barcza, who happened to have an apartment in the same building as his, in
the Avenue Emile de Beco. When Margarete's Czech husband died in March 1940, she moved in with Guryevitch and
subsequently introduced him to friends whom he persuaded
to join the board of Simexco, his import-export company,
thus lending it an air of respectability when it was registered
in March 1941. Despite a magnetic personality, and all his
undoubted skills as an illegal, Guryevitch never shook off his
peasant origins. He was fascinated by sumptuous restaurants, where he invariably drew attention to himself by
ordering too much food and drinking the equivalent of half a

bottle of spirits before a meal. He never got used to leather shoes and often bought several identical pairs at a time, apparently convinced of some impending scarcity.[3]

When the Germans swept through Belgium in May 1940, Trepper's network was unprepared. Makarov's Ostend branch of the Excellent Raincoat Company was bombed out by the Luftwaffe, and Trepper was forced to make a hazardous journey to the resort town of Knokke-le-Zoute to retrieve a wireless transmitter hidden in a seaside villa. A measure of protection for Trepper's party, which included Grossvogel, was afforded by the presence of the (apparently innocent) Bulgarian Consul, who drove the car in an attempt to trace Bulgarians isolated on the coast by the fighting. Another motive for the dangerous trip was to obtain accurate information about the Wehrmacht's advance through Belgium. Having survived the German invasion, Makarov moved to Brussels and, early in July, Trepper fled to France, leaving his network in the hands of Guryevitch.

Once in France, Trepper made contact with General Susloparov, the Soviet Military Attaché in Vichy, and arranged for his wife and son to return to Moscow via Marseilles. After their departure in August 1940, Trepper established himself in Paris as a businessman named 'Jean Gilbert' and opened the Société Import-Export (Simex) with Grossvogel. Once Simex had begun operating, Trepper ventured back to Brussels under his French identity to liaise with Guryevitch and to see his beautiful American mistress, Georgie de Winter, who had borne him a son, Patrick, in September 1939. De Winter played no direct part in Trepper's network, but she had believed the story he had told her, that he was a secret agent working for British Intelligence. Meanwhile, Guryevitch continued to run Simexco without any adverse interference from the Germans and succeeded in negotiating several useful contracts with the occupation forces. Simex/Simexco's business relationship with the enemy flourished and not only provided useful cover for Trepper and his network, but also gave them travel facilities.

The first major problem experienced by the network occurred during the night of 12/13 December 1941, when the

German Abwehr, guided by radio direction-finders, raided 101 rue des Attrebates in the Etterbeck district of Brussels and arrested an illicit wireless operator who gave his name as de Smets. In fact, de Smets was Lieutenant Anton Danilov of the GRU, who had been posted to Paris as an assistant military attaché in 1938 and had subsequently worked in that capacity in Vichy. In mid-1941, he had moved to Brussels to work for Guryevitch as a communications expert. Danilov had been transmitting early in the morning of 13 December as the Germans burst into the house and, in a fierce struggle, was injured and overcome. A few hours later Trepper, who happened to be visiting Brussels, called at the house and was questioned by the Germans, but he was sufficiently well equipped with authentic permits from the Nazi construction agency, the Todt Organisation, to bluff his way out of a potentially very awkward situation. Alerted to Danilov's arrest, Trepper succeeded in warning Guryevitch of what had happened, and he promptly fled to Paris. Unfortunately, Makarov was not so lucky; he also called at the house on the day of Danilov's arrest and was taken into custody.

The discovery of Danilov's safe-house was to prove of exceptional value to the Germans. Although he himself gave minimal co-operation, and was to be executed two years later, the woman who was the principal tenant in the building, Rita Arnould, immediately turned informer and revealed her role as a courier and wireless operator in a ring headed by Guryevitch. Recently widowed, she also disclosed that her lover, a Belgian diamond merchant named Isadore Springer, was an important Soviet agent, a member of the German Communist Party with experience of operating in Palestine, France and the International Brigade in Spain. Like Guryevitch, Springer evaded arrest and moved to France, where he started a new network in Lyons.

The other occupant in the house, also a member of Guryevitch's cell, was Sofia Posnanska, a Polish Jewess whose husband was later to work with Springer in Lyons. She had been one of Trepper's subordinates in Paris in 1940 and had received cipher training in Moscow before the war. Rather than collaborate with her captors, like her friend Rita, she committed

Chart 1 Trepper's group at the time of the arrest of Makarov and Danilov (December 1941)*

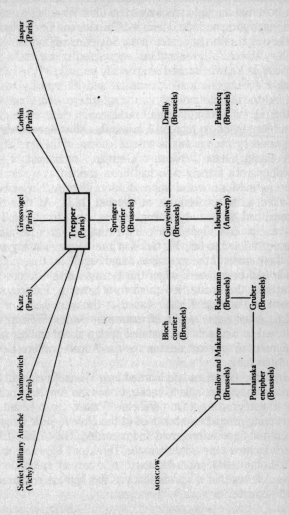

* Charts 1–7 are from MI5's report, *The Rote Kapelle*, by Michael Serpell and Robert Hemblys-Scales.

suicide in St Gilles prison, Brussels. Meanwhile, Rita Arnould betrayed a forger's workshop concealed in her house and, from passport photographs recovered in this Aladdin's cave of espionage paraphernalia, identified Trepper and Guryevitch as the key figures at the centre of the Soviet organisation.

The Abwehr's investigation, conducted under the code-name *Rote Kapelle*, stalled temporarily because of the intransigence of Danilov and Posnanska, and its inability to put names to the network's two ringleaders who had disappeared. Its next significant breakthrough came some eight months later, on 30 July 1942, when the Abwehr radio direction-finders closed in on the attic of a house in Laeken. There they found Johann Wenzel, a German Communist of long standing from Danzig who had been trained as a wireless operator in Moscow and was in Belgium illegally, having been expelled as an undesirable in October 1937. At that time Wenzel had been studying engineering, but early the following year he had slipped back into Brussels. After his arrest Wenzel refused to help his German interrogators in any way, but their study of the messages found beside his transmitter, which had been warm when the German investigators had burst into the house, led them to a hitherto undiscovered branch of the *Rote Kapelle* based at the very heart of the Reich. After eight weeks of torture in Berlin, Wenzel was returned to Brussels and installed with a guard and his radio equipment in an apartment in the rue Aurore, where he co-operated fully.

Once the Germans had learned how Wenzel's ciphers had worked, they were able to backtrack and the Abwehr's principal cryptographer, Dr Wilhelm Vauck, succeeded in decrypting around two hundred of the *Rote Kapelle*'s signals which had been intercepted and recorded. On 15 July 1942, Vauck tackled a message from the 'Direktor', Moscow, dated 10 October 1941 and addressed to a certain KENT, one of several texts that disclosed data of the highest significance to the counter-espionage investigators:

KL 3 DE RTX 1010–1725 WDS GBT FROM DIREKTOR TO KENT PERSONAL:

Proceed immediately Berlin three addresses indicated and determine causes failure radio connections. If interruptions recur take over broadcasts. Work three Berlin groups and transmission information top priority. Addresses: Neuwestend, Altenburger allee 19, third right; Coro Charlottenburg, Frederiastrasse 26a second left, Volf-Friedenau, Kaiserstrasse 18 fourth left. Bauer. Call name here 'Eulenspiegel'. Password: 'Direktor'. Report before 20 October. New plan repeat new in force for three stations GBT AR KLS RTX.[4]

It did not take the Gestapo long to establish the identities of the occupants of these three suspect addresses, who were placed under surveillance. They were Harro Schulze-Boysen of the Air Ministry; Arvid von Harnack, a respected university lecturer who ran a widespread organisation with sources in both the Abwehr and the Kriegsmarine; and Adam Kuckhoff, a film producer. Another of these compromising messages, decoded by Vauck, referred to Saalestrasse 36, the Berlin address of a young woman named Ilse who was also of some importance. If the Germans had any doubts about her identity, the grotesque indiscretion that had compromised so many agents was compounded by a signal dated 28 August 1941, decrypted retrospectively, which made it clear that Ilse was her true name: 'An important agent known as ILSE will in the future be designated under the cover name ALTE . . .'

Gestapo enquiries showed that Ilse Stoebe was working for Theodor Wolff at the German Foreign Ministry and that before the war she had been a correspondent for various Swiss newspapers. She was arrested by the Gestapo in Hamburg and, under interrogation, revealed that she had been the mistress of Rudolf Herrnstadt, the notorious *Berliner Tageblatt* journalist who had defected to Moscow in 1933. Despite the seniority and sensitivity of her post, Ilse had kept in touch with Herrnstadt, who became a senior GRU officer supervising clandestine air drops into Germany, and had even allowed her address to be given to GRU parachutists as a safe-house. Before her execution on 22 December 1942, she had implicated the three most important members of the German *Rote Kapelle*: Schulze-Boysen, von Harnack and Rudolf von Scheliha, a diplomat in the information section of the German Foreign Ministry. Once Ilse had named

Schulze-Boysen and von Harnack, their entire network amounting to eighty sub-agents was rounded up and either hanged or beheaded without delay.

The subsequent RHSA (the Reich security agency) investigation concluded that von Harnack and Schulze-Boysen, both Communist activists for many years, had only been recruited by the GRU as recently as 1941. They had been given a wireless transmitter by Alexander Erdberg of the Soviet Trade Delegation in Berlin before its withdrawal in June 1941, but they never achieved direct contact with Moscow, as intended. In August 1941, Viktor Guryevitch had given them another set, but again they failed to establish direct contact and instead had relied upon couriers to pass messages to the Soviet Embassy in Stockholm and to Wenzel in Brussels. This was the fatal flaw in an otherwise well-organised network, for Wenzel's arrest and the capture of his ciphers compromised the rest. Certainly, the quality of the material reaching Moscow from Berlin was unprecedented, for among the members of the ring were Herbert Gollnow, an Abwehr liaison officer at OKW headquarters responsible for supervising clandestine air operations on the eastern front; Leutnant Wolfgang Havemann of naval intelligence; and Horst Heilmann, an Abwehr cryptographer who was having an affair with Schulze-Boysen's wife, Libertas. All were interrogated and then hanged at Ploetzensee prison.

Von Scheliha, a more experienced Soviet agent, suffered the same fate. He had been recruited while serving at the German Embassy in Warsaw in 1934 and had been paid for his information through a Swiss bank. As well as being compromised by Ilse Stoebe, he was incriminated by Heinrich Koenen, a German Communist who parachuted into Osterode in east Prussia in October 1942 with instructions to contact Ilse; by the time Koenen landed, she was already in the hands of the Gestapo. When he was arrested on 22 October, he was found to be carrying a receipt confirming a transfer of $7,500 to von Scheliha's bank account.

Simex and Simexco survived the German occupation until November 1942, when raids were mounted simultaneously

Chart 2 Schulze-Boysen's network

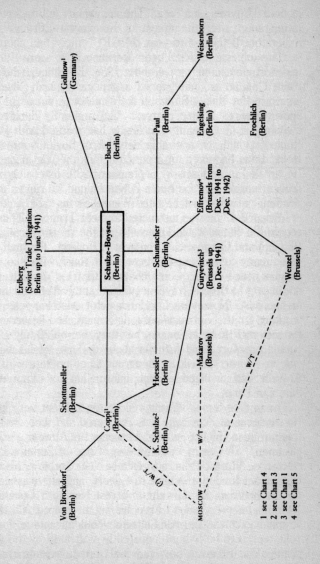

1 see Chart 4
2 see Chart 3
3 see Chart 1
4 see Chart 5

in both Brussels and Paris. The companies fell under suspicion soon after the arrest of Konstantin Effremov, an
experienced, thirty-two-year-old GRU officer and chemical
warfare expert, who had been operating in Western Europe
under student cover since about 1936. Effremov, who had
trained as an engineer, used a genuine Finnish passport
issued in the United States in the name of Jernstroem, but,
shortly before Wenzel's arrest, had prudently decided to
switch to a new identity. Effremov had worked with Henri
Robinson, had run a sizable network of Soviet sources in
Holland and had lived for a period before the war in Zurich.
He arrived in Brussels in September 1939, ostensibly as a
student enrolled at the Ecole Polytechnique, to run an independent network, but he used Wenzel as his radio link and
in March 1942 he was instructed to meet Trepper. Thus he
acquired a considerable knowledge of the rings operating in
Belgium and Guryevitch's contacts in Holland. Through one
of his many contacts he had been put in touch with a corrupt
Belgian police officer, Chief Inspector Charles Mathieu, who
had access to Belgian travel documents and had proved useful
in the past. However, Chief Inspector Mathieu was also
working for the Germans as an informant, and he arranged
for Effremov to be arrested when they met on 22 July 1942.
Under pressure, and anxious about the fate of his young
wife in Russia, the Ukrainian agreed to co-operate with the
Abwehr and divulged enough information to compromise
Simex in Paris.

The raid on Simex initially yielded the Abwehr very little.
No evidence of espionage was recovered and there was no
trace of 'Jean Gilbert', who had become the Abwehr's principal target. However, interrogation of one of Simex's Paris
directors, Alfred Corbin, suggested a clue. Corbin or his wife
had recommended a dentist to Gilbert, and surveillance on
the surgery led the Abwehr to arrest him on 5 December
1942 as he prepared to have his teeth treated. Catching
Trepper gave the Germans a tremendous advantage, for he
volunteered to help them, apparently motivated by the very
justifiable fear that the Soviets would execute his entire family
if they learned of his arrest. While the Sicherheitsdienst (SD)

Chart 3 Von Scheliha's network

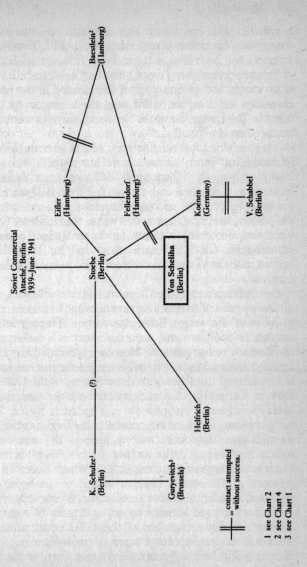

Soviet Commercial Attaché, Berlin 1939–June 1941

Baestlein[2] (Hamburg)

Eifler (Hamburg)

Fellendorf (Hamburg)

Koenen (Germany)

V. Schabbel (Berlin)

Stoebe (Berlin)

Von Scheliha (Berlin)

Helfrich (Berlin)

(?)

K. Schulze[1] (Berlin)

Guryevitch (Brussels)

╪ = contact attempted without success.

1 see Chart 2
2 see Chart 4
3 see Chart 1

negotiated with Trepper, it took elaborate steps to prevent
the news of his arrest from leaking. Most of the *Rote Kapelle*
suspects had been kept in the isolation cells in a special wing
of Fresnes prison, but Trepper was held separately in a suite
of rooms on the ground floor of the building in the rue des
Saussaies which formerly had been the headquarters of the
Sûreté. The remainder of the Sonderkommando was accommodated on the fifth floor.

Trepper's capture came only a fortnight after the arrest in
Marseilles of Viktor Guryevitch and his mistress, Margarete
Barcza. Unwisely, Guryevitch had opened a branch of
Simexco in Marseilles after he had fled from Belgium following the arrests there, and once Effremov had started to help
the enemy, the Simex cover was worse than useless. Guryevitch was escorted to Berlin for interrogation, where he
admitted his GRU codename KENT and, in March 1943,
agreed to transmit to Moscow from Paris as MARS, under SD
control.

By Christmas 1942 the Germans had unravelled an extraordinary series of interlocking networks and had taken control
of most of the senior Soviet personnel. Trepper seemed
entirely co-operative and, agreeing to act as a double agent,
initiated a wireless link with Moscow codenamed EIFFEL. He
ensured Robinson's arrest and arranged for the entrapment
of Grossvogel, together with three others, at the Café de la
Paix in Paris. He also denounced Springer and thereby
betrayed an entire independent ring based in Lyons. Trepper's help was of critical importance to the Germans because,
through him, they were able to recover the now famous
Robinson papers, a virtual archive of Soviet illegal activity in
Europe dating back to the 1920s. When Robinson was
arrested in December 1942, a search of his hotel room
revealed a briefcase hidden under the floorboards, full of
documents, forged identity papers and texts of messages.
Among the many branches of the GRU compromised by
Robinson was an important wireless transmitter run by Dr
Hersog Sokol for the French Communist Party at his home
in Le Rancy, through which Trepper had relayed messages
to Moscow via London. Although Polish in origin, Sokol was

a physician prominent in the Belgian Communist Party. He and his wife Mariam were arrested on 9 June 1942 and both later died in captivity.

As well as scrutinising the veritable goldmine of the Robinson papers, and obtaining Trepper's apparently enthusiastic assistance, the Germans also persuaded Konstantin Effremov to change sides and work as a double agent. A jealous anti-Semite from Sawotzki, Effremov hated being subordinate to the Jews who dominated the GRU and lost no time in making radio contact with Moscow, codenamed PASCAL, under the direction of the Germans. He also lured two of his contacts into a trap. The first, Herman Isbutsky, had been running his own organisation in his native Antwerp and had relied upon Johann Wenzel for his communications. He was executed soon after his arrest in late July 1942 and a radio link, codenamed BOB, developed in his absence. Effremov's second victim was Maurice Peper, a Jew from Amsterdam who had been recruited into the GRU while a seaman in the Dutch merchant marine. Both Peper and Isbutsky were arrested together at a meeting called by Effremov, but only Peper agreed to help the Germans. He admitted his role as a liaison officer with a separate Dutch network codenamed HILDA and led his captors to its leader in Amsterdam, Anton Winterink. A prominent Dutch Communist, Winterink was arrested in an Amsterdam restaurant in August 1942 and, after two weeks of interrogation, agreed to re-establish a wireless link to Moscow, codenamed TANNE by the Germans, on the radio that had been discovered at his home. The Abwehr regarded Winterink's capture as a significant coup because they had already correctly suspected him of being TINO, the head of a dangerous Communist Party cell.

Winterink's attempt to deceive the GRU appeared initially to fail because Moscow had been warned of his capture by other members of HILDA who had witnessed his arrest, but TINO seems to have persuaded the Soviets that he had escaped. Accordingly, Moscow maintained the wireless link with him until March or April 1944, when he was instructed to stop transmitting and join the resistance. This order

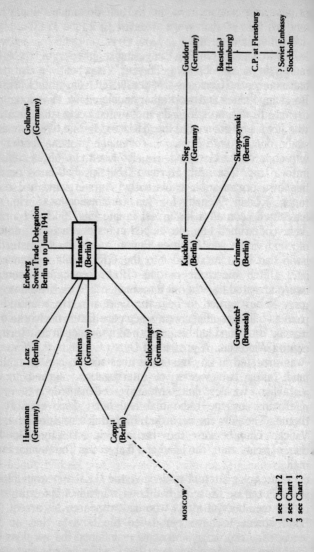

Chart 4 Harnack's network

Gollnow[1]
(Germany)

Erdberg
Soviet Trade Delegation
Berlin up to June 1941

Harnack
(Berlin)

Sieg
(Germany)

Guddorf
(Germany)

Baestlein[3]
(Hamburg)

C.P. at Flensburg

? Soviet Embassy
Stockholm

Skrzypczynski
(Berlin)

Kuckhoff
(Berlin)

Grimme
(Berlin)

Guryevitch[2]
(Brussels)

Lenz
(Berlin)

Havemann
(Germany)

Behrens
(Germany)

Schloesinger
(Germany)

Coppi[1]
(Berlin)

MOSCOW

1 see Chart 2
2 see Chart 1
3 see Chart 3

proved to be a death sentence as the Germans no longer had any use for him and he was executed.

With Winterink, Effremov and EIFFEL in radio contact with Moscow, and Guryevitch promising to co-operate, the Germans had much to be pleased about. They believed that they had taken control of most of the GRU's illegal networks in Belgium, France and the Netherlands, and had eliminated the organisation's entire branch in Germany, but the situation was actually rather more complicated. In fact, Trepper had succeeded in both winning the confidence of the Germans, who thought that he had genuinely switched sides, and alerting Moscow Centre to his arrest. Similarly, Wenzel eluded his German captors in November 1942 and sent a message to the Soviet Embassy in London that Effremov was in enemy hands and that his radio was operating under control. Although Trepper appears to have betrayed a large number of his subordinates to the enemy, he kept a single contact at liberty and used this line of communication to keep Moscow informed of developments. The GRU responded by protecting its star agent and participating in a complicated triple game of wireless deception, a *funkspiel*, which may have been part of a sophisticated contingency plan but certainly one that was to be maintained until Trepper's escape from German captivity in September 1943.

Trepper was later to insist that his escape had been prompted by his discovery that the Abwehr had closed down a previously unknown transmitter run by the French Communist Party near Lyons, and recovered a large quantity of backtraffic which was to be scrutinised by the celebrated Dr Vauck. Trepper had used this undisclosed channel for his communications to Moscow and feared that the Sonderkommando was on the point of learning how he had duped his captors. Accordingly, Trepper eluded his escort while under guard in the centre of Paris and went into hiding for the rest of the war. Intriguingly, Trepper wrote four letters to the Sonderkommando, in which he pretended to have been the victim of an abduction, and reassured Heinz Paulsen, a senior SD officer, that Moscow remained ignorant of the *funkspiel*.

Notwithstanding Trepper's escape, and despite the

Abwehr's confidence that the *Rote Kapelle* had been eliminated, the network continued to function, albeit under German
supervision. Effremov, for example, ran the PASCAL radio link
from Breendonck prison until April 1944, when he was moved
to a house at 63 rue de Courcelles, where Guryevitch was
being held. Similarly, Guryevitch had operated the MARS
transmitter since March 1943 from a ten-bedroomed villa at
40 avenue Victor Hugo in Neuilly, which was the residence
of Sturmbannführer Karl Boemelburg, the head of the SD in
Paris. That Guryevitch and his mistress, Margarete Barcza,
enjoyed a considerable degree of freedom is evident from the
birth of their son, Michel, in April 1944. The German decision
to develop MARS was rewarded on 14 March 1943, when
Guryevitch was instructed by Moscow to make contact with
a hitherto undiscovered network run by Waldemar Ozols, a
former Latvian general who had fought with the International
Brigade in the Spanish Civil War. Guryevitch found him at
the address supplied by Moscow and learned from Ozols that
he and his small organisation had been run by the Soviet Air
Attaché in Paris; however, when the Soviets withdrew from
France in 1940, he had been left with a wireless transmitter
but no operator. Accordingly, Ozols had gone underground,
waiting to be contacted. Under Guryevitch's directions, Ozols
reformed his network and linked up with MITHRIDATE, a resistance group in Marseilles headed by Colonel Bressac and an
elderly captain in the reserve, Paul Legendre. In consequence, MITHRIDATE effectively came under German control,
but only one of its members, Marcel Droubaix, seems to
have realised what had happened. Droubaix, a Frenchman
who had been educated in England and had served in the
Royal Horse Artillery during the Great War, suspected German penetration in June 1944, but was arrested the following
month while attending a meeting with Guryevitch in Paris
and was to die at Buchenwald in February 1945.

The German villa in Neuilly also accommodated various
other captured GRU personnel. Trepper stayed there until
his escape in September 1943, and his colleagues there
included his assistant, Hillel Katz, whom he had betrayed
almost as soon as he was arrested. Like Trepper, Katz was

a Polish Jew and had been a member of the Communist Party in Palestine. He was an important figure in the *Rote Kapelle* as he had acted as Trepper's link between Grossvogel, Simex and Henri Robinson. He too willingly co-operated with the Germans, as did Otto Schumacher, a German who had fought for the Republicans during the Spanish Civil War. It was at Schumacher's house in Laeken that Johann Wenzel had been arrested in June 1942, and from that moment he was a marked man. He had promptly fled to Lyons, where he had joined Isadore Springer, but after Trepper's arrest he had been moved to Paris, where he was caught early in 1943.

Although it would appear that the Germans had gained the upper hand in the *funkspiel* conducted with Moscow, there remains some doubt about both the fate of those involved and the loyalties of those known to have survived. Trepper, for example, remained in hiding in Paris until the end of the war, when he emerged and reported to Colonel Novikov, the head of the Soviet military mission in Paris. Novikov arranged for Trepper to be flown to Moscow on 6 January 1945, where he was thrown into the Lubyanka, only to emerge in March 1953 after the death of Stalin. He returned to Poland, where he became a leader of what was left of the Jewish community, but he remained the subject of suspicion until 1973, when, after a lengthy international campaign, he eventually received permission to emigrate to Israel. His controversial memoirs, *The Great Game*, were published in Paris in 1975, but only after he had successfully sued Jean Rochet, the director of the French domestic security agency, the Direction de la Surveillance du Territoire (DST), for defamation when the latter had accused Trepper of having collaborated with the enemy.

Guryevitch suffered much the same experience as Trepper and, having been released from the KGB prison at Vorkonta in 1956, now lives in his native St Petersburg. Anton Danilov, Henri Robinson and Leon Grossvogel died in German captivity, as did Isadore Springer and Otto Schumacher. Johann Wenzel reportedly ended the war in Holland, having escaped from the Germans in mid-November 1942 by knocking out the guard on his apartment in Brussels, but was imprisoned in Moscow by an ungrateful NKVD after he had made his way to Moscow. According to the most recent estimates, 217 arrests were made in connection with the *Rote Kapelle* investigation, of whom 143 committed suicide, died in captivity or were executed.

At the end of the war Allied investigators seized many of the German records of the *Rote Kapelle* investigation, and in later years a determined effort was made to piece together the fragments of the story. Guryevitch and Trepper maintained their silence for many years, but some of the Germans who had supervised the *funkspiel* were traced and interrogated. It became clear that in July 1942, when the scale of the Soviet network emerged, a special joint counter-intelligence unit, a Sonderkommando, was formed under the leadership of an SD officer, Karl Giering. Unfortunately, Giering had died of cancer in a Paris hospital in 1943, and his chief, Karl Boemelburg, died after an accident in Germany in December 1946, but there were others to be found. The first arrests, of Danilov and Makarov in November 1941 in Etterbeek, had been made by Captain Henri Piepe of the Ghent branch of the Abwehr IIIF. Piepe had also been responsible for catching Wenzel and was later transferred to the Sonderkommando in Paris. Much later, when he had become a businessman in Hamburg, he was to describe Trepper's interrogation to the CIA.

Piepe's version of events was largely confirmed by Wilhelm Berg, who had been Trepper's escort when he had slipped away, but the British suspected that the former Kriminal-inspektor, who had served as Ribbentrop's bodyguard in Moscow, may have fallen under the influence of the Soviets and might even have been recruited by Trepper (a charge he denied). Other useful SD sources were Horst Kopkow, who was interrogated in 1947, and Heinrich Reiser, a former prisoner of war in England during the First World War, who had been Giering's deputy. Obersturmbannführer Reiser was transferred from the Paris Sonderkommando to a Gestapo job in Karlsruhe during the summer of 1943, following the arrival of Heinz Paulsen, and later wrote a book about the *Rote Kapelle*. He retired to Stuttgart and was interviewed.

Paulsen, who called himself Pannwitz, was posted to Paris in March 1943 following his investigation into the assassination of Reinhard Heydrich in Prague. Paulsen took charge of the Sonderkommando from Giering, who was in failing health. He remained in Paris until 16 August 1944, when he withdrew with Guryevitch and the rest of the Sonderkommando to Hornberg in the Black Forest and then to Wurzberg in the Tauber valley, where they burned what remained of their records. In May 1945, he and Guryevitch, who had moved into a chalet near Budenz in Austria, surrendered to the local French occupation troops and were returned to Paris. On 7 June 1945, they were flown to Moscow on Stalin's personal plane, interrogated by the head of Smersh, the notorious Viktor S. Abakumov, and imprisoned. Paulsen was sentenced to twenty-five years' imprisonment, but was released in 1954. After his return to Stuttgart, he became a banker and also undertook some contract work for the West German intelligence agency, the Bundesnachrichtendienst (BND).

The view commonly held by the German survivors was summed up by Paulsen, who remarked to the CIA that, 'the Germans succeeded not only in locating and liquidating the clandestine networks in Brussels, Berlin, Amsterdam and Paris, but also in doubling the Soviet agents, and by virtue of the *funkspiel* in intoxicating the Soviets with false information'.[5]

However, this is sharply contradicted by Trepper, who maintains that it was the Germans who were the victims of an elaborate deception campaign. He insists that he betrayed no one and that 'the Centre made perfect use of the Great Game to ask, constantly, for more military information. After February 1943, the Germans were forced to give Moscow information that a normally functioning network, however powerful, would have had trouble obtaining.'[6]

The issue of Trepper's loyalties is central to the consideration of the relative success of the GRU and the SD. In November 1943, Moscow alerted Guryevitch that Trepper was a traitor, but was this an authentic warning or another dimension to an increasingly complex deception? From the analysis undertaken by the CIA, it is clear that the Agency

Chart 5 Effremov's network

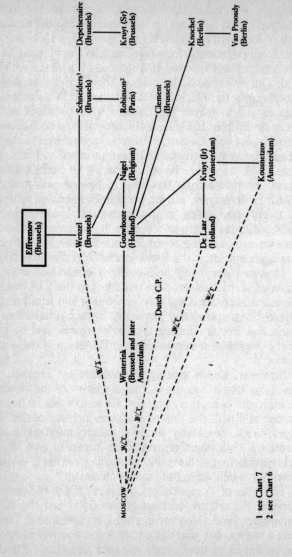

Effremov (Brussels)

Wenzel (Brussels)

Gouwlooze (Holland)

De Laar (Holland)

Schneiders[1] (Brussels)

Depelsenaire (Brussels)

Kruyt (Sr) (Brussels)

Robinson[2] (Paris)

Nagel (Belgium)

Clement (Brussels)

Knochel (Berlin)

Van Proosdy (Berlin)

Kruyt (Jr) (Amsterdam)

Kousnetzov (Amsterdam)

Winterink (Brussels and later Amsterdam)

Dutch C.P.

MOSCOW

W/T

1 see Chart 7
2 see Chart 6

Chart 6 Robinson's network

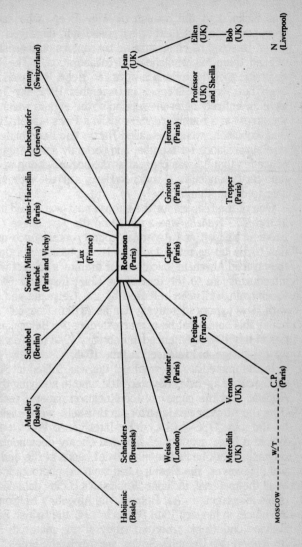

was inclined to the opinion of Willy Berg, who said that 'Trepper appeared neither surprised nor dismayed by his arrest. Instead he congratulated his captors on their skill and offered them his wholehearted collaboration.'[7] The CIA is emphatic that the evidence points to Henri Robinson having been 'betrayed by Trepper' in December 1942, but Trepper gave an entirely different version of the events which led to the arrest at a routine rendezvous in a Paris street. He says that Robinson, whom he called Harry, had been under German surveillance for months, and certainly since August. He concedes that he was present at the scene, sitting in a Gestapo car in handcuffs: 'I watched Harry's arrest without being able to do anything.'[8]

One of the reasons for the intense post-war Allied interest in the *Rote Kapelle* was a desire on the part of the British, French, Belgian and American counter-intelligence authorities to tie up as many loose ends as possible. In doing so they traced Abraham Raichmann, Effremov's contact who had introduced him to the duplicitous Chief Inspector Mathieu. Raichmann had been released by the Germans and issued with new papers identifying him as Arthur Roussel. It was under this name that he was arrested by the Belgian authorities in July 1946, sentenced in February 1948 to twelve years for espionage and released in June 1956.

In the immediate aftermath of the war, Allied intelligence and security agencies devoted little time to studying the *Rote Kapelle*, and the copies of the Robinson papers, recovered from the Abwehr headquarters in Brussels, were mislabelled by the joint OSS–SIS Counter-Intelligence War Room and lost in a huge quantity of captured enemy documents. The original papers had fallen into Soviet hands at the end of the war. However, the Gestapo had supplied photostatic copies of all the material, including Robinson's coding data and texts of his messages, to Ast Belgien, the Abwehr's Belgian satellite office, in January 1943. When in 1947 the British Security Service undertook a belated study of this material, headed by Robert V. Hemblys-Scales and Michael Serpell, of the hundreds of documents which made up the Robinson papers, it was realised that the German dismemberment of the *Rote*

Kapelle not only offered a unique insight into Soviet intelligence operations, but also represented an opportunity to complete many of the pre-war investigations and to give clues to current activities. There were references to the code-names of dozens of individual agents, some of whose true identities could be deduced. In a report completed as recently as 1966, MI5 concluded that, apart from the single case of Ernest Weiss, the Robinson papers

did not give any positive lead to spies in situ in the UK. They do, however, indicate that Robinson played an important part in the running of Russian operations in the UK in the 1930s, and it seems . . . that even at this late stage there are a number of points arising out of the Robinson papers worthy of further study on both sides of the Atlantic.[9]

During the war itself comparatively little work had been done on Soviet operations, the security agencies having been inhibited by political considerations. In Britain a ban had been placed on the analysis of the Soviet Embassy's cipher traffic, and it was not until the Gouzenko case in Canada, and the defection of Allan Foote in Berlin, that the evidence materialised of a continued espionage offensive in the West. In subsequent years it transpired that the *Rote Kapelle* had amounted to a snapshot of a vast, worldwide series of inter-locking clandestine networks. Names from the *Rote Kapelle* turned up in the most unexpected contexts. In February 1970, Hans Voelkner was sentenced in Paris to twelve years for espionage; it emerged during the trial that his mother had been Kathe Voelkner, one of Trepper's key agents, who had been arrested in January 1943 and executed. Shortly before Melinda Maclean disappeared from Switzerland in September 1953, following the defection to Moscow of her husband two years earlier, she had been contacted by Mrs Lubszynski, whose son Hans had been identified as a pre-war member of the British branch of the *Rote Kapelle*. Harry Gold, who was convicted of being a member of the Rosenbergs' atomic spy ring in the United States in 1950 and sentenced to thirty years' imprisonment, turned out to be a cousin of Louis Kapelowitz, a director of Trepper's Excellent Raincoat Company.

Alexander Erdberg, the member of the Soviet Trade Delegation in Berlin who supplied radios to the Berlin branch of the *Rote Kapelle*, subsequently played a role in the Gouzenko case in 1946 under the name of Sergei M. Kudriavtsev. Malvina Gruber, who had been Abraham Raichmann's mistress and had been arrested by the Germans in October 1942, was convicted in February 1949 by a Belgian court-martial and sentenced to ten years' imprisonment. Rudolf Roessler and Xavier Schneiper were both charged with espionage in 1953, having previously escaped imprisonment when their first network was closed down by the Swiss police in 1943. Ursula Kuczynski, who had been recruited by Richard Sorge in Shanghai before the war, later turned up in Switzerland as a GRU radio operator and defected to East Berlin in 1950 from England after the arrest of Klaus Fuchs, the atom spy for whom she had acted as case officer.

It was the evidence of these connections with the *Rote Kapelle* that persuaded Allied counter-intelligence agencies that prolonged study of the GRU's wartime networks would prove their relevance to more recent espionage[10]. In particular, it was hoped that the previous Soviet practice of mixing illegals and local Communist Party cells would make future illegals vulnerable to detection.

3 · Sorge's Contacts

Sometimes the apparatchiks were called *'illegale'* (illegals) and their work *'illegale arbeit'* (illegal work). These terms were used from habit or nostalgia, chiefly by older foreign communists whose memories and activities went back to the times before the Russian Revolution.

Whittaker Chambers in *Witness*[1]

While the Allied intelligence agencies in Europe attempted to reconstruct the complexities of the *Rote Kapelle*, American military authorities concentrated on a similar exercise in Japan, where the Kempei'tai's work on the Soviet network led by Richard Sorge promised to reveal more details of the Soviet use of illegals. The American research, summarised in a 25,000-word report entitled *The Sorge Spy Ring*, was sponsored by Major-General Charles Willoughby, Douglas MacArthur's German-born G-2 Chief of Intelligence in the US military government, who later published a version of it in *The Shanghai Conspiracy* in 1952.[2] This was essentially the first unclassified case history of a Soviet illegal, but there was much about Sorge which made him a highly unconventional illegal, not the least being the comprehensive statement he had given to his Japanese captors and the investigation conducted into his background by the Gestapo at Tokyo's request.

As well as attracting Willoughby to the case, the mass of

documentary material relating to Sorge prompted Sir William Deakin to research his 1966 biography, *The Case of Richard Sorge*,[3] which was completed with acknowledged help from David Footman, an SIS veteran who had retired to St Antony's College, Oxford.

Unlike most illegals, Sorge never made any attempt to conceal his identity or his origins. He had been born in Baku, on the Caspian, to a German oilfield engineer, and had been wounded twice while fighting with the Kaiser's forces during the First World War. He became an active member of the German Communist Party (KDP), attending its Second Congress in 1921 as an official delegate, and contributed to a Leftist newspaper, *The Voice of the Mineworkers*, based at Solingen in the Ruhr. Despite leaving a trail of evidence concerning his political beliefs at Aachen University, in the mines where he had worked as an agitator, in the police files of Hamburg which recorded his Party membership, and in the economic textbooks he had written, Sorge joined a Soviet intelligence network in around 1924. Ostensibly he cut his links with the KDP and with his schoolteacher wife Christiane, who was later to emigrate to the United States, but in reality he went to Moscow for training and reportedly attended a radio course given by Nikolai Yablin. According to Alexander Orlov, Sorge had been 'recruited and trained' by Aleksandr Karin,[4] a highly experienced illegal who had operated in Europe with a Latvian and later an Austrian passport, but was liquidated in 1937, with his wife. Orlov also recalled that Karin had been the beneficiary of a ruthlessly authentic 'legend' provided by Artur Artusov, then the head of the NKVD's Foreign Intelligence Directorate:

Artusov had lived in Switzerland before the Russian Revolution. He had known a well-to-do couple there, whose daughter went on a trip to Russia at the beginning of the century, and had met and married a young Russian teacher. In 1903 she gave birth to a boy. When the child was seven, the mother died. The grandparents in Switzerland showed great concern for their grandson and were in constant correspondence with his father. When in 1917 the country was swept by the Revolution and civil war was accompanied by mass migration of the population, the old people lost track of their grandson. The letters they wrote to Russia remained unanswered. Artusov sized up this drama and suggested that Karin impersonate the grandson, enter into correspondence with the family of 'his' late mother, and express a desire to emigrate to Switzerland. Meanwhile, the grandfather died, and the old lady was still alive. Her two sons were wealthy businessmen with respectable positions in Swiss society. In accord with Artusov's plan, a touching correspondence sprung up between the grandson (Karin) and his grandmother. He sent her the old photographs and letters of his 'poor mother', and hinted that he would like to emigrate to Switzerland if this were possible. The Swiss family at once mobilised all its connections among the diplomatic and business circles in Europe inviting them to use their influence with the Soviet authorities and persuade them to allow the young man to leave Russia. The Soviet authorities, that is, Artusov himself, proved sympathetic toward the Swiss family and granted an exit visa to the young man, his wife and little daughter. Karin was greatly depressed by the ignominious role he played and the warmth with which he was received by the Swiss family. The experience proved too great for the frail old lady. She died a couple of months later, happy in the belief that God had heard her prayers and fulfilled her cherished wish to see her grandson before she died. She bequeathed to Karin her house and a little estate, and soon, thanks to the unflagging solicitude of his uncles, Karin obtained a genuine Swiss passport, the authenticity of which no authorities would be able to dispute.[5]

Sorge's first overseas mission appears to have taken him to Hollywood, where he wrote articles on the American movie industry for a German magazine. He used the same journalistic cover in Scandinavia and Holland, but in 1929 he was interviewed by a Metropolitan Police Special Branch detective in London which, although a routine encounter at his hotel concerning the registration of aliens, had the effect of terminating his visit. It appears to have lasted just ten weeks, supposedly for the innocent purpose of studying British politics and economics, but Sorge was either unforthcoming on this topic under Japanese interrogation, or the Kempei'tai was relatively uninterested in his activities in Britain. Sorge subsequently turned up in Shanghai as correspondent for *Sozialogische Magazin*, and it was here that he established his reputation as an unusually gifted intelligence officer. With the help of a radio operator named Seber Weingarten, Sorge developed a large ring for the GRU and was responsible for the recruitment in November 1930 of Ursula Kuczynski, her husband Rudi Hamburger and the veteran left-wing American journalist, Agnes Smedley. Ursula was later approached by a parallel group, run by the Comintern, but she remained committed to Sorge. 'I did stay with Richard and his group, but did not give much thought to what its specific tasks might be. Only two years later did I know that it operated under the intelligence department of the Red Army General Staff.'[6] Occasionally, Ursula translated articles for Agnes Smedley and she recalled that the reporter had 'told me that she was with us in thought and in deed, but would find it too difficult to submit to our party discipline. Perhaps during those years of illegality she did not wish to admit her membership even to me.'[7] Another of Sorge's contacts was Gerhardt Eisler, later a senior Soviet intelligence officer in the United States. When General Willoughby attempted to reconstruct the cosmopolitan membership of Sorge's ring in Shanghai, he identified only sixteen suspects, including Ozaki Hozumi, the local correspondent of the Tokyo daily, *Asahi Shimbun*, who was to return to Japan in 1932 and organise a separate network.[8]

Sorge's ring in Shanghai was one of several parallel organisations that had been established by the Soviets, and scrutinised by the International Settlement Police, in which the British ran a very effective Special Branch. Almost all the European residents in the enclave had large Special Branch files and a high proportion related to suspected Soviet agents. The British and French contingents were very wary of the Comintern and much evidence had been accumulated to suggest the existence of a Soviet ring. Connections between various Far Eastern Communist Parties were routinely monitored, and in June 1931 a raid on a man named Ducroux, a French member of the Communist Party in Singapore, by the colony's British police led to the discovery of an address in Shanghai for the Comintern's regional representative, a Belgian named Hilaire Noulens. He worked as a languages teacher, but a search of his home revealed identity papers, including Canadian and Belgian passports, in nine different names. At first the police believed him to be a Swiss, Paul Ruegg, who had been a prominent member of the Communist Party until 1924 when he had disappeared to Moscow, but he made no admissions concerning his origins. He and his wife Gertrude were handed over to the Chinese authorities for trial and, at a court-martial in Nanking in October 1931, he was sentenced to death and his wife given life imprisonment. After a long campaign for their release conducted by an international defence committee, in which Agnes Smedley and Sorge played important roles, the couple were released in June 1932 and deported to the Soviet Union. However, during the period they were held in Shanghai, the international police had an unprecedented opportunity to study the contents of three steel trunks which proved to be the Comintern's regional accounts for 1930–31. Using the Pan Pacific Trades Union as a convenient front, Noulens had liaised with the Chinese Communist Party, run a clandestine system of couriers and maintained contact with a range of political activists in Indochina, Japan, Hong Kong and Malaya through various sub-agents, one of whom was Gerhardt Eisler.

When Elisabeth Poretsky, the widow of Ignace Reiss, was asked about Noulens, she recalled that he had once been based at the Soviet Embassy in Vienna, where he had used the surname Luft. 'He was then about thirty-five years old, not unattractive-looking but extremely tense, forever moving about and switching from one to another of his three languages apparently without noticing.'[9] He had married the daughter of a Russian aristocrat in Rome, where she had been working as a secretary at the Embassy, and after the birth of their son they had been assigned to the Far East. Although the international campaign to gain their freedom was successful, Poretsky asserted that the story of Noulens/ Luft had ended in predictable tragedy:

When he came out Luft learned that the Left opposition had been defeated and that Trotsky had gone into exile. We heard from friends that on his release Luft expressed the desire to return to the USSR but said that he would like to talk to Trotsky first. We were not too surprised, it was just the kind of thing Luft could be expected to say. He did not see Trotsky but returned to the Soviet Union. No doubt he was dealt with immediately, for no one ever heard of him again. [10]

As a result of the Settlement Police's analysis of the Noulens accounts, a Comintern correspondent named Nguen Ai Quac was arrested by the Special Branch in Hong Kong. He had travelled widely, having left Saigon as a ship's steward, and had worked in restaurants in London and Paris. His arrest prompted another international campaign to prevent his deportation to the French authorities in Saigon, and after his release he dropped from sight, only to emerge eight years later in French Indochina under the nom de guerre Ho Chi Minh.

When word spread that Noulens had been taken into custody, Sorge left Shanghai, but returned soon afterwards, apparently confident that he had not been jeopardised. Although he discouraged Ursula Kuczynski from helping the Noulens campaign, so as to avoid compromising her, many of those who lent their support, including Smedley and Ozaki, were actively engaged in espionage. Quite apart from his skills as a clandestine operator, Sorge proved himself to be a survivor in a critical period of Soviet history. When Sorge's Comintern colleagues in Europe, like Ignace Reiss, were being summoned to Moscow for execution, he escaped the purges and switched to the GRU. Even though some of those Sorge had worked with in Shanghai disappeared, Sorge himself was undeterred and, in May 1933, travelled to Berlin via Moscow to join the Nazi Party and to take a staff job with the *Frankfurter Zeitung*. Sorge's transformation into a local supporter of the regime was completed with his cultivation of the Reich Propaganda Minister, Joseph Goebbels, and his introduction to Hitler. According to Leopold Trepper, Sorge had contacts with his network in Brussels in 1938.

When Sorge arrived in Tokyo, in September 1933, he did so as a respected German journalist equipped with authentic Nazi credentials. He was popular in the local expatriate community's club and established an extremely useful friendship with Colonel Eugen Ott, with whom he had served in the same regiment during the Great War. An artillery expert on attachment to the Imperial Army, Ott was later appointed Military Attaché at the German Embassy and, in 1940, succeeded Herbert von Dirksen as Ambassador. Apparently, Ott never suspected his friend, and it was on his recommendation that Sorge became the Embassy's unofficial Press Attaché, a post which gave him useful access to German diplomatic cables, upon which he reported to Moscow. Evidently neither the Foreign Ministry in Berlin nor the Gestapo raised any obstacle to Sorge's appointment, vindication apparently of the wisdom of the GRU's decision to allow Sorge to use his own name while operating as an illegal. According to Trepper, Sorge himself raised this issue with his GRU controller, the legendary Jan Berzin, who allegedly replied that 'a man walks better in his own shoes'.[11]

Sorge's network in Japan fell under suspicion in June 1941 following the arrest by the Kempei'tai of Ito Ritsu, a prominent member of the Japanese Communist Party in November 1939. Under interrogation he implicated Miyagi Yotoku, an American-educated Japanese artist, who in turn led the Kempei'tai to Ozaki Hozumi. By the end of October thirty-five members of the ring were under arrest, including Sorge himself and his radio operator, a KDP activist named Max Klausen. Among the others taken into custody were Branko de Voukelitch, a Yugoslav who represented the French magazine La Vue, and Sorge's Japanese mistress, Mikaya Hanako.

Sorge and Ozaki were hanged on 7 November 1944, leaving only the summaries prepared by their principal interrogator, Yoshikawa Mitsusada, for study by post-war Allied investigators. De Voukelitch died serving a life sentence in 1945, but Max Klausen survived his imprisonment and was repatriated to Vladivostok, where he was promptly rearrested by the NKVD and taken under escort to Moscow for interrogation and to face charges of duplicity.

The Sorge case was to be the subject of much study in the West and became celebrated in the Soviet Union, where postage stamps were eventually issued bearing his face. The phenomenon of the illegal was still not entirely understood by Western security and intelligence agencies although there had been other indications of how Soviet espionage was developing. In 1940, the defector Walter Krivitsky had undergone a very comprehensive interrogation at the hands of Jane Archer, MI5's Comintern expert. The fact that he had been instrumental in exposing John King as a Soviet mole in the Foreign Office added weight to his statements, as did the depth of his undoubted knowledge of Soviet intelligence operations in Europe. Krivitsky, who had worked for the Comintern and the GRU since 1920, described how he had been assigned to head Soviet military intelligence in Western Europe in September 1936, while based in The Hague, and equipped with Austrian papers for himself, his wife and his child. He was an illegal *rezident*, concentrating on building and running Soviet networks in Germany. His experience dated back to his involvement with revolutionary movements in Germany in 1923, which had compromised him with the police and had led him to spend two months in hiding in the Soviet Embassy in Berlin in 1926 and a spell in prison in Austria. However, in July 1936, at the outbreak of the Spanish Civil War, his role had changed and he had been directed to switch his attention to Franco's forces. The OGPU had established a veteran officer, 'Nikolsky, alias Schwed, alias Lyova, alias Orlov', to head the local organisation from Madrid. Ominously, Krivitsky described how the travel documents of Communists volunteering for service in the International Brigade were routinely removed for future use:

All the volunteers' passports were taken up when they arrived in Spain, and very rarely was a passport returned. Even when a man was discharged, he was told that his passport had been lost. From the United States alone about 2,000 volunteers came over, and genuine American passports are highly prized at OGPU headquarters in Moscow. Nearly every diplomatic pouch from Spain that arrived at the Lubyanka contained a batch of passports from members of the International Brigade. Several times while I was in Moscow in the spring of 1937 I saw this mail in the offices of the Foreign Division of the OGPU. One day a batch of about a hundred passports arrived; half of them were American. They had belonged to dead soldiers. That was a great haul, a cause for celebration. The passports of the dead, after some weeks of inquiry into the family histories of their original owners, are easily adapted to their new bearers, the OGPU agents.[12]

Krivitsky's disclosure prompted the State Department to replace every red-jacketed US passport in circulation with a specially printed version with a green cover. As well as giving a fascinating account of Soviet personalities deployed across Europe, Krivitsky was able to clear up several of the mysteries surrounding previous investigations. For example, in the case of Lydia Stahl he disclosed that she 'had joined our secret service while a refugee in Finland in 1921. She was one of the best we had.' He also revealed that one of the Soviet controllers who had supervised Robert Switz was Alfred Tilton, whose wife Maria was serving a ten-year sentence in Finland for espionage. Tilton himself had escaped suspicion and had returned to an administrative post in Minsk. Krivitsky also revealed that Adolph Rubens, alias Donald Robinson, who had disappeared in Moscow in December 1937, 'had served many years as an officer in the Soviet Military Intelligence, both in the United States and abroad'. Rubens had been purged, Krivitsky asserted, as had Valentin Markin, the OGPU chief ostensibly killed in a bar-room brawl in 1934. According to gossip circulating in Moscow, Markin had been assassinated on Stalin's personal order.

The extent of Stalin's paranoia was breathtaking, according to Krivitsky, who claimed that some 350,000 people had been arrested during the purge, with at least 36,000 executed. Whether he too fell victim to a murder squad, or whether his death was a suicide, is still unclear.

Krivitsky's contribution, recognised only after his death, was to indicate the size and scope of Soviet intelligence operations in the West. Two further defectors, Hede Massing and Elizabeth Bentley, were to give a more detailed account of Soviet illegal operations in the United States, based on their own experiences. Like Krivitsky, Massing had returned to Moscow during the height of the terror and had survived. Austrian by birth, and married at seventeen to Gerhardt Eisler, one of the KDP's leading figures and a friend of

Sorge's, she had travelled to the United States in 1926 and
stayed, working in an orphanage in Pleasantville, New York,
until she acquired her citizenship in December 1927. According to the statement she made to the FBI in late 1947, she
had returned to Europe in January 1928 and, while studying
in Berlin, had met and been recruited by Sorge. A year in
Moscow followed, where she was indoctrinated into the Comintern, ready for her new role as an illegal based in Berlin.
Supervised by Ignace Reiss, Massing had worked openly for
the KDP, on one occasion travelling to London to help audit
the accounts of the CPGB, but also undertaking clandestine
work for the Soviets. She had operated a mail-drop for Reiss
and, in 1932, had been introduced to Krivitsky, who apparently had rejected her as unsuitable for a particular mission
he had had her in mind for.

In October 1933, Massing returned to New York aboard
the *Deutschland* as a correspondent for the *Weltbuehne* and
moved in with Helen Black, the representative of the Soviet
Photo Agency. She took her orders from Valentin Markin,
whose cover was that of a director of a small cosmetics company owned by a CPUSA member named Hart. During this
period Massing acted as a courier, taking microfilms to Paris,
and as a recruiter, successfully persuading Noel and Herta
Field to join her network, but failing to acquire his State
Department friend, Alger Hiss, who, Massing discovered,
was already involved with a separate ring in Washington.
After a single, preliminary encounter with Hiss, Massing was
warned to keep away from him. 'Never see him again. Stay
away from him and forget him,' she was told by her controller.

I understood, of course. There had apparently been a reprimand
and these were urgent, emphatic instructions. I had met a member
of another apparatus. I had had a conversation with him in which I
had disclosed that I was working in a parallel apparatus. That was
strictly taboo, and disliked by the big boss here and by the bigger
bosses in Moscow. [13]

Following the murder of Ignace Reiss, Massing expressed
doubts about her own commitment to her new controller,
who she subsequently learned was Elizaveta Zubilin, the wife

of Vassilli, the *rezident* in New York, and was summoned to Moscow. She arrived in November 1937 and underwent months of interrogation to confirm her continued loyalty, but she was too disillusioned to continue. The following year she returned to New York and broke off contact with Helen Black and the Zubilins. When the FBI approached her, after the war, in regard to its investigation of Gerhardt Eisler, she agreed to give evidence against Alger Hiss and her testimony secured his conviction on a charge of perjury, following his denial on oath of charges made by another defector, Whittaker Chambers.

Chambers, a senior editor on *Time* magazine, was one of several CPUSA supporters who had become disaffected with the Party and had abandoned the cause in April 1937. Married to an active Communist, he had been an editor on the *Daily Worker*, but by 1948 his ideological conversion was complete. He publicly denounced Alger Hiss as a Soviet source and revealed that when he had first made the accusation to the State Department in 1939 no action had been taken. Hiss denied the charge and tried to bring an action for slander against Chambers, who had given a detailed account of his work as a courier carrying classified State Department documents between Hiss and a Soviet contact, whom he later identified, with Krivitsky's help, as Colonel Boris Bykov. Fortunately for Chambers, he had kept as an insurance policy a batch of State Department documents typed on Hiss's own typewriter and annotated in his handwriting. This evidence was to prove damning for Hiss and to ensure his ultimate conviction and imprisonment, albeit on the relatively minor charge of perjury, and not espionage.

When Chambers met Krivitsky in New York in 1939, he was told that 'Krivitsky had worked underground with Bykov in Italy'. Chambers recalled that 'in 1937 and 1938, I knew Colonel Bykov as "Peter" – Peter, nothing more. Wherever possible, underground Communists are known to each other by such simple first-name pseudonyms.'[14] He also learned from Krivitsky that the contact he had known as 'Herman', and with whom he had been on bad terms, was really Valentin Markin.

Although Chambers was to become a star witness for the federal authorities and to name dozens of members of his old apparatus, his co-operation was won over a period of time. When he was first interviewed by the FBI, as part of the investigation into Gerhardt Eisler, Chambers initially had denied knowledge of him. Later he was to give a more candid account of his clandestine activities, describing how he had handled six important sources who had operated independently in the US Treasury Department, the State Department, the Bureau of Standards and the Aberdeen Proving Ground in Maryland, where a sympathetic mathematician had betrayed the technical data of an experimental bombsight. Like Elizabeth Bentley, Chambers had been taught the technique of acquiring false US passports, and at one stage it had been intended that he and his family should adopt new identities to run an illegal network in London, hidden by a convenient commercial front, a literary agency sponsored by a willing CPUSA member in New York who was anxious to expand his business into Europe. The method of applying for passports, he admitted, 'was ghoulishly simple':

The head of the underground section of the American Communist Party had organised two teams of researchers. They were Communists. In the Genealogical Division of the New York Public Library, both teams were engaged in studying vital statistics. One team studied the dates of the birth of infants. The other team concentrated on the infants' deaths. The results were compared, and when it was discovered that a baby had died shortly after birth, the name of the dead child and its parents was listed.[15]

Using the data gleaned from the records, an application was made in the name of the deceased for a passport. By roughly matching the year of birth with that of an agent requiring an identity, an entirely authentic passport would be issued to the fraudulent applicant. Provided the issuing authorities did not cross-refer the names of applicants with the register of deaths, which was an administratively difficult task, the system was virtually foolproof. However, once the authorities had learned of the Soviet methodology, the FBI was able to convict Earl Browder, the Secretary-General of the CPUSA, on a charge of passport fraud, for which he served a term of imprisonment in the federal penitentiary at Atlanta, Georgia.

According to Chambers's testimony, he had not actually met Hede Massing, but he knew of her network based in Washington by reputation and recalled that the Fields had been key figures in the parallel Soviet network centred in the same city. Similarly, he had not known Elizabeth Bentley, but she too had become disenchanted with her clandestine activities and had switched sides in August 1945 by volunteering a statement to the FBI. The daughter of a newspaper editor, Bentley had been a scholarship student at Vassar, and was recruited from the CPUSA and run by Jacob Rasin, a Jewish Ukrainian and veteran Party activist who called himself Jacob Golos and headed World Tourists Inc., a travel agency set up by the CPUSA to supervise the movement of volunteers to Spain during the Spanish Civil War. Golos and Bentley became lovers, but their relationship was detected by the FBI which placed Golos under surveillance after he had been spotted at a series of seven clandestine meetings held with Gaik Ovakimian in early 1941, not long before the latter's arrest and deportation in July. In poor health and under heavy pressure from the Soviets and the FBI, Golos had succumbed to a heart attack in November 1943, leaving Bentley to take his place as organiser of his apparatus. Bentley's promotion was confirmed by her new Soviet contact, Anatoli B. Gromov, a Lithuanian case officer whose real name was Gorsky and who, until recently, had been the Second Secretary at the Soviet Embassy in London. Now he held a similar diplomatic post in Washington DC.

Although Bentley could not offer the kind of documentary evidence that Chambers had produced, she was able to identify more than eighty of her contacts, including several who had wormed their way into America's secret wartime intelligence organisation, the Office of Strategic Services (OSS). For example, she named J. Julius Joseph and his wife Bella as being 'of invaluable use'.[16] He had been placed in OSS's Japanese Section, where he 'knew in advance the Americans' plans concerning Japan', while his wife worked 'for the OSS's

Movie Division, which made confidential films for the use of the United States General Staff'.[17] Bentley also confirmed the complicity of an OSS translator, Leonard Mins, who was a well-known Communist Party activist; and Donald N. Wheeler and Duncan C. Lee, a personal assistant and a legal adviser to the head of OSS, General Bill Donovan. Helen Tenney, of OSS's Spanish Section, was compromised by Bentley, as was Maurice Halperin, head of the Latin America Division of the Research and Analysis Branch. Another contact was Cedric Belfrage, then employed by British Intelligence in New York, and of particular interest was Fred Rose, a Canadian MP who had corresponded with Golos through a mail-drop run by Bentley. His name was to hit the headlines in 1945, not long after the defection of Igor Gouzenko, a GRU cipher clerk based at the Soviet Embassy, who had accumulated enough incriminating evidence to justify Rose's arrest and prosecution.

Although the FBI's attempt to reintroduce Bentley to the Soviets as a double agent, by means of an intimate dinner held with her Soviet controller, proved a failure, she was to continue to give sworn testimony about her undercover activities for most of the decade following her initial interview with the FBI. Despite the lack of any documentary material, she made a convincing witness and her recollection neatly dovetailed with the picture of Soviet illegals portrayed by Chambers, Massing and Krivitsky. Furthermore, it corroborated aspects of the FBI's first penetration by a double agent of a Soviet network of illegals.

The original target of what had been initiated as a surveillance operation had been Vassilli Zubilin, the man believed by the FBI to be the Soviet illegal *rezident* in New York. In July 1943, Zubilin had been spotted holding a clandestine meeting with a Hollywood movie producer named Boris Morros. When interviewed, the Russian-born Morros admitted that he had been recruited by Zubilin in 1936, but at that time he had known Zubilin not as a Soviet diplomat, but as an Amtorg official named Edward J. Herbert. Morros explained that Herbert had persuaded him to provide authentic Paramount Studios cover as a movie talent scout for Herbert so that he could travel freely in Nazi Germany. In return, Morros's two brothers, who had been in danger of being prosecuted, were freed by the Soviet authorities, his father was allowed to emigrate, and he had arrived in the United States from Moscow in January 1943. It was at a rendezvous soon after this that the FBI had first latched on to Boris.

According to Morros,[18] Zubilin had operated in the United States as an illegal for several years before his official arrival in San Francisco with diplomatic status in December 1941. After his father's release Boris had agreed to allow his independent movie production company to be used by Zubilin's organisation, and it had been financed by Alfred Stern, a wealthy New York Communist and Soviet sympathiser. Boris was also assigned a partner, Jack Soble, who was Lithuanian by birth and had operated in Germany as a journalist until he had been withdrawn to Moscow in 1940. Ostensibly his occupation in America, while his naturalisation application was being processed, was that of manager of a grocery store in Manhattan, but in reality Soble, his wife Myra and his brother Dr Robert A. Soblen were key illegals, supervising a network of other agents in Europe. Among them were George Zlatovsky, a former US army intelligence officer, and his wife Jane Foster. A naturalised US citizen originally from Kiev who had come to America with his parents as a child, Zlatovsky had fought with the Abraham Lincoln Battalion during the Spanish Civil War and had served in the US army in Austria until 1948. Jane Foster had joined OSS in December 1943 as an expert on Indonesia, having lived in Java for four years before the war. A committed Communist who had become a Party member in the Dutch East Indies, she was strongly suspected of having passed OSS secrets to her future husband while based in Salzburg in 1947.

After a decade of continuous surveillance the FBI arrested the Sobles in 1957, together with Jack's successor, Jacob Albam. Morros's testimony ensured convictions for Albam and the Sobles, but the Zlatovskys resisted attempts to extradite them from France, while the others identified by Morros also remained out of reach.

Under interrogation Jack Soble admitted his espionage and, as well as providing evidence against his brother Robert, implicated Martha Stern, *née* Dodd, who he claimed had spied as a Soviet agent in her father's Embassy when he had been the US Ambassador in Berlin for four years before the war. Alfred and Martha Stern were both indicted but moved to Mexico and then used Paraguayan passports to travel to Prague. They remained in Czechoslovakia until 1979, when, following the death of Morros, all charges against them in the United States were dropped. Suffering from cancer, Dr Robert Soblen disappeared to Israel in 1962 when the Supreme Court rejected his appeal against a life sentence, and in September 1962 he committed suicide in London soon after he had been deported from Tel Aviv. His first attempt, on the aeroplane to England, failed, but a second one, when his plea for political asylum had been rejected by the British authorities, was successful. Soble also identified one of his Soviet handlers in Paris as Pavel S. Kuznetsov, a KGB officer who had since been compromised in an espionage case which occurred in London in June 1952.[19]

At the conclusion of the Soble case the FBI reconstructed much of Zubilin's career, and positively identified him as a veteran illegal who had worked in Germany before being posted to China as a diplomat. His true name was said by defectors to be Vassilli Zarubin, and his wife was believed to be Liza Rosenberg, who had not only accompanied her husband to the United States while he masqueraded as Edward Herbert, but had also applied for a US passport under the name Sara Herbert. The defector Georges Agabekov recalled that he had known the beautiful Liza Rosenberg as Lisa Gorskaia, when she had been married to a Soviet intelligence officer named Gorsky, and asserted that she had betrayed one of his colleagues, Jacob Blunkmine, then the 'illegal OGPU resident for the whole of the Levant'[20] to his OGPU assassins. Blunkmine had been a famous revolutionary and had acquired considerable celebrity as the murderer of the German Ambassador to Russia, Count de Mirbach, in 1918, and Lisa Gorskaia had denounced him in Moscow as a Trotskyite in August 1929. Blunkmine, then aged thirty, had been arrested while being driven in a car with Lisa Gorskaia and had later been shot on orders from Stalin. Agabekov's account, published in his 1931 autobiography, told how shots had been fired in a Moscow street as Blunkmine had attempted to escape his captors, and his version was subsequently confirmed by Alexander Orlov in his memoirs when he retold much the same story, but referred to Lisa Gorskaia as 'Liza G.' and, more accurately than Agabekov, to Blunkmine as 'Blumkin'.

Yagoda summoned an employee of that department, Liza G., a beautiful young woman toward whom Blumkin had displayed at one time a romantic interest, and asked her to become friendly with Blumkin and, feigning disappointment with the party, act as if she sympathised with the Trotskyite opposition. Yagoda hoped that when Liza G. had wormed her way into Blumkin's confidence, he would tell her about his meeting with Trotsky and name the former leaders of the opposition whom he had seen since his return from Turkey. Liza was given to understand that she must in the interests of the party drop all 'bourgeois prejudices' and try to become intimate with him.[21]

Thus 'Liza G.' was the same Elizaveta who had run Hede Massing so many years later, and Massing had noticed

her strange beautiful eyes – large, and dark, heavy-browed, with long, curled eyelashes. They shone from a face of small, delicate features, dark skinned and narrow of mouth. Her warm and engaging smile, which she gave so sparingly, exposed large, beautiful teeth. The exquisite head belonged to a small, frail body. Her posture was poor, however, and she had large, painfully bad feet, and ugly hands. She was polite and completely self-assured. She had an authoritative air about her without being annoying or aggressive. Her English was flawless as was her German. She carried herself like an emissary of a great country, but she was ready and willing to talk and understand the problems of smaller people. She was too clever to be patronising.[22]

She was also remembered by Elisabeth Poretsky, who 'had known Lisa Zarubin when she was still Liza Rosenberg and was Zaporozhet's secretary at the Embassy in Vienna in 1925, and had distrusted her even then':

Since that time she had always worked for the NKVD. So did most of her family, including her brother Victor, a photographic specialist, and his wife who in 1935 was saved in extremis from a suicide attempt . . . The particular reason everyone avoided Lisa Zarubin was because of the role she had played in the betrayal and eventual death of Jacob Blumkin.[23]

Elizaveta and her husband left the United States for the last time in August 1944 by air. Apparently upon his arrival in Moscow, he reverted to his true name and was promoted to the rank of general with responsibility for the supervision of illegals in the West. Certainly another defector, Ilya Dzhirkvelov, who fled the KGB in 1980, recalled that in May 1947 he had been assigned a new post abroad by 'General Zarubin, the officer in charge of *nelegaly* [illegals]'.[24] But according to Morros, who made an extensive tour of Europe in mid-1948 accompanied by his FBI handler, Zubilin had not lasted long as the controller of Soviet illegals. His drinking had led to his banishment to Siberia, and he had been replaced by Pyotr V. Fedotov, 'a soft-spoken intellectual, who had been Stalin's bodyguard at both Potsdam and Yalta'.[25] Fedotov's deputy, whom Morros met in Switzerland in August 1948, was Aleksandr M. Korotkov, 'a stern-looking man',[26] broad-shouldered and over six feet tall.

Morros's information about Fedotov and Korotkov was subsequently confirmed by Ilya Dzhirkvelov. Lieutenant-General Fedotov, he recalled, had been the popular head of the NKVD's foreign intelligence directorate during the war, becoming head of the First Chief Directorate in 1946. He had remained a senior KGB officer until his removal in a purge in 1956, when he was head of the KGB's Second Chief Directorate in charge of domestic counter-intelligence. Colonel Korotkov

had risen from the ranks, starting as a footballer and then becoming a courier, carrying papers from one office to another with the KGB. At the same time he was teaching himself German. Having attracted the attention of his superiors, he was finally promoted to be a case officer and spent several years doing illegal work in Germany, first in the Hitler years and later in the Western sector of occupied Germany.[27]

In April 1954, Vladimir and Evdokia Petrov, the two most senior KGB personnel in Australia, defected and, in the course of their extensive debriefing, identified 'General Aleksandr Korotkov' as the head of the illegals' network of 'the Fourth Directorate of the *Komitet Informatsyi*'[28] at the time of their last visit to their Moscow headquarters, in January 1951.

Unlike most double agents who enjoy only a limited shelf-life, Morros was hugely successful for more than a decade. He provided an invaluable insight into Moscow's commitment to illegals and positively identified senior Soviet handlers whose names were later confirmed by other well-placed sources. In addition, Morros supplied the FBI with a continuous commentary on the current anxieties of his case officers. For example, in March 1949 Soble had confided that he had been greatly concerned by the recent arrest of Valentin A. Gubitchev in New York, whom he had apparently met several times. Morros duly passed this item on to the FBI, which was delighted by the news. An employee of the United Nations Secretariat, but not the Soviet delegation, Gubitchev did not enjoy diplomatic immunity and had been entrapped after a lengthy surveillance operation established that he had been in receipt of classified material from a member of the US Department of Justice since his arrival in New York at the end of July 1946. The culprit was Judith Coplon, a long-time Soviet sympathiser who had been compromised by the interception and decryption of a Soviet cable by the US Armed Forces Security Agency (AFSA). Based on AFSA's tip, the FBI had placed Coplon, who had been in her post since 1945, under observation and had identified Gubitchev as her handler in January 1949 when they had dined together at an Italian restaurant near Broadway. Two further meetings were monitored, and the FBI moved in as she was in the act of passing a batch of secret documents, including some specially prepared counter-intelligence reports, to Gubitchev. Three items in particular, ostensibly internal memoranda that actually had been fabricated by the FBI, were considered to be irresistible bait, for they purported to suggest that the FBI possessed at least four moles inside Amtorg, one of whom was identified by name:

We are presently using, on a confidential basis, two highly placed officials of the Amtorg Trading Corp. One of these is Isadore Gibley Needleman, the Amtorg legal representative, with whom we have been maintaining a rather indirect contact through an intermediary. We have not been entirely satisfied with the arrangement, as to the extent of the information supplied by Needleman, and for that reason, in order to check his sincerity, we desire to obtain from him more complete information on a variety of matters. [29]

Gubitchev fell for the ploy, and when he was searched he was found, in an uncharacteristic breach of security, to be carrying Dr Robert Soblen's name and address. Gubitchev was sentenced to fifteen years' imprisonment and deported, while Coplon, who deployed the bogus defence that she had only been Gubitchev's lover, was convicted of espionage but later freed on a technicality relating to the FBI's interception of her telephone calls without a warrant.

The importance of the Coplon case centred in part on the type of material she had been passing to Gubitchev, which clearly the Soviets attached considerable importance to. By virtue of her position in the Justice Department section dealing with the registration of foreign agents, she had received regular reports from the FBI on the current status of Soviet espionage. In particular, the Soviets were apparently anxious to know the extent of the FBI's knowledge of the ring headed by Victor Perlo, a member of the War Production Board, first exposed by Elizabeth Bentley. To exploit this appetite for FBI material, Coplon's attention was drawn deliberately to the false document which alleged that the FBI had succeeded in planting an informant inside Amtorg. The exercise not only proved Coplon's guilt, but also served to confirm that Amtorg was still considered an intelligence asset by the Soviets, and that Moscow had been worried about Bentley's disclosures. In fact, the Soviets had been unduly concerned about Bentley, for her testimony only resulted in a single prosecution, that of William W. Remington, of the War Production Board, on a charge of perjury. In that prosecution the FBI received additional help from Remington's ex-wife, who had corroborated aspects of Bentley's evidence. Nevertheless, Bentley supplied significant details about the work of Abraham Brothman, a brilliant chemical engineer who ran his own company, his mistress Miriam Moskowitz and the Rosenbergs, all of whom were to be imprisoned.

The scope of Soviet espionage, as demonstrated by the many arrests and prosecutions of the early 1950s, brought home to the American public the very real threat posed by the Russian intelligence service. The realisation that Soviet advances in the nuclear field, manifested dramatically by the successful tests of atomic weapons, had been enhanced by illicit access to American technology also served to highlight the strategic implications of large-scale hostile espionage. Initially based from the relatively safe havens of Soviet diplomatic missions, these activities had been expanded through the use of political sympathisers and then illegals. As the Western security investigators probed deeper into the origins of the networks, the more it became clear that considerable responsibility had been given to just a handful of key individuals, the so-called 'great illegals', who had not only operated skilfully on their own account, but had also used their charismatic personalities to recruit sub-agents and build independent organisations. The mysterious Arnold Deutsch and Theodore Maly had been just such stars of the NKVD, and Richard Sorge had been another. Sorge's activities were to extend well beyond his own work in Shanghai and Tokyo, for he had exercised tremendous influence on other agents whom he had persuaded to work for the cause. Among them were Agnes Smedley, Leopold Trepper and the vital figure at the heart of the Swiss networks, Ursula Kuczynski, who had been despatched from China to develop a cell in Geneva.

4 · The Swiss Networks

From my youth on I have belonged to the revolutionary
working-class movement, spending years, indeed decades,
in exile doing party work of a conspiratorial nature. This
was my training; it was this that enabled me to graduate to
the more complex and difficult task of running an intelligence
group.

Sandor Rado in *Codename Dora*[1]

Analysis of the Robinson papers captured in Brussels at the
end of the war revealed numerous links to an important Swiss
branch of the *Rote Kapelle*, but it was not until an Englishman
named Allan Foote presented himself to the British occupation authorities in Berlin in March 1947 that MI5 could not
only reconstruct the membership of an entire network of
GRU illegals, but also interview the West's first post-war
illegal defector.

Allan Foote's appearance in Berlin had been entirely
unexpected, and his story was even more extraordinary. He
explained that although his papers identified him as a repatriated German prisoner of war called Albert Mueller, he was
a Briton working under Soviet instructions to travel to
Argentina and then build a network in the United States
for the GRU. As well as having undergone eighteen months
of training in preparation for his mission, Foote was able to
describe in detail to his MI5 debriefer, Courtney Young, his

participation in the GRU's wartime ring in Switzerland in which he had been known by the codename JIM.[2] Until Foote's defection, knowledge of the Swiss network had been limited to the interrogation reports of suspects kept by the Swiss Bundespolizei, an impressive quantity of Soviet radio signals which had been successfully deciphered by Marc Payot, a Swiss cryptographer, and an analysis of nearly 5,500 clandestine wireless signals exchanged between Moscow and three illicit transmitters in Switzerland intercepted by Wilhelm F. Flicke, a thirteen-year veteran of the Abwehr's communications branch. In addition, there had been a considerable British connection with the organisation apart, of course, from Foote's involvement. One tantalising clue to that link, dating back to 1943, was found buried deep in SIS's archives. At that time the head of the SIS station in Berne was Frederick Vanden Heuvel, and one of his agents had been Louis Suss, originally from Alsace-Lorraine, who had worked as Press Attaché in the Vichy French Legation in Berne. In early November 1943, Suss had approached Vanden Heuvel with a curious request: would the British give asylum to an important Soviet agent in the event of 'an emergency'? Nothing more had come of the enquiry, but Foote had provided an explanation. According to him, Suss had operated for the GRU as well as SIS, and his enquiry had been prompted by his GRU controller, a respected Hungarian cartographer, Alexander (Sandor) Rado, who was then in imminent danger of arrest by the Swiss security police.

The GRU's operations in Switzerland were considered sufficiently important to justify SIS conducting its own independent investigation, headed by Nicholas Elliott, a former MI5 officer now assigned to Berne as Vanden Heuvel's successor as head of SIS's Swiss organisation, and his principal local asset, Klop Ustinov.[3] Together Elliott and Ustinov obtained all the dossiers compiled by the ever-thorough Bundespolizei and produced a very comprehensive overview of the GRU's wartime activities. On the basis of the Swiss network's reports addressed to 'the Centre', it was clear that the GRU had run a large and cosmopolitan organisation which had handled accurate information of a kind that could only have come straight from exceptionally reliable sources in Germany. In contradiction of Trepper's subsequent recollection that 'the heads of the Comintern decided that Soviet Intelligence would no longer use Communist militants. There would be a total separation between the secret service and the party – a decision that was overdue but justified,' Elliott discovered[4] that most of the GRU's key figures were lifelong Communist activists. In this regard, Foote was no exception.

Born in Kirkdale, Liverpool, in 1905, Foote had been discharged by the Royal Air Force because of his failure to disclose his membership of the CPGB. He had volunteered to fight in the Spanish Civil War and in December 1936 arrived in Spain as a member of the British battalion of the International Brigade. Upon his return to London in September 1938 he was recruited as a courier by a lady in St John's Wood, London, and despatched to Geneva, where he was met by another woman in the central post office. MI5 identified the first woman as Birgette Lewis, *née* Kuczynski, and later established that the second was her sister, Ursula. For the next three years, until his arrest at his apartment in Lausanne by the Bundespolizei in November 1943, Foote had worked first as a spy based in Munich, where he had fallen in love with a beautiful young KDP courier, and later as a radio operator for a Soviet network that had succeeded in penetrating Germany. If his commitment to the cause needed any further support, it was provided by the Nazis when his girlfriend received a savage beating from the Gestapo.

While living in Lausanne Foote had played the role of a wealthy Englishman in poor health who was disinclined to return to London while the war continued. During lengthy interviews with Courtney Young, which later became the basis of his memoirs, *Handbook for Spies*, Foote accurately identified almost all the other members of the Soviet network with whom he had come into contact, and not unnaturally enhanced his own importance in the ring to the detriment of those members he had disliked. After his release from a Swiss jail in September 1944, he had reported to the Soviet military mission in Paris where Colonel Novikov of the NKVD had arranged for him to be flown to Moscow, accompanied by two other agents scheduled for repatriation: Leopold Trepper and Alexander Rado. However, their flight had been routed through Egypt and Persia, requiring a forty-eight-hour stop in Cairo, where Rado had disappeared, leaving Foote and Trepper to complete the journey on their own. The GRU, ever suspicious of treachery, had put the worst possible interpretation on Rado's reluctance to rejoin the flight and had subjected Foote and Trepper to months of harrowing interrogation. Eventually, Foote was able to satisfy his inquisitors and was sent to a GRU training centre at Sehjodia, twenty-five miles north-west of Moscow, in preparation for a new assignment, supposedly to Mexico and the United States. Trepper, meanwhile, was not so lucky and remained in Soviet prisons until May 1954. As for Rado, although he had tried to defect to the British in Cairo in January 1945 and then had attempted suicide, he was handed over to the Soviets in July and persuaded to complete his journey to Moscow. Upon arrival he was arrested and remained in Soviet prisons until 1955, when he was released to take up an academic post in Budapest.

Of special significance to MI5 was Foote's identification of Birgette Lewis as the person who had originally recruited him into the GRU in 1937, for at the end of the war she and the rest of her family were still resident in England. Foote underwent weeks of debriefing at the hands of the Security Service, during which he described his wartime activities in Switzerland, ending in his arrest, and his subsequent release and recall to Moscow for a new assignment. Many of the key personalities who featured in the Serpell/Hemblys-Scales report were known to Foote, who, having experienced an ideological conversion, was enthusiastic in his co-operation with the British authorities. In his book he revealed that Ursula Kuczynski, codenamed SONIA, was the GRU's leading organiser, but only after MI5 had traced her and her British husband, Leon Beurton, to their Oxfordshire home at Great Rollright and had interviewed them there in November 1947. Whatever optimistic hopes MI5 might have entertained about Ursula following Foote's example, they were to be dashed.

She asserted that her espionage on behalf of the Comintern was all in the past and that she had no wish to discuss it. Without any evidence to the contrary MI5's interrogator, Jim Skardon, had been obliged to take her at her word, although his visit had come at an embarrassing moment for her network which was in fact far from defunct. Not only was she active in running Klaus Fuchs, the nuclear physicist then still engaged on classified work and stationed at the atomic research establishment at Harwell, which was no great distance from her home, but her brother Jurgen, an economist by profession, had also played a part in enabling the GRU to maintain contact with Fuchs. Apparently satisfied that Skardon's visit had no sinister implications, Ursula, Jurgen and Leon Beurton remained in England until February 1949, when they decamped to East Germany, where they now live.[5]

In many respects Foote's story dovetailed with data gleaned from the Robinson papers and the post-war interrogation of German personnel, among whom was the cryptographer, Wilhelm Flicke. When compared to the Bundespolizei reports and the very substantial quantity of Soviet wireless messages deciphered by the Swiss, it became clear that, apart from a few memory lapses and a tendency to inflate his own significance, Foote's recollection was entirely accurate. The SD had been aware of the existence of a Swiss branch of the *Rote Kapelle* and had made several attempts at penetration, but each had been detected and rejected. Nevertheless, the German records gave further clues to the Soviet network, which evidently had been remarkably cosmopolitan in its membership and had been run with virtually no contact from the Soviet Embassy or the Communist Party, and there was a suspicion that such a valuable asset was very likely to be active still. Whereas the French, Belgian and German branches of the *Rote Kapelle* had been decimated by the SD, virtually all the components of the Swiss branch had survived the war, even if they had endured a few months of imprisonment.

The key figure in the Swiss network was a Polish Jewess named Rachel Duebendorfer, who had worked as an

Chart 7 Rado's network

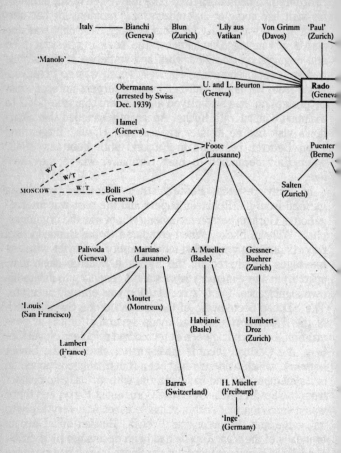

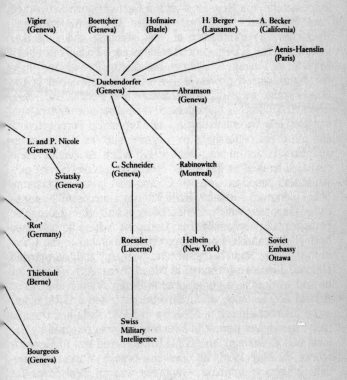

Vigier
(Geneva)

Boettcher
(Geneva)

Hofmaier
(Basle)

H. Berger
(Lausanne)

A. Becker
(California)

Aenis-Haenslin
(Paris)

Duebendorfer
(Geneva)

Abramson
(Geneva)

L. and P. Nicole
(Geneva)

Sviatsky
(Geneva)

C. Schneider
(Geneva)

Rabinowitch
(Montreal)

'Rot'
(Germany)

Thiebault
(Berne)

Roessler
(Lucerne)

Helbein
(New York)

Soviet
Embassy
Ottawa

Bourgeois
(Geneva)

Swiss
Military
Intelligence

interpreter and typist with the International Labour Organisation in Geneva since 1934. She had married Henri Duebendorfer in about 1932, apparently for the sole purpose of obtaining Swiss citizenship, for they had separated almost immediately; she then lived with a German journalist named Paul Boettcher, who had adopted the same surname. Boettcher, a Communist of long standing and a former member of the KDP's central committee, who had once been Minister of Finance in Saxony, had fled to Switzerland when the Nazis seized power in Germany. He appeared in the Soviet traffic as PAUL, while Rachel was codenamed SISSY. The Duebendorfers had operated their own independent network in Geneva, consisting of local Communist Party activists and members of Rachel's own family, such as her daughter and French son-in-law, until 1941, when Alexander Rado revealed himself as the leader of another parallel Soviet network also based in Geneva. Codenamed DORA, an anagram of his (adopted) surname, Rado had run a successful business called Geopress which distributed maps and other geographic paraphernalia. Originally from Budapest, where he had been born Radolfi and had been a prominent member of the Communist Party, Rado had studied in Germany and had married Helene, Lenin's secretary, in Moscow in 1923. Thereafter he had worked as a geographer in Berlin, Vienna and Paris. An old acquaintance of Richard Sorge's, and a GRU agent since his recruitment in Moscow in 1935, Rado had tried to gain a residency permit in Brussels but was rejected by the local police. Instead, the GRU had directed him to Geneva, where, in May 1936, he opened a branch of the map publishing agency, Impress. Geopress was an ideal cover for espionage, the front for the GRU's operations mounted against Italy and supervised from the Soviet Embassy in Paris, and Rado had proved an exceptionally talented illegal, with Helene acting as his wireless operator. When Ursula Kuczynski was ordered to England in 1941, she had passed Allan Foote on to Rado and, although the two men often clashed, they had continued to work together until Foote's arrest in November 1943.

On 14 October 1943, the Bundespolizei seized two illicit

Soviet transmitters in Geneva and, a little over a month later, caught Foote in his apartment in Lausanne. Enough crypto-graphic material had been recovered in the three raids to compromise Rado, who promptly disappeared from sight, and one of his principal sub-agents, Rudolf Roessler, who was taken into custody in June 1944.

The Swiss network was dubbed '*Der Rote Drei*' ('The Red Three') by the Bundespolizei because of the three wireless transmitters confiscated in the raids of October and November 1943. Although the Swiss agreed to hand over copies of almost all their files to SIS and the CIA soon after the war, they never pursued every clue uncovered, partly because of a reluctance to appear to be collaborating too closely with the Western allies, but mainly because a branch of Swiss military intelligence had been implicated as Roessler's main source of high-grade information from inside Germany. When examined by the analysts, it became obvious that Foote's messages had come from Rado, who had received the infor-mation from Roessler, apparently without asking its prov-enance. The compelling question was, where had the former German journalist acquired it? The quality and volume of Roessler's material, which is clear from the intercepted wire-less traffic studied after the war, has made the Swiss network an issue of great controversy and continuous speculation. The unpalatable truth for the supposedly neutral Swiss was that their intelligence personnel had been far from unpartisan in the conflict and had given both the British and the Soviets generous access to their quite impressive sources. Whilst the Swiss military intelligence apparatus had actively and enthusiastically participated in this unofficial assistance, their security counterparts had not been indoctrinated into the arrangement, which had led to two awkward episodes: the arrest and imprisonment of some *Rote Drei* members during the war, and the collapse of a prosecution against some of their collaborators soon after the war. This conclusion could be reached because, unusually, several senior figures in the Soviet organisation published accounts of their wartime work, including Alexander Rado, Ursula Kuczynski and Allan Foote. Their stories, together with the decrypted Soviet texts and the Swiss police files, combined to produce a unique opportunity to study illegal methodology and the evolvement of what was arguably the war's most important intelligence apparatus.

The network's architect was Maria Poliakova, who was known to Foote as VERA. A Russian Jewess and a dedicated Communist, even though her brother, husband and father had perished in Stalin's purges, she spoke several languages fluently and had arrived in Switzerland in 1936 to supervise Rado. In 1941, she had returned to Moscow, but her continued involvement in the network was evident from her distinctive Marxist style, which manifested itself in so many of the signals that were exchanged between Moscow and Switzerland, and which were intercepted.

Before the war Poliakova had served as the GRU's illegal *rezident* in Germany and Belgium, and had operated independently in France and Switzerland. When the senior GRU organiser, Ismail Akhmedov, had undertaken tours of inspection in Europe, Poliakova had acted as his deputy in Moscow. Even though many of her colleagues disappeared during the purges, Poliakova survived, probably because her knowledge of the GRU's files was regarded as indispensable. According to Foote, Poliakova was switched to head the GRU's Spanish section in 1944, and when he and Trepper reached Moscow in January 1945, they were interrogated by her. She remained at her post until April 1946, when she fell ill. Soon afterwards, she disappeared and was probably liquidated 'in about May 1946 . . . The Centre has only one penalty for failure.'[6]

Poliakova had laid the foundations of the *Rote Drei* in 1936 when she had supervised the activities of the GRU's network in Switzerland, which at that time had consisted of Rachel Duebendorfer and Otto Puenter in Berne, and Alexander Rado in Geneva. In April 1938, Rado had been put in touch with Puenter, a generously proportioned lawyer codenamed PAKBO, who worked as a journalist reporting parliamentary proceedings in Berne for his own INSA Socialist press agency. An experienced GRU agent with a useful cover, Puenter had maintained good contacts with the Swiss military establishment and had run some sources into Italy, whence he received reports on Italian naval movements. His main source was GABEL, a Yugoslav former pilot who acted as the Spanish Consul in Susak, a port on the Yugoslavian coast close to the Italian frontier. Although GABEL harboured Republican sympathies, he had been in regular touch with General Franco's official representative in Belgrade and had acquired some interesting intelligence concerning Spain and Italy for Puenter. As well as GABEL, Puenter had also managed Georges Blun, a French political correspondent based in Zurich codenamed LONG, who had learned his tradecraft from the Deuxième Bureau and the British SIS during the First World War. Despite his contacts with numerous intelligence agencies, including the Polish and the American, his first loyalties had always been to the Comintern and the GRU, and in 1920 he was expelled from Switzerland for Communist agitation. His return in 1939, following a considerable period as a journalist in Berlin, had enabled him to cultivate a wide range of Swiss and German contacts from whom he extracted some very worthwhile intelligence. Blun spent most of 1942 in Germany or German-occupied territory and often featured in the *Rote Drei*'s traffic. Among the many contacts he milked were journalists, an SS lieutenant-general, a director of a Swiss airline, various German nobles and Austrian financiers, some Hungarian diplomats and a few Swedish industrialists.

Puenter's third source was a former German Social Democrat codenamed POISSON, who had taken Swiss nationality after fleeing from his home in the Saarland, where he had participated in the League of Nations administration before the 1935 plebiscite. After the war, when an effort was made to find Puenter, it was discovered that he had moved to East Berlin. When interviewed on the subject of the *Rote Drei*, Puenter proved highly unreliable, making statements that were obviously untrue, such as his claim that Field Marshal Jodl had been one of his collaborators. Nevertheless, despite his disinformation, Puenter had been an important figure in the GRU's organisation, not least because he had obtained considerable financial support for the network by the expedient of promising Swiss businessmen lucrative post-war contracts with the Soviets in return for immediate cash aid. One

person who had co-operated with Puenter by giving money
and information was Emil Guehrle, a director of the Oerlikon
arms manufacturer, who featured in a couple of messages
and had made a regular contribution to the *Rote Drei*'s dwin-
dling funds.

In December 1939, Rado had been joined in Geneva by
Ursula Kuczynski, who as SONIA had been assigned the task
of facilitating Rado's communications in the event that his
channel, via microfilm carried by couriers, to the Embassy
in Paris was interrupted. She in turn handled Rachel Duebendorfer and ran the GRU's two British volunteers, Allan Foote
and Leon Beurton, both veterans of the International Brigade. 'She taught them the rules of conspiracy, how to use
secret codes and operate a radio, and in fact everything an
intelligence agent needs to know,' recalled Rado.[7] Ursula
married Beurton, a CPGB member whose French father had
become a naturalised British subject and had been killed on
the Western Front in 1914, so as to obtain a British passport.
Although the marriage was initially a sham to allow Ursula to
stay on in Switzerland and then travel to England, they have
remained devoted to each other to this day in Berlin, where
they live in reduced circumstances. Always an ideological
zealot, Ursula had travelled widely even before she had been
recruited into the GRU by Richard Sorge. At the age of
twenty-two she had moved to New York, where she helped
to run the Henry Street Settlement to accommodate poor
Jewish families with the legendary Lillian Wald.

Although the *Rote Drei* must have provided Moscow with
some useful items of information, including some from Belgrade where Rado had been despatched briefly in October
1940, the organisation did not produce any really strategically
significant intelligence until the autumn of 1942, when Rudolf
Roessler started supplying high-quality material to Rado via
Puenter. Rado has identified most of his agents and has disclosed the true names of many of the sources which appeared
in his wireless messages disguised by cryptonyms: Louis
Suss, of the French Legation in Berne, was SALTER; Dr Eugen
Bircher, of the Swiss medical delegation to Germany, was
another key source;[8] PETER was a director of the Bosch works

and a frequent visitor to Zurich laden with data about German munitions; and LOUISE was a generic cover for the Swiss General Staff. According to Rado, 'Rudolf Roessler only became "Lucy" in November 1942 when we established contact with him on a regular basis. Before that, all we had received from him were bits and pieces that TAYLOR (Christian Schneider) had passed on to us without telling Roessler he was doing so.'[9]

A German political refugee, Roessler had settled in Lucerne in 1933 and opened a small publishing business, which, in the summer of 1939, had attracted the attention of Dr Xavier Schneiper of the Swiss military intelligence service. While the Swiss had been anxious to exploit Roessler's many anti-Nazi contacts still in Germany, the publisher was motivated primarily by money, and by the end of 1942 he was receiving a regular salary from the Swiss via Schneiper, and from Rachel Duebendorfer through a GRU intermediary, or 'cut-out', Christian Schneider. Roessler had gained access to exceptionally accurate Swiss assessments of German troop movements and there is reason to believe that his Swiss contacts had known he was relaying their material to the Soviets. In any event, when the Bundespolizei finally intervened on 14 October 1943 and seized two of Rado's wireless operators, it found documents that could be traced to Roessler and to the Swiss General Staff.

The Bundespolizei's first move against the *Rote Drei* had been a raid on the home in Geneva of Edmond and Olga Hamel, timed to coincide with the arrest of Margaret Bolli and a search of her flat. The Hamels and Bolli had been Rado's radio operators, and the fact that he had needed three different transmitters to send his material to Moscow is an indication of the volume involved. The Bundespolizei had been listening to the traffic for a considerable period and in the raid recovered two transmitters, a partial record of Rado's accounts, and enough information about Soviet cipher techniques for Marc Payot to begin decrypting the thousands of signals that had been intercepted. As soon as he learned of the raids, Rado dropped from sight by checking himself into a clinic and asking Louis Suss to approach the British for help.

However, before he could obtain a reply, Moscow vetoed the idea. On 20 November, Foote was arrested in his flat in Lausanne in the act of receiving a lengthy message from Moscow, and suddenly the *Rote Drei* came to an end. The detainees underwent six months of solitary confinement and interrogation, and on 19 April 1944 Rachel Duebendorfer, Paul Boettcher and Christian Schneider were taken into custody. A month later Roessler was arrested and charged with espionage.

With the help of some unofficial assistance from the Abwehr, the Bundespolizei reconstructed much of Rado's network and identified its members from photographs taken covertly during a lengthy surveillance operation. Payot succeeded in deciphering a large quantity of Rado's messages and most of those imprisoned gave statements that either incriminated themselves or their contacts. The result was that the Hamels were released on bail in July 1944, having received a suspended prison sentence and a fine, paid by Otto Puenter, who was himself never charged. Rado escaped to Paris in September 1944, where he was reunited with Foote, who had been released earlier in the month. Rachel Duebendorfer was released soon after her arrest in June 1944 and promptly disappeared, reportedly to Paris and then to Moscow, where she was imprisoned again. In her absence she was sentenced by the Swiss to two years' imprisonment and fifteen years of exclusion from Switzerland. Her lover, Paul Boettcher, received a similar sentence and was transferred to a refugee camp at Sichem, but he escaped in July 1945 and was apparently spotted with Duebendorfer in Paris in August 1945. Thereafter, neither was seen again. In contrast, Christian Schneider co-operated with his interrogators and was set free within a month. The GRU made no attempt to re-establish contact with him and, in 1948, he moved to Paris to work for UNESCO.

While the Geneva end of the *Rote Drei* seems to have posed few problems for the Swiss, the arrest of Roessler early in June 1944 had proved highly embarrassing because he turned out to enjoy close links with Swiss military intelligence. He spent three months in custody and was then released without charge, after managing to persuade the authorities that it would not be worth prosecuting either him or Rachel Duebendorfer, whose arrest had taken place at about the same time. He was eventually charged with espionage in October 1945, but was acquitted. Short of money, he was lured back into espionage in mid-1947, this time ostensibly by the Czechs, and was prosecuted again in November 1953 and sentenced to twenty-one months' imprisonment.

For the West's security agencies, the *Rote Drei* presented a fascinating glimpse of how the GRU operated and offered several tangible clues to post-war espionage. Evidently, the Swiss network had been part of a much larger organisation, and its contacts extended across Europe to Canada and beyond. The GRU controller, Viktor Sukolov, who had operated from Brussels, had once appeared at Rado's home to give him instructions from the 'Director' at the 'Centre' in Moscow, and Rachel Duebendorfer was in touch with at least one member of the network betrayed by Gouzenko in Ottawa in 1945. While the Belgian branch had concentrated on German troop movements in Northern Europe, and the Canadian and American networks had focused on technical intelligence, the *Rote Drei* had been able to provide Moscow with accurate information of a strategic significance from inside Germany. Quite how Rado had achieved this was to become a matter of much speculation not only by historians, but also by some of the participants themselves who had never been allowed to learn the truth.[10]

The crucial watershed had been the autumn of 1943, when Roessler's material came on stream. Before that time Rado's signals had contained relatively trivial data, which, as we have seen, had emanated from a handful of Leftist sources who were personal contacts developed by Puenter. Attempts to determine the identity of the source of Roessler's material have been complicated by several factors, not the least of which were the many changing cryptonyms assigned to particular sources in the intercepted traffic, and the inexplicable Soviet reaction to the survivors of the *Rote Drei*, who, far from being greeted as heroes in Moscow after the war, were treated as though they had collaborated with the enemy and had willingly participated in an elaborate deception campaign. An additional complication was the possibility that some of the *Rote Drei*'s sources were identical to individuals who had made separate contact with the American OSS or the British SIS, or both, and even the Czech intelligence service. Whatever the case, post-war analysis of the *Rote Drei*'s messages has confirmed the authenticity of their content and the extraordinary speed with which they had reached the Soviets. Much of it could be traced back to Roessler, codenamed LUCY, but he had resisted all the attempts made by Moscow Centre, and evident in the traffic, to make him identify them. In his signals LUCY had referred constantly to four sub-agents, WERTHER, TEDDY, OLGA and ANNA, and both the CIA and the Swiss have devoted considerable resources to finding names for these cryptonyms. The CIA obtained copies of 437 signals, calculated to be around eight per cent of the total messages exchanged, in which fifty-five separate sources are indicated. Regrettably, there was minimal internal evidence to suggest the identities of the sources, for the intelligence conveyed was of an extraordinarily diverse nature. Statistically, the 437 texts were considered sufficiently large to make some deductions, the most important of which was that LUCY's four key sources had been responsible for forty-two and a half per cent of the radio traffic passing from Switzerland to Moscow. After lengthy study the CIA had positively identified fifteen of the cryptonyms and had put possible names to a further sixteen, leaving twenty-four unaccounted for. Nor was this the complete picture, for there were certainly people on the periphery of the *Rote Drei* who had never merited a mention in a signal to Moscow. Of the 332 texts traced to Rado, WERTHER had appeared in twenty per cent, making him by far the most important and productive source, with TEDDY at ten per cent, and OLGA and ANNA trailing in at eight per cent and three and a half per cent respectively.[11]

The CIA concluded that the speed with which the German data consistently reached Switzerland meant that the original German sources must have had access to some official communications channel. Considering that shortly before he died Roessler himself had hinted to a friend that Hans Oster and

Hans Bernd Gisevius, two well-known anti-Nazi conspirators who also happened to have been Abwehr officers, had been among his contacts adds weight to the theory that they had misused the Abwehr's internal channels for their own purposes. Certainly both had been in ideal positions to do so as, prior to his arrest in March 1944, Major-General Oster had been deputy chief of the Abwehr and had given very categoric and well-documented warnings to the Allies, via the Dutch Military Attaché in Berlin, of the imminent Nazi invasions of Holland and Norway. Gisevius, who had operated from the fall of Paris under vice-consular cover in Berne until his complicity in the 20th of July plot against Hitler in 1944 had made his position impossible, was also a likely candidate. He had been the recipient of a thrice-weekly diplomatic pouch to the Consulate from Abwehr headquarters in Berlin, and had been in touch with Allen Dulles of OSS, SIS and the Swiss authorities, as well as with Roessler and Georges Blun. In his memoirs Gisevius never admitted having been a source for the Soviets, despite his sympathies with the Kremlin's cause, but he had emphasised that 'Oster seemed to be organising an intelligence service of his own, within the counter-intelligence service . . . One of the most important of his activities was to instal his own confidential agents in the most diverse positions.'[12] Before becoming a key source for OSS, Gisevius had kept SIS well supplied with Nazi secrets, so there could be no doubt about his willingness to help the Allies.

The CIA research into LUCY's sources also produced the name of Colonel Fritz Boetzel, head of the High Command's cipher department until 1939 when he was transferred to the South-East Army Group's intelligence evaluation office. He had been known to Oster and Admiral Canaris, and had fitted the anti-Nazi profile of Roessler's contacts. Another candidate was Carl Goerdeler, formerly the Lord Mayor of Leipzig, who was Reichchancellor for price control until his execution in October 1944 for involvement in the plot to assassinate Hitler.

One person positively linked to Roessler's espionage was Ernst Lemmer, the German-born Berlin correspondent of the *Neue Zuercher Zeitung*, who was implicated in Roessler's second brush with the Swiss authorities after the war. A friend of the Swiss Military Attaché in Berlin, Lemmer was granted the cryptonym AGNES by LUCY. He was eventually elected to the Federal Bundestag and appointed a cabinet minister.

The conundrum of LUCY's sources is further complicated by the knowledge that as well as dealing with the Swiss and the *Rote Drei*, Roessler was also in touch with the Czechs. Colonel Karel Sedlacek had operated under journalistic cover in Zurich as a correspondent for the Prague daily *Narodni Listy*. Using the name Karl Selzinger, Sedlacek had cultivated Roessler and became friendly with a Swiss intelligence officer, Major Hans Hausamann. Both gave information to Sedlacek, who transmitted it to his superior in London, Colonel Frantisek Moravec, over a period of three years. Proof that Sedlacek and Hausamann had relied almost entirely upon Roessler for their information can be deduced from the fact that when LUCY was detained by the Bundespolizei, between June and September 1944, the quality of Sedlacek's reports to Moravec deteriorated markedly. In his memoirs Moravec recalled Sedlacek's success:

Reports arrived almost daily, giving details of men and material. We passed on these reports to the British, producing almost daily changes in the huge War Office maps on which the deployments of the German forces were plotted. The information was mainly rather technical data, such as movements of armies and divisions, changes in command, transportation and supply problems, innovation in equipment, but there were also comments and forecasts concerning the German invasion of the West.[13]

There were, however, two complications inherent in this extra channel of intelligence. One was the suspicion that in London Moravec, ostensibly a staunch anti-Communist, was acting for the Soviets as well as his British hosts, and secondly that Sedlacek himself may have been serving more than one master. After the war he was declared the Czech Military Attaché in Berne and had wasted no time in recruiting Roessler as his agent.

Since Moscow Centre knew from Moravec (and perhaps

other sources) that Roessler had been acting for the *Rote Drei* on a non-exclusive basis, this may well have been the foundation for the GRU's obvious paranoia and post-war determination to discover who had been working for whom. It was a puzzle that only the participants themselves were able to solve, and some of the key players were more inclined to perpetuate the *Rote Drei*'s mythology than to elicit the truth. One aspect that gave the network some of its notoriety was the claim that, much like Sorge's warning to the Kremlin which had been ignored, the GRU in Switzerland had given advance notice of the Nazi invasion of Russia in June 1942. In reality, as the CIA learned through its study of the Swiss intercepts, no such signal had been sent, and in any event LUCY had not become a conduit for the *Rote Drei* until after BARBAROSSA. However, even if the *Rote Drei* had not alerted Moscow to the German intentions in 1942, it had provided intelligence in April the following year which correctly predicted the Nazi offensive on the Kursk salient, an advantage that was fully exploited and had tipped the balance in the resulting tank battle in favour of the Red Army. Indeed, some strategists have characterised this single event as the turning-point of the war when the tide finally moved against Hitler.

5 · Atomic Secrets

Even after many years of experience with captured illegals, Western security services remain puzzled by the extent of this parallel system. In the late sixties, estimates based on the testimony of defectors, the size of illegal training classes in Moscow, and the confessions of arrested illegals ranged from several hundred to a thousand dispatched to the West.

Harry Rositske in *KGB: The Eyes of Russia*[1]

No Western intelligence agency was to get a hint of what had happened to Rachel Duebendorfer until September 1945 and the defection of a GRU cipher clerk in Canada. Igor Gouzenko was himself of only minor importance, apart from his help to the RCMP in filling in some useful details regarding the personalities within the Soviet Embassy in Ottawa, but the 109 documents he removed from the closely guarded secret suite in the Embassy, the *referentura*, in anticipation of his escape, were to inflict a mortal blow to Soviet intelligence operations in North America.

Among the papers stolen by Gouzenko was an exchange of messages between the Assistant Military Attaché, Lieutenant-Colonel Motinov, and Moscow over how to handle a plea for help from a crippled woman named Hermina Rabinowitch. Study of Gouzenko's documents revealed that in November 1943 Rachel Duebendorfer had written to her friend Rabinowitch asking for $6,700. The letter had been passed through the internal mail of the International Labour Organisation, where both women worked, Duebendorfer in Geneva and Rabinowitch in Montreal. Prior to her transfer to Canada in 1940, the Lithuanian-born Rabinowitch had been a close colleague of the Duebendorfers, and before her work as a researcher for the International Labour Organisation she had been employed by the Soviet Trade Delegation in Berlin. From Gouzenko's file it became clear that after her first plea in November 1943, Duebendorfer cabled Rabinowitch *en clair* in January 1944 and sent another letter in April. Motinov had responded in May 1944 by assigning the Soviet First Secretary, Sergei M. Kudriavtsev, codenamed LEON, to handle Rabinowitch. Kudriavtsev's passport photograph showed him to be identical to Alexander Erdberg, the GRU officer who had played a key role in the development of the *Rote Kapelle* in Berlin in 1941. Kudriavtsev and Rabinowitch met in Montreal on 4 May and he arranged for $10,000 to be sent by her to Duebendorfer in Geneva, via a company in New York which imported Swiss watches.

The RCMP pursued these clues with Rabinowitch, who, very reluctantly, gave evidence to the Royal Commission established to investigate Gouzenko's revelations. She admitted that, on Kudriavtsev's instructions, she had travelled to New York and received $10,000 from a man subsequently identified as Pavel P. Mikhailov, the acting Soviet Consul-General in Manhattan since 1941. According to the CIA, Mikhailov's true name was Pavel P. Menshikov, and he had been the deputy chief of the GRU's Section IV until his arrival in the United States with diplomatic status. Having received the cash, Rabinowitch had handed it to William Helbein, a fifty-six-year-old Russian who had become a naturalised American citizen and was a director of Helbros, a watch company based in New York City at West 48th Street. Helbein had transferred the dollars to Geneva, where they were collected by another International Labour Organisation employee, a Lithuanian named Alexander Abramson, who in the autumn of 1944 happened to be seconded to a Soviet military mission inspecting internment camps in Switzerland.[2]

Although the scent went dead with Abramson, who was

sacked by the International Labour Organisation when his name was made public in Canada, and who subsequently took a job with a French trade union in Paris, there was no further trace of Duebendorfer, but the paper trail had established a clear link between the GRU's wartime network in Germany, Switzerland and Canada. Mikhailov was revealed to have been a senior GRU officer, who, according to some of Gouzenko's material, had headed the GRU's network in North America and had supervised the activities of Major Sokolov in Canada. Sokolov, who appeared in the cable traffic as DAVIE, had been the Commercial Counsellor at the Soviet Embassy in Ottawa before the arrival of Colonel Nikolai Zabotin in June 1943. As for Hermina Rabinowitch, five of Gouzenko's stolen documents referred to her and described her contacts with Motinov and Kudriavtsev. The Royal Commission, which noted her impressive linguistic skills and academic achievements, concluded:

It was evident during the early part of her testimony that she had come prepared to tell a certain story based on her assumption that what she had thus read comprised all the information with regard to her in the possession of the Commission. When faced with all the documents she became embarrassed and stood mute. She was then asked whether she wanted to consult with her Counsel, who was present throughout the examination, to decide her line of conduct. Both of them withdrew, and after a short recess she changed her story and reluctantly admitted the substance of the documents and furnished many details which they did not mention.[3]

The Commission took lengthy testimony in secret from Gouzenko and analysed the material he had provided, and on 14 February 1946 thirteen suspected Soviet agents were taken into custody: two engineers working for the National Research Council, Edward Mazerall and Philip Durnford Smith; Professor Raymond Boyer, an academic from McGill University, who had researched the development of high explosive and was the NRC's explosives expert; Squadron-Leader Fred Poland of the RCAF; Lieutenant David Shugar, a naval radar specialist; J. Scott Benning from the Department of Munitions and Supply; Captain David Lunan of the Canadian army; Professor Israel Halperin, a speech-writer, and Emma

Woikin, a code clerk, both in the Department of External Affairs; Eric Adams, an economist with the National Selective Service; and Kathleen Willsher of the British High Commission. As Gouzenko named others whose cryptonyms appeared in the stolen documents, more arrests were made and the suspects were taken to the barracks of the RCMP's training division at Rockcliffe for interrogation. The next to be detained was Harold Gerson, who was Scott Benning's brother-in-law and who also worked in the Department of Munitions. A graduate of McGill University, he had been born in Montreal of Russian parents. Squadron-Leader Matt S. Nightingale, a telephone specialist, was arrested soon afterwards, under similar conditions of great secrecy so as to avoid tipping off other members of the Soviet network, and no public announcement was made for nearly three weeks while the Commission cross-examined the detainees.

Some of the suspects were easily identified from Gouzenko's documents, while the true names of others had been protected by codenames. One vital Soviet source, codenamed ALEK, was described as a scientist at the Chalk River atomic research facility who was about to return to England to take up an appointment at London University. This clearly was a reference to the physicist Allan Nunn May, who did fly home in September, only to be arrested on 6 March 1946. Dr Nunn May, who had been placed under surveillance by MI5 in the vain hope of entrapping him when he conformed with Zabotin's instructions and met his Soviet contact in London, readily admitted that he had been a Communist since Cambridge and that he had passed numerous atomic secrets, including two tiny samples of enriched Uranium-235, to Lieutenant Pavel Angelov, Zabotin's Assistant Military Attaché. According to Gouzenko's papers, this material was considered so important that Motinov had taken it straight to Moscow. Under interrogation, Nunn May confirmed every detail about his case already disclosed by Gouzenko and was sentenced to ten years' imprisonment.

Of the original thirteen arrests, two suspects had initially evaded the RCMP. Fred Rose, the Communist MP for the Cartier Division of Montreal, who had been on the first list of arrests, was not caught until 14 March when he was surprised at his apartment. Sam Carr, the secretary of the Communist Party, who had been born Schmil Kogen in the Ukraine and was known to have completed a course at the Lenin Institute in Moscow, had disappeared and was believed to have escaped abroad. This was the second time that he had gone to ground since his arrival in Canada as an emigrant in 1924. As editor of the Communist Party newspaper, the *Clarion*, he had fled to Philadelphia in 1940 to write anti-war articles. It was only after the Nazi invasion of the Soviet Union that he had surrendered to the RCMP in Toronto in September 1942 to face a charge of sedition. Following his second disappearance, he was not to be caught until January 1949, when he was arrested in New York and sentenced to six years' imprisonment.

Once the Gouzenko papers had been translated, they were circulated to Allied counter-intelligence agencies and a comprehensive analysis was undertaken to reconstruct the Soviet networks in Canada and to trace their contacts overseas. Fred Rose and his mistress, Freda Linton, were revealed as vital links between the Canadian sources and Zabotin. Rose was identified as her recruiter by Kay Willsher, while Freda, who had been born Fritzie Lipchitz in Montreal of Polish parents and had recently worked for the Film Board of Canada, apparently had acted as a go-between for Rose and Professor Boyer. Similarly David Lunan, the Scottish-born army officer who edited the military journal, *Canadian Affairs*, supervised Durnford Smith, Mazerall and Halperin, and reported to Major Rogov, Zabotin's Air Attaché.

Some of those arrested gave detailed statements and thereby both implicated other conspirators and served to give added credibility to Gouzenko. Kay Willsher, for example, the London School of Economics graduate working in the British High Commission, who was an active Communist and had been betraying information since 1935, named her contacts as Fred Rose and a Bank of Canada official, Eric Adams. Similarly Emma Woikin, the clerk in the Department of External Affairs, who had been born in Canada of Russian Dukhobor parents, admitted that she had routinely left secret

documents in a hiding-place where they were collected by
Zabotin's driver, Captain Gorshkov. She had also been in
close contact with Major Sokolov's wife and had even
requested Soviet citizenship.[4] Lunan's evidence to the Royal
Commission not only incriminated himself, but also compromised Halperin, Mazerall and Durnford Smith. However, in
the subsequent trials, Halperin, Adams and another Bank of
Canada employee, Agatha Chapman, pleaded not guilty and
were acquitted. Born in England, Chapman had moved to
Canada as a child and had graduated from the University of
British Columbia. At the time of her arrest she was a committed Marxist and had been seconded by the bank to the Bureau
of Statistics.

A total of twenty-one were charged; prosecutions followed
in fifteen of the cases and twelve convictions were obtained.
Of those incriminated by Gouzenko, the charges against Captain Jack Gottheil and Freda Linton, of the International
Labour Office, were withdrawn. Norman Veall, an English
chemist and Young Communist League activist, who had
worked with Allan Nunn May at Cambridge, also escaped a
charge. According to Gouzenko's documents,[5] he had asked
Nunn May's advice about passing information from the Chalk
River atomic research facility to the Soviets, but had been
warned against such a move. According to Nunn May, Veall
was in too junior a post to be useful and his radical politics
were too well known. When Major Samuel Burman was
cross-examined, he simply denied that he was the individual
referred to in one of Gouzenko's dossiers, specifically the
text of a lengthy signal from Colonel Motinov to Moscow
concerning one of Fred Rose's sources known as 'Burman'.
In the absence of any collateral evidence of Burman having
attended a secret rendezvous outside Canada House in
London in October 1944, as described in Motinov's instructions, Burman was not charged. In the case of J. Scott
Benning, his conviction was quashed on appeal. His only link
to the ring was an entry in one of his own notebooks listing
two of Fred Rose's telephone numbers in Ottawa, and an
entry on a card index under the codename FOSTER which
suggested that Scott Benning had been supplying war pro-

duction data to Zheveinov, one of the TASS agency correspondents in Ottawa.

The Commission also reported that five Soviet cryptonyms, all members of Zabotin's GRU ring, had not been positively identified. They were GALYA, a housewife living next to Major Sokolov; GINI, the Jewish owner of a drugstore and a photographic laboratory; GOLIA, a young artist in a photographic studio; GREEN, an assistant to a superintendent dealing with procurement contracts in a tank assembly plant, all in Montreal; and SURENSEN, a source in naval intelligence who was believed to be Lieutenant Henning I. Sorensen, who gave evidence to the Commission on a voluntary basis.[6]

Nine of those sentenced to terms of imprisonment were, despite their names, either of Polish or of Russian origin and had arrived in Canada decades earlier as immigrants. Fred Rose, for example, the senior Canadian Communist Party figure who had been elected to the Canadian Parliament in 1932 and was demonstrably a key figure in Zabotin's spy ring, had been born Fred Rosenberg to Russian parents in Lublin, Poland. After serving their sentences those of foreign origin were deported.

Gouzenko's testimony, combined with his stolen papers, revealed no fewer than four separate Soviet intelligence networks operating in Canada, two of which extended to the United States, where the defector identified Elizabeth Bentley in Washington DC and Anatoli A. Yakovlev, based in the New York Consulate, as key organisers. Vitali G. Pavlov was the NKVD *rezident* in Canada, with Zabotin as his GRU counterpart. A naval intelligence network had operated in Halifax and Vancouver, masterminded by a Captain Patzerney from New York, but, according to Gouzenko, two other diplomats at the Embassy in Ottawa undertook an intelligence function: the Commercial Counsellor, Ivan Krotov, and the Second Secretary, Goussarov, who headed the political section. The documentation was compelling, as was illustrated by Zabotin's highly compromising, handwritten notes regarding a request for relevant information he had made to Sam Carr about the use of illegals, a concept hitherto only vaguely understood in the West:

Chart 8 The Canadian network

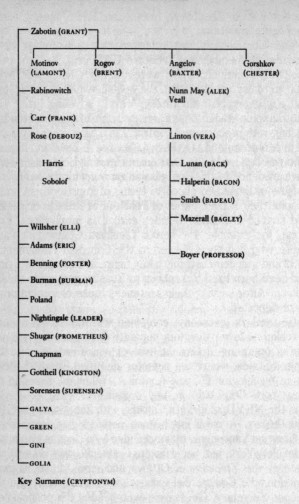

Zabotin (GRANT)

Motinov (LAMONT) Rogov (BRENT) Angelov (BAXTER) Gorshkov (CHESTER)

Rabinowitch Nunn May (ALEK) Veall

Carr (FRANK)

Rose (DEBOUZ) Linton (VERA)

Harris Lunan (BACK)

Sobolof Halperin (BACON)

Smith (BADEAU)

Mazerall (BAGLEY)

Willsher (ELLI)

Adams (ERIC)

Benning (FOSTER) Boyer (PROFESSOR)

Burman (BURMAN)

Poland

Nightingale (LEADER)

Shugar (PROMETHEUS)

Chapman

Gottheil (KINGSTON)

Sorensen (SURENSEN)

GALYA

GREEN

GINI

GOLIA

Key Surname (CRYPTONYM)

Task No. 3 of '1.8.45'

1. Requirements which a person living as an 'illegal' must meet (nationality, citizenship, occupation, education, knowledge of languages, family and financial considerations etc.).

2. Ways of legalisation (organisation of a commercial undertaking, joining a business firm as a partner, what kind of firm, joining as a member any office, joining the army as a volunteer, accepting employment).

3. Documents which an 'illegal' must possess (passport, different kinds of certificates, references, recommendation letters, etc.).

4. More expedient methods to slip into any country.

5. To provide for secure living quarters and financial means during the period when the 'illegal' gets acquainted with the local set-up and conditions.

6. To reveal the channels of influence of the English government on the foreign policy of Canada.

7. Conditions of entry into the country and of moving about in the country.

8. Conditions of adoption and living in the country.

9. Methods of work of the counter-espionage. The organisation of the Federal and provincial counter-espionage services.[7]

Zabotin's preoccupation with illegals, which reflected Moscow's interest in the topic, was highlighted by more of his correspondence concerning his efforts to obtain a passport for an agent who was to adopt the identity of Ignacy S. Witczak, an unmarried farm labourer and naturalised Canadian from Poland who had fought on the Republican side with the Mackenzie Papineau Battalion of the International Brigade in 1937 during the Spanish Civil War. While in Spain Witczak had lost his passport and had reported this upon his return to Halifax in February 1939. As far as the real Witczak was concerned, this had been the end of the matter, and he had simply applied for a copy of his original naturalisation papers.[8] Unknown to him, his original passport had been used by an illegal, Zalamon Litvin, accompanied by his wife Bunia, to land at New York from the ss *Veendam* in September 1938. Litvin was an experienced intelligence officer, who had already served in China, reporting on the Japanese invasion, under cover of a Finnish businessman based in Teitsin. Having described himself as a merchant, Litvin the impostor had passed through the US immigration controls without incident, but Witczak's original passport had expired after five years, in March 1942, a matter that was to inconvenience Litvin, who had established himself in Los Angeles and, according to the GRU's messages, was anxious to have the document revalidated for a further five years. According to Litvin, who still lives in Moscow, he was operating as a contact for a hitherto undisclosed spy in America's atomic weapons programme.

Moscow seemed to have shared Litvin's anxiety, for the subject of the renewal was mentioned by the head of GRU's illegals branch, Ilya Milstein, who had visited Zabotin on a tour of inspection in June 1944, masquerading as a diplomatic courier named Milsky, and had sought a meeting with Sam Carr to discuss the best way of acquiring Canadian passports. As a result of Milstein's discussion with Carr, complex arrangements had been made to accommodate Litvin, who was highly valued by the GRU and had found a job as a lecturer in politics at the University of Southern California in Los Angeles and was considering taking a PhD at a foreign affairs institute in Washington DC. Since neither the handwriting nor the photo on Litvin's renewal application would match the original deposited in Ontario in 1937, Carr had recruited an agent inside the Canadian Passport Office and had bribed him with $3,000 to replace Witczak's application with a back-dated version which fitted Litvin and included his wife, Bunia. Gouzenko's documentation also indicated that the illegal's original, stolen passport had been brought back to Ottawa in case the Passport Office demanded to see it. To deliver the passport to Carr, Zabotin's elaborate security procedures required it to pass from Major Rogov to a physician, Dr Henry Harris, who relayed it to Carr. Harris was Carr's optometrist in Toronto and proved to be of Russian extraction. He had been born in New York of Russian immigrant parents and had become a naturalised Canadian citizen at the age of five. His sentence of five years' imprisonment for his part in the passport transaction was later quashed on appeal. Unfortunately, Carr's recruit in the Passport Office had inserted the replacement into the right file, but neglected to extract and destroy the original, so when the RCMP followed up the clues to Witczak in Gouzenko's papers, they discovered both applications. Of particular interest to the Canadian investigators was the attached documentation supporting Litvin's application for a renewal. The counter-signatory, for example, was Dr John Soboloff, a medical practitioner of Toronto, who, when confronted with the evidence, admitted that he had completed the statutory declaration as a favour for his friend and patient Sam Carr. He also gave evidence to the Commission and subsequently was convicted of passport fraud and fined $500. The RCMP's investigation eventually led to a corrupt clerk in the Passport Office, W. M. Pappin, who denied switching Witczak's file and thereby narrowly escaped prosecution.

The RCMP's enquiries inevitably alerted Litvin to Gouzenko's betrayal, and the FBI's discreet surveillance of him, following a tip from Ottawa, proved ineffective. His movements across the United States were monitored, to New York and back to Los Angeles, and his mail to his wife intercepted, until he simply disappeared by slipping aboard a Soviet freighter in Oregon. Examination of his letters revealed a very crude clear language code in which Litvin had explained to his wife that 'Harry' had fallen ill and had been obliged to seek the help of doctors. To the FBI, this was further proof that the illegal, referring to himself in the third person, had spotted the surveillance and had made emergency contact with his Soviet case officer in New York. The FBI had exercised restraint at the request of the RCMP and, after Litvin's escape, had been obliged to content itself with approaches to all the illegal's contacts in the hope of extracting limited confessions. When interviewed, most expressed astonishment at the university lecturer's duplicity, and a few admitted confiding information of an unclassified nature to him. As for the original Ignacy Witczak, who was still farming in Ontario, he willingly gave evidence to the Commission and satisfied the RCMP that he had been an innocent party to the Soviets' misuse of his passport, which he had believed lost in Spain.

With comprehensive documentation of this kind, it is hardly

surprising that Gouzenko's revelations were to have a profound impact on the West's appreciation of Soviet legal networks, run from diplomatic premises in much the same way the British had been operating for the past two decades. Gouzenko's purloined papers documented twenty separate agents, each ascribed a different codename, and linked sixteen Soviet diplomats to espionage. In addition, there were vague references to numerous other individuals in Gouzenko's papers, many of whom were regarded by the counter-intelligence investigators as credible espionage suspects. Clearly the most effective counter-measure was the introduction of an adequate order-of-battle analysis designed to identify the intelligence personnel adopting diplomatic cover, and the intensive surveillance of diplomatic missions to detect clandestine communications with individual agents. These lessons were learned, perhaps belatedly, and applied in those cities with facilities to support such action. In countries that enjoyed no security infrastructure, of which Canada and Australia were but two, the respective governments were persuaded by MI5 that a definite threat existed, and supplied with detailed advice on the training and development of suitable police special branches.

The evidence deployed to great effect by MI5 consisted of the Serpell/Hemblys-Scales report, the British assessment of the wartime investigation conducted by the Gestapo into the GRU's illegal network in Europe, together with a highly classified analysis of Soviet signals traffic intercepted by AFSA. This was to be the basis of many productive investigations and represents convincing proof that the GRU and the KGB had adopted a long-term policy of establishing illegal networks across the globe. There was also collateral confirmation that many of these networks were interconnected, with the same personalities turning up in different cells, often in different parts of the world. This may have been an economic deployment of that most scarce resource, the skilled and ideologically committed illegal, but it did have implications for security and offered investigators the chance of breaching the compartmental integrity of the networks. Thus some names which had been found in the Japanese files, relating to the pre-war Comintern apparatus in Shanghai, were found to have a European relevance, and clear links were traced between Soviet illegals in North America and other parts of the world.

Gouzenko's defection provided eloquent proof of the Soviets' dependency on the local Communist Party infrastructure to supply sources and organisers. Fred Rose, indisputably a key GRU agent for many years, had been a senior member of the Party in Canada and had served a year's imprisonment for sedition in 1931 and, as recently as 1942, had been interned for 'disloyal activities'. While the West's counter-intelligence agencies noted the inherent insecurity of the obvious connection between the Party and the illegal apparatus, the Soviets resolved to remedy the situation henceforth by distancing their future activities from the Party membership. Evidence of this measure was later to be given by Rupert Sigl, an Austrian illegal who defected in 1969 and who, during his subsequent debriefing, recalled that he had been instructed by the KGB to avoid contact with 'the party level'.[9] Similarly, Alexander Orlov explained the Soviet determination to separate the illegals from the Party:

Each time a spy ring operating for the Soviets was exposed, the trail led straight to the Soviet embassy with all the resulting adverse publicity. And when some of the arrested spies turned out to be Communists, the press would raise a bitter campaign against the local Communist party, branding it as a gang of Soviet spies masquerading as a legitimate political party. What the Soviet government wanted was to reorganise its intelligence operations on foreign soil in such a manner that if some of its agents were caught, the trail would not lead to the Soviet embassy, and the Soviet government would be able to disclaim any connection with the exposed spy ring. The answer to this dilemma was the creation of the so-called 'illegal *rezidentura*'.[10]

Whilst the KGB and GRU sought to improve their security by developing new networks isolated from the Party membership, they were handicapped by two specific disadvantages. Firstly, the vulnerability of their existing illegal organisation, which was heavily reliant upon ideological sympathisers who inevitably had once enjoyed an overt Party link, ranging from

full card-carrying membership to potentially suspicious
association with front organisations of varying transparency.
Secondly, the difficulty of recruiting suitable personnel in the
post-war era from beyond those individuals who had already
demonstrated a political commitment to the cause, and
thereby probably had come to the attention of the local security service. Thus, although the Soviets felt compelled to
develop sources outside their conventional pool of talent, the
task was fraught with difficulty. Quite apart from the inherent
improbability of finding non-Russian collaborators with the
appropriate motivation to adopt the lifestyle of an illegal, there
was the prevailing economic and political climate to be taken
into account. Whereas the depression of the 1930s had helped
to create an environment in which intellectuals and others
had looked favourably upon the Soviet experiment, the revelation of Stalin's excesses and the continuing confrontation
of the Cold War had made the challenge of recruitment very
unrewarding.

While the GRU and KGB grappled with the implications
of Moscow's new policy, there must have been an acknowledgment that some of the remaining illegal networks in North
America were vulnerable to the FBI's continuing investigation. For example, Professor Halperin, the Canadian born
of Russian parentage who was acquitted of the charges arising
out of Gouzenko's revelations, had been linked to Klaus
Fuchs, the nuclear physicist who was not to be identified as
a Soviet agent for a further three years. Although Halperin
had never met Fuchs, he did know his sister, Kristel Heine-
man, and had mailed magazines and newspapers to Fuchs
while the scientist was interned in Canada in 1940. When
Halperin was arrested, Fuchs's name and current address in
Edinburgh were found in his address book. Fuchs was
eventually to be arrested in February 1950, but only after a
batch of retrospectively decrypted Soviet signals had in-
directly identified him as a GRU source. An intercepted GRU
cipher text had referred to an agent who was obviously a
physicist with access to some of the Manhattan Project's
most highly classified secrets. A lengthy and ingenious comparison between the known movements of the spy, who had

apparently visited Boston in February 1945, and the journeys declared by members of the atomic bomb team revealed a similarity. By a process of elimination, Fuchs was discovered to have visited his sister then living in Cambridge, Massachusetts, just outside Boston, at a time that had coincided with the incriminating GRU coded message. Under subtle interrogation by MI5, which succeeded in protecting the cryptographic origin of the evidence against him, Fuchs was to admit his espionage and to identify by name one of his contacts as Jurgen Kuczynski of the KDP. He was unaware that his GRU case officer, the woman whom he had met secretly in some of Oxfordshire's lanes during the war, was Kuczynski's sister Ursula. There were, in short, plenty of avenues of investigation for the FBI and MI5 to follow in their search for illegals.

In the aftermath of Gouzenko's revelations, the FBI concentrated on the pursuit of Anatoli Yakovlev, his contacts, and the occasional lead offered by the AFSA's decryption programme. Yakovlev himself remained at his post in New York until the end of 1946, when he narrowly escaped indictment in another espionage case, that of Abraham Brothman, which had been brought as a result of testimony from Elizabeth Bentley. Yakovlev subsequently spent two years at the Soviet Embassy in Paris, and his true name, Anatoli Yatskov, was later given by a defector. Although there was plenty of circumstantial evidence to link Yakovlev to a network of agents operating across North America, it was not until Klaus Fuchs identified a chemist named Harry Gold as one of his contacts that the FBI's investigation achieved a long-awaited breakthrough. After his arrest Fuchs was entirely cooperative with the British Security Service and explained that he had taken the initiative in offering his services to the Soviets. He implicated Jurgen Kuczynski as his link with a London-based Embassy official, who was identified from MI5 photographs as Simon D. Kremer, the Military Attaché's secretary. He never knew the name of the woman to whom he had subsequently reported, but gave an accurate description of his contact in America, where he had worked during 1944 and 1945, before his final appointment to the British atomic research establishment at Harwell. Soon after his arrival in England, Fuchs said, he had held a rendezvous with a Russian at the Nag's Head pub in Wood Green, north London. From photographs, Fuchs identified this man, whom he was to meet every three months for the next two years, as Aleksandre Fomin, an NKVD officer whose true name was Aleksandre S. Feklisov. He had arrived in London in 1946 with the rank of third secretary, and at their first meeting had reprimanded Fuchs for having compromised himself with an old KDP friend from before the war, whom he had used to re-establish contact with the Soviets.

Under interrogation in Wormwood Scrubs prison Fuchs admitted that at the end of 1943 his female case officer had met him at the roadside near Banbury and had given him instructions on how to resume contact with the GRU after his arrival in the United States. Fuchs had been transferred to the Allied atomic research project at Los Alamos and was scheduled to land in New York early in December 1943. Soon after his arrival he had followed her very precise directions and in January 1944 met a man who introduced himself as 'Raymond'. When confronted with movie stills shot in secret by the FBI of Harry Gold, Fuchs confirmed that Gold was the Soviet contact he knew as 'Raymond', whom he had met several times: five times in New York, twice in Boston and once in Santa Fe, New Mexico, not far from the Los Alamos site where Fuchs had been a part of the team developing an atomic weapon. The positive identification of Gold by Fuchs was enough for the FBI to arrest him on suspicion of espionage.

Born in Berne, Switzerland, as Heinrich Golodnitsky to Russian parents who emigrated to the United States four years later, Gold admitted that he had been a Soviet agent since 1935. When his antecedents were examined, it was realised that his cousin was Maurice Kapelowitz, one of the founder directors of the Excellent Raincoat Company in Brussels back in 1924. Coincidentally, when the FBI interviewed Gold in August 1950, he was described not as a chemist, but as an official of Pago Originals Inc., a supplier of rainwear based at 222 West 37th Street. His previous employment

LEFT Ernest Weiss, the organiser of a GRU network in Britain, who survived undetected throughout the war. When confronted by MI5 in 1945, he readily admitted his espionage and subsequently pursued a successful career as a concert pianist.

RIGHT Zalamon Litvin, the key illegal who operated in California between 1938 and 1945 and ran several hitherto undiscovered agents inside the Anglo-American atomic research project at Los Alamos.

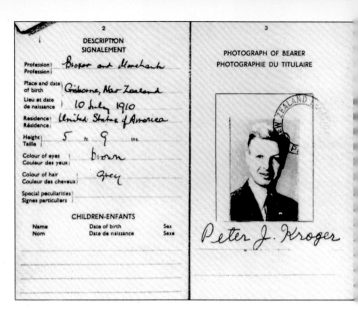

ABOVE AND BELOW The New Zealand passports issued in the names of Peter and Helen Kroger by Paddy Costello in Paris to Morris and Lona Cohen.

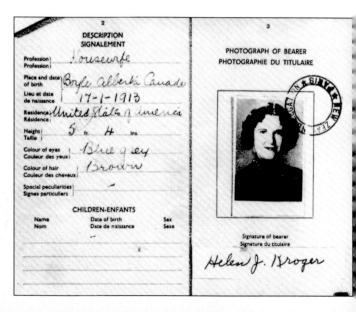

Profession / Profession: ~~MECHANIC~~ COMPANY DIRECTOR

Place and date of birth / Lieu et date de naissance: COBALT, ONTARIO, CANADA 27 AUGUST 1924

Residence / Résidence: CANADA

Height / Taille: 5 FT. 8 INS

Colour of eyes / Couleur des yeux: GREY

Colour of hair / Couleur des cheveux: DARK BROWN

Visible peculiarities / Signes particuliers:

CHILDREN — ENFANTS

Name / Nom | Date of birth / Date de naissance | Sex / Sexe

PHOTOGRAPH OF BEARER
PHOTOGRAPHIE DU TITULAIRE

ABOVE Gordon Lonsdale's Canadian passport. When the document was given to the Black Museum, Lonsdale's signature was obliterated for security reasons.
BELOW Konon Molody, alias Gordon Lonsdale (second left), entertaining friends from his London University course. Next to him is Charles Elwell's wife, Anne Glass, herself a distinguished MI5 officer.

RIGHT An enlargement of a microdot message addressed to Konon Molody's wife and found among the espionage paraphernalia recovered from the Krogers' home.

BELOW LEFT The death notice published in the *Los Angeles Times* of Emil Goldfus, the identity adopted by William Fisher, the illegal *rezident* who called himself Rudolph Abel. By the time of his arrest in New York, he had become Mark Collins. The FBI never realised that his strange English accent was typical of someone born in Newcastle-upon-Tyne.

BELOW RIGHT A portrait of Colonel Abel, by Sheldon Fink.

DEATHS REPORTED OCT. 11.

Mannattan.

Ages of one year or under are put down one year.

Name and Address.	Age in Yrs.	Date Dth. Oct.
BUCHLER, Henry, 2,129 Madison Av	1	10
BROWN, William J., 33 E. 83d St...	53	10
BERGSTEIN, Joseph, 157 Ludlow St.	1	9
BRAUN, Charles, 319 E. 78th St.....	42	10
BLUM, Lina, 25 Avenue B..........	66	9
CIHLAR, John, 456 E. 77th St.......	53	10
COHEN, Fannie, 119 Delancey St..	1	10
CHEITMAN, Charles, 3 Goerck St...	1	10
COHEN, Lillie, 174 Clinton St......	1	11
DUFFY, Peter J., 165 E. 90th St.....	53	9
DE MARTINE, Sarcrio, 827 E. 11th St	1	10
FAY, Michael, 244 1st Av...........	63	9
FREEDMAN, Ernest, 1,842 2d Av...	1	10
FIELD, Dennis, 117 West St........	84	10
FELDMAN, Isidor, 33 E. 122d St...	6	11
GOLDBERG, Itosie, 354 E. 84th St...	80	9
▶ GOLDFUSS, Emil, 120 E. 87th St...	1	9
GOLDENBERG, Isidor, 10 Stanton St	42	10
HELFSTEIN, Tillie, 145 Ridge St...	1	10
HENNESSY, Kate, 415 W. 56th St...	28	10
HAMISH, Gottlieb, 413 E. 69th St...	70	9

A PORTFOLIO OF ABELS
Drawings, paintings and photographs of Rudolph Abel, 1954–1957

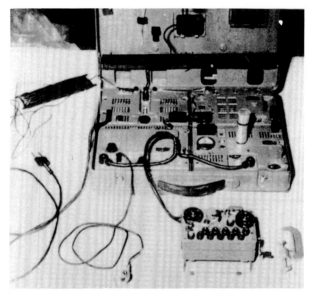

The shortwave radio transmitter and high-speed magnetic tape-recorder which was seized from the Krogers and was recognised as standard issue to KGB illegals.

BELOW Konon Molody and Rudolph Abel reunited at KGB headquarters. Both men were regarded as embarrassing failures because of their capture in the West, but they were rehabilitated in an attempt to enhance the KGB's reputation.

Yuri Loginov, pictured in his flat in Johannesburg shortly before his arrest, and (below) his Canadian birth certificate in the name of Edmundas Trinka.

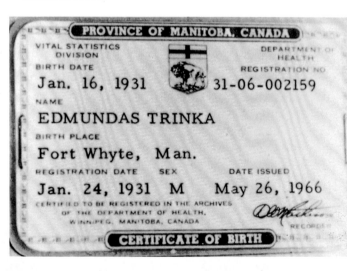

PROVINCE OF MANITOBA, CANADA

VITAL STATISTICS
DIVISION

DEPARTMENT OF
HEALTH

BIRTH DATE

Jan. 16, 1931

REGISTRATION NO

31-06-002159

NAME

EDMUNDAS TRINKA

BIRTH PLACE

Fort Whyte, Man.

REGISTRATION DATE   SEX   DATE ISSUED

Jan. 24, 1931   M   May 26, 1966

CERTIFIED TO BE REGISTERED IN THE ARCHIVES
OF THE DEPARTMENT OF HEALTH,
WINNIPEG, MANITOBA, CANADA

RECORDER

CERTIFICATE OF BIRTH

ABOVE LEFT The front cover of Alexander Orlov's KGB file, as photographed in the KGB's archives, Moscow.

ABOVE RIGHT Alexandre Sokolov at his trial in 1963. An experienced illegal, his brother turned out to be a retired British intelligence officer.

RIGHT Dmitri F. Polyakov, the senior GRU officer who was executed in March 1988 after his exposure as an American source for the past twenty-five years.

ABOVE LEFT Vassilli Dozhdalev, the Line N specialist who supervised Konon Molody from the London Embassy *rezidentura*, worked as George Blake's case officer and later was appointed head of Directorate S's training branch, where he still works.

ABOVE A rare picture of Vadim A. Kirpichenko, formerly the long-serving head of Directorate S, taken in Moscow in 1992. Before his appointment to run the KGB's illegals in 1974, he had served as KGB *rezident* in Cairo.

LEFT Erwin van Haarlem in a snap taken in the Kremlin when he travelled to Moscow in support of refuseniks. A DNA test eventually proved that he did not have the Dutch parents he claimed and in 1993 he was released from a ten-year prison sentence and deported to Prague.

had been with the Lecap Rainwear Company, which was dissolved in 1948, and had been run by various cousins with connections to the original firm that had played such a key role in *Der Rote Kapelle* (see chapter 2).

Under interrogation Gold compromised Abe Brothman and Brothman's secretary and mistress, Miriam Moskowitz. Both previously had been named by Elizabeth Bentley, but no charges had been brought. Although Bentley had insisted that Brothman had supplied her with technical data on chemical processes, and that Harry Gold had worked as a courier for Yakovlev, there was no other evidence of espionage. Brothman, Moskowitz and Gold had denied Bentley's version and had insisted that their relationship with Amtorg, and with Jacob Golos who was supposedly its representative, was entirely legitimate. Although the FBI disbelieved the trio, and was convinced that they had betrayed industrial secrets, no further action had been taken against them.

Fuchs's positive identification of Gold in May 1950 undermined the latter's claims to innocence and proved that the evidence he had already given under oath to a grand jury in 1947 had been perjured. Accordingly, Gold underwent a change of heart and, together with Elizabeth Bentley, gave evidence for the prosecution against Brothman and Moskowitz, who were convicted and imprisoned. Gold's confession, which resulted in a thirty-year prison sentence, was also to lead the FBI directly to a major spy ring that had penetrated the Allied atomic weapons programme.

Gold's statement corroborated Fuchs's recollection in almost every respect, except in regard to the two meetings held in Boston. Fuchs had deliberately misled his FBI and MI5 interrogators on this specific point because he wished to shield his sister Kristel from his activities. Kristel had succumbed to a mental illness and was in no condition to be questioned, a view endorsed by the FBI. However, Gold's most interesting disclosure did not directly relate to the physicist or his sister, for he recalled for the FBI that when, in June 1945, he had held a meeting with Fuchs at Santa Fe, he had also visited the home in Albuquerque of another important source, a young soldier who had also been based at Los Alamos. Gold remembered enough of his home for the FBI to find the address and its resident was identified without much difficulty as David Greenglass, who, in the face of Gold's evidence, opted to assist the FBI. Greenglass and his wife Ruth were Communists of long standing, and he confirmed his involvement in espionage and named several others, including his brother-in-law, Julius Rosenberg, an electrical engineer who had been discharged from the Signal Corps in 1945 because of his Communist affiliations. Greenglass was a machinist by trade who had been posted to Los Alamos in 1944 and had been given access to some of the most secret aspects of the plutonium bomb project. According to Ruth, who was never charged, she had been asked by Julius Rosenberg to extract classified information concerning her husband's work, and had done so. Although Greenglass initially was reluctant to incriminate his sister Ethel, he gave damning evidence against her husband, who not only appeared to fit the profile of another cryptonym for a Soviet spy mentioned in the texts of several KGB intercepts, but was also a probable candidate for a suspect named Julius who had been described first, years earlier, by Elizabeth Bentley. The FBI was naturally anxious to protect its cryptographic source and, accordingly, relied upon testimony from Gold, Greenglass and Bentley to obtain convictions against the Rosenbergs and their accomplice, Morton Sobell. David Greenglass was rewarded with a fifteen-year sentence, of which he served two-thirds before his release in 1960. Sobell, who was linked to an agent codenamed STONE in the Soviet intercepts, denied knowledge of nuclear espionage but was convicted of conspiracy and sentenced to thirty years' imprisonment.

It had been the FBI's intention to obtain Julius Rosenberg's co-operation by putting his wife under pressure, a tactic that had ensured the assistance of David Greenglass, but even after they had both received a death sentence neither Rosenberg was willing to confess. From the testimony of Gold and the Greenglasses, and the secret data extracted from the Soviet intercepts, it was clear that Julius Rosenberg was not just one part of a minor husband-and-wife team, but a key figure who could implicate many other members of his ring. In particular, the FBI was interested in tracing Joel Barr and Alfred Sarant, two former CPUSA activists and technicians who had worked on classified contracts and had fled to Mexico when Gold's arrest was announced, and Morris and Lona Cohen,[11] who had also suddenly disappeared from their East 71st Street apartment in New York at about the same time. Altogether half a dozen of Julius Rosenberg's Communist friends had vanished, and the FBI remained convinced that they fitted the cryptonyms of unidentified spies mentioned in the KGB wireless signals. However, despite the certain prospect of execution in the electric chair at Sing Sing, neither Julius nor Ethel made any admission and went to their deaths in silence.

With the loss of the Rosenbergs the West's counter-intelligence agencies were left with numerous loose ends. There were several codenames in Gouzenko's papers that were never positively identified, including ELLI, GINI and GOLIA. Some years later, following his defection to Moscow in September 1950, the Jewish source known as GINI was named tentatively as Bruno Pontecorvo, a talented nuclear physicist from an Italian family with strong Communist associations. Both Pontecorvo and his Swedish wife were Jewish and Marxists, and three of his brothers and sisters were Communist Party activists. He had spent six years at the Chalk River installation and in 1949 had taken up a senior post at Harwell, having become a naturalised British subject. While on vacation with his wife and three children he flew to Helsinki and disappeared, only to emerge at a press conference held in Moscow in March 1955 at which he announced that he had become a Soviet citizen and was engaged in the research of nuclear energy.

Of the other open files, Morris and Lona Cohen were to be discovered living as illegals in London in 1962, and Joel Barr was to return to New York from Moscow in 1992, to draw a state pension, following the collapse of the Soviet Union and having spent forty years in the Soviet electronics industry using the name Joe Berg. His friend Alfred Sarant changed his name to Filipp Staros and lived in Vladivostok working on computers for Soviet submarines until his death.

Throughout the late 1940s and early 1950s, the FBI expended tremendous resources into the investigation of Soviet illegal networks in the United States. Apart from the cryptographic evidence indicating the existence of other spies, the alarming rapidity of Soviet progress with atomic weapons was a powerful incentive to plug the leaks. Scrutiny of KGB files in Moscow suggest that several key sources remain undetected, including those codenamed BULL, CAT, SHOT and TIFF. According to Leonid R. Kvasnikov, the NKVD officer who collated all the atomic information in Moscow, the crucial leads were provided in October 1941 through Donald Maclean, who was then handled in London by Anatoli Gorsky, and by the Manhattan Project spies, supervised from New York by Anatoli Yatskov. As well as the familiar names of the Rosenbergs and Klaus Fuchs, Kvasnikov asserts that he received vital information from other Soviet sympathisers at Los Alamos, including HURON, who was close to the project's director, Robert Oppenheimer. Yatskov confirms Kvasnikov's recollection and recalls that from 1942 he ran a hitherto unsuspected agent, a physicist codenamed PERSEUS, and that his wife made two trips to Albuquerque to collect messages from him. 'Only half, perhaps less than half' of his network was identified by the FBI, says Yatskov.[12]

After Maclean's departure in April 1944 to the British Embassy in Washington, closely followed by his contact Gorsky, Kvasnikov continued to receive scientific intelligence from London via Vladimir B. Barkovsky, who was posted to the Embassy with the rank of third secretary especially to run OLD MAN, MAUR, KELLY and YORIK. Despite references to these and other agents in signals transmitted to Moscow by Boris M. Krotov, the acting legal *rezident* in London, some of which were later deciphered, none of these four has been positively identified.

An effort to put real names to the cryptonyms prompted counter-espionage enquiries conducted in Canada, France, Germany and Britain, and very gradually some of the pieces of what sometimes appeared to be a complicated mosaic were placed in the right position. Co-operative, well-informed witnesses were few and far between, especially among the veteran illegals who had escaped Stalin's purges and had subsequently transferred their operations to the United States. Jack Soble had been a rare convert, and his testimony had not only compromised his brother but had also produced numerous other leads in Europe, where they were known by the surname Sobelivicius. However, in April 1953 the FBI learned from no more improbable source than *Life* magazine that an illicit alien calling himself Igor K. Berg was actually General Orlov, a lifelong Soviet illegal with an encyclopaedic knowledge of illegal operations in the United States and across Europe, who had been mentioned in reverential terms by Walter Krivitsky. To the undisguised embarrassment and fury of J. Edgar Hoover, Orlov had entered the country undetected from Canada in August 1938 and had remained in hiding with his wife and daughter ever since. He had emerged only because he had run short of funds and had sold the serialisation of his book, *The Secret History of Stalin's Crimes*, to raise cash. After verifying his credentials as the most senior Soviet intelligence officer ever to seek refuge in the West, *Life* had edited excerpts from Orlov's memoirs and then, belatedly, arranged for him to be interviewed by the FBI.

Prior to his receipt of a sinister summons to Antwerp in 1938, Orlov had been one of the most experienced of Soviet intelligence officers, having worked in France under trade delegation cover between 1926 and 1928, and later in Switzerland, Prague and Berlin as an illegal. After a three-year posting to Moscow, he had undertaken another illegal assignment in Austria and, in 1937, had been appointed the Soviet 'security counsellor' or NKVD *rezident* to the rebel Republican government in Barcelona. This, at least, was the version of his career that Orlov gave to the FBI in 1953, but recently evidence has emerged to indicate that Orlov's rejection of Stalin had not amounted to a full commitment to the West. Indeed, at the time of his death in April 1973 he was negotiating with the KGB to return to Moscow, and in his lengthy interviews with the FBI in New York he had failed to disclose much of what he had known about Soviet illegals in Europe. The fact that no fewer than sixty of the KGB's sources in the West known to Orlov, including Guy Burgess, Donald Maclean and Kim Philby, had gone undisturbed, had suggested to the KGB that he remained loyal and accordingly, unlike other defectors, he was never tried on charges of treachery by a Soviet court *in absentia*. This was the message conveyed to Orlov's wife, Marya Vladislavovna, when she was eventually traced by the KGB in November 1969 to their modest home in Ann Arbor, Michigan. The first contact was made by Georgi Feoktistov, a Soviet diplomat based at the United Nations in New York, but Marya prevented him from speaking directly to her husband. A second meeting followed in Cleveland, Ohio, in August 1971, but Marya died three months later. Orlov also succumbed to heart disease on 7 April 1973, his wish to return to Moscow, as expressed in his first letter home for thirty-five years, unfulfilled.[13]

When the FBI and CIA interviewed Orlov, he always appeared co-operative and, after the success of his exposé of Stalin's crimes, he published a second book, a *Handbook of Intelligence and Guerrilla Warfare*, in 1963. Orlov claimed that he had based it on a document he had prepared in 1936 for the Central Military School in Moscow, and he expounded at length on the role of the illegal, using numerous anecdotes to illustrate the need to maintain security. So many appeared to relate to Orlov's experiences in Paris that the DST, the French domestic security agency, asked the CIA to re-interview the defector to put names to some of the cases mentioned. When confronted with the French demand, Orlov suffered a characteristic memory lapse.

In fact, Orlov took numerous secrets to his grave, not the least being what he had done during two moments in his career as an illegal: the two months he had spent in the United States between September and November 1932 when he was registered at a Columbia University language course, and the period after his return to Moscow from Vienna in June 1934. Although two years apart, they were linked by a single item, passport number 566042, which he had acquired in New York in the name of William Goldin, issued on 23 November 1932 to a Russian immigrant who described his occupation as a salesman. While Orlov had been born in August 1895, Goldin's birthdate was not too dissimilar, July 1899, an acceptable difference in age of only four years. In his interviews with the FBI Orlov acknowledged that he had used the false name Lev N. Nikolaiev during the assignment and pretended that the purpose of his first visit to the United States had been unrelated to espionage, and that he had been part of an innocuous trade mission sent to negotiate with General Motors. When checked, Orlov's story had sounded reasonable. US Immigration records confirmed the arrival of Nikolaiev on the ss *Europa* on 23 September 1932 and his departure on the ss *Bremen* on 30 November. The industrial background to his cover also stood up to investigation, and there was internal evidence in Orlov's *Handbook* to support his assertion that his career as an illegal in Europe had been handicapped by his membership of the Soviet Trade Delegation in Paris. He had deliberately exaggerated the difficulties of an illegal maintaining a false cover when already having compromised himself by working overtly for an organ of the Soviet Government, such as a trade delegation, a scenario that had appeared to fit neatly his own situation.

I remember the case when D. Smirnov, a former secretary of the Soviet embassy in Paris, was detained by the Polish border police when he was passing through Poland on the way to the Soviet Union with a Greek passport. The reason for the detention was that two Polish police officers recognised Smirnov as the man who a year before had travelled from the Soviet Union to France, through Poland, with a Soviet diplomatic passport.[14]

In reality, Orlov had been obliged to admit his 1932 trip, which he would otherwise probably have preferred to omit from his statement to the FBI, partly because Elisabeth Poretsky had positively identified the person using the nom-de-guerre 'General Alexander Orlov', the NKVD *rezident* in Barcelona in 1937, as the same illegal named 'Orlov-Nikolsky, alias Schved or Lova',[15] the former *rezident* in Paris. This neatly coincided with Krivitsky's memory of 'Nikolsky, alias Schwed, alias Lyova, alias Orlov'.[16] Even if Orlov could not be certain what Elisabeth Poretsky had disclosed about him, he could have had no doubt that he had been compromised by Krivitsky, for Orlov would have been bound to have read this second statement, which had been published before the author's mysterious death in Washington DC in 1941. Accordingly, Orlov must have felt that he had little option but to acknowledge his 1932 visit, but in doing so he had been careful to neglect to mention 'William Goldin', and neither the FBI nor the CIA had suspected that it had been duped.

Disclosure of 'Goldin' by Orlov would have rendered him vulnerable to scrutiny of the journeys he had undertaken using Goldin's authentic passport. More significantly, Orlov had travelled across Europe at a time he had told the FBI that he was non-operational, languishing in Moscow in an obscure branch of the NKVD responsible for the security of the Soviet railways. Actually, during the crucial period between his departure from Vienna in June 1933 and October 1935, Orlov was operating as an illegal, in parallel with Ignace Reiss and Theodore Maly, running a network in Britain. If MI5 or the FBI had been able to study the Goldin passport, they would have discovered that Orlov had made several journeys that he would have had difficulty describing, or reconciling with his stated sojourn in Moscow. At this time Orlov went to Vienna to learn English and then moved to Paris masquerading as the American, William Goldin. In December 1933, he undertook a short assignment in Rome, but in April he was forced to abandon Paris because he had been spotted by a contact who had previously known him as Lev Nikolaiev. He returned to Vienna, where he received instructions to proceed to England. An entry visa was granted to 'Goldin' in Stockholm on 14 July 1934, and Orlov landed at Harwich the following day. According to British immigration records, his visit lasted exactly ten days. However, he was to return four times, arriving at Newhaven on 18 September and again at Plymouth on 16 November. This third trip was long enough for him to register with the police as an alien on 14 January 1935, but he entered the country again on 13 March and 26 April. During some of his time in London Orlov was accompanied by his wife, who travelled on an Austrian passport issued to 'Maria Feldbene'. In all, Orlov as 'Goldin'

came to Britain five times and during that period was associated with a company based in Regent Street importing
refrigerators from America. What had he been doing and why
had he deliberately concealed the visits from MI5 and the
FBI? Undoubtedly the answer lies in the need for the Soviets
to service their agents. Considering that Orlov was fishing
in the same pool as that used by Ignace Reiss, Willy Brandes,
Ernest Weiss, Henri Pieck, Waldemar Ozols, Theodore Maly
and Henri Robinson, not to mention the ten weeks spent in
England by Richard Sorge in 1929, all this clandestine activity
would seem to suggest that the Soviets possessed an embarrassing wealth of agents with whom they needed to communicate in 1934–5. Yet to date only a very limited number of
spies have been revealed. Weiss, of course, ran Major Wilfred Vernon and Frederick Meredith until their arrest in 1937,
and both Pieck and Maly had controlled John King until he
was taken into custody in 1939. Glading had worked with
Brandes and Maly, so who were the rest? Not members of
the Cambridge ring, for Donald Maclean, the first of the
'ring-of-five' to achieve access to Whitehall's secrets, was
not to start passing material from the Foreign Office until
January 1936.

When MI5 belatedly attempted to tackle this conundrum
in the early 1960s, when the danger of moles had manifested
itself dramatically through the defection of Guy Burgess and
Donald Maclean in 1951, it had relied upon two main sources
of information. The first was a confession written by Kim
Philby in January 1963 in which he asserted that he had been
recruited into the NKVD by Maly, who had subsequently
been replaced in 1936 by a Soviet illegal known to him only
as OTTO. In return for the offer of a formal immunity from
prosecution, and confronted by the weight of denunciations
from defectors, Philby had admitted his guilt in an interview
conducted in Beirut. He claimed that when he had been
stationed in Washington DC in 1949, he had taken the
opportunity to study the FBI's files on Soviet illegals and
had identified OTTO from an FBI photograph as an Austrian
academic, Arnold Deutsch. While this sequence of events
seemed entirely plausible, a check with the FBI revealed

that the Bureau had only acquired Deutsch's picture after Philby had been sacked from SIS. Had Philby lied, or had he sought to protect some other illegal? The most likely explanation is that Philby knew his principal contact in London during 1934 and 1935 was still, in January 1963, at liberty in the West and, therefore, vulnerable. Apart from whatever covert meetings they had held together in London, Orlov had met Philby on a regular basis during the Spanish Civil War, when Orlov was the NKVD *resident* in Madrid. Orlov had taken up his appointment as security adviser to the Republican government in the capital in September 1936, and Philby had been supplying intelligence from the Nationalist lines since February 1937, while working as a war correspondent for *The Times*. Initially Philby had posted his information, concealed in secret writing in letters addressed to the Soviet Embassy in Paris, but after a rendezvous in Biarritz in mid-September 1937, Philby and Orlov had met in Narbonne once a fortnight. Thus, when Philby came to concoct his 'confession', which was to be eagerly studied by MI5, he had taken the precaution of shielding Orlov from suspicion, no doubt conscious that Orlov had for years paid him the same service by remaining silent about the moles he had run in London. Indeed, when Philby released his memoirs, *My Silent War*, in 1968, he drew a veil over the exact circumstances of his recruitment in London, pleading they were 'operational matters'. The only operational reason for such discretion, so many years later, was the continuing need to keep someone out of harm's way. That person, of course, must have been Orlov.

Given the nature of their relationship, one is bound to wonder whether Philby was ever informed, when Orlov vanished from his post in Spain in July 1938, that he might be in some jeopardy. Certainly none of Orlov's colleagues was told that he had disappeared, leaving Stalin a letter threatening to expose his crimes if he allowed the NKVD to take reprisals against his family in Russia. To a man, his subordinates accepted that the *resident* had been recalled, and they had drawn their own conclusions. Although some considerable time would elapse before Philby was invited to join Special

Operations Executive as an expert on propaganda, and then switch to SIS, his exposure as a Soviet source in 1938 would have been a considerable embarrassment to himself and *The Times*, and would have handicapped him in his future career. However, it may well be the case that Philby only realised his potential predicament, and the risk he had run of betrayal since 1938, when he learned that Orlov had surfaced in the United States in 1953. Whatever the circumstances, Philby must have owed Orlov a debt of gratitude, a debt that he was to repay in full.

MI5's other key witness to the Soviet network in Britain in the mid-1930s was Anthony Blunt, who confessed to his espionage in April 1964 after having accepted a deal similar to that given to Philby. The homosexual art expert had accepted an immunity from prosecution and had appeared to give his full co-operation to his Security Service inquisitors. Under lengthy interrogation Blunt confirmed that Maly had recruited Philby and then had been run by the mysterious OTTO, now positively identified as Arnold Deutsch, who had entered England under his own name in January 1934 to conduct research into his chosen subject, psychology, at London University, which was to last more than three years until his final departure in September 1937, when his student visa expired. A graduate of the University of Vienna, Deutsch had visited Moscow in 1932 and had been recruited first by the Comintern, and then by the NKVD. In the middle of his time in London, in February 1936, when he lived in Lawn Road, Hampstead, he was joined by his wife, Josefine, alias 'Liza Kramer', who had completed a course in clandestine radio techniques. Deutsch's file in Moscow suggests that during this period he had been responsible for the recruitment of no fewer than seventeen agents in England, a total that goes some way to explain the extraordinary concentration of illegals in London during the mid-1930s. Among them are three spies whose identities have yet to be disclosed: a London University academic, codenamed PROFESSOR, and two sources in Whitehall, BEAR and SUCCESSOR. As for Deutsch, he was to die in the Atlantic when the ship on which he was sailing to America was sunk by a U-boat in November 1942.

According to Blunt, OTTO had not been replaced and the ring of spies who had all been up at Cambridge together, namely Burgess, Maclean, Philby and Blunt, had temporarily lost touch with their NKVD controllers. After a long delay, contact had been re-established through Philby's Austrian wife, Litzi Friedmann, with the Soviet Embassy using one of Litzi's Viennese friends, Edith Suschitzky, as a cut-out. Some aspects of this chronology MI5 could confirm, for Suschitzky was a veteran Communist who had come to Britain in 1933 as the wife of a senior member of the CPGB, Dr Alex Tudor Hart. As leading Communist activists, both Tudor Harts had been the subject of routine surveillance by MI5, but, although interviewed, neither had volunteered any helpful information.[17] The Security Service was also sure that at some point Philby and his fellow conspirators had been run by the Soviet Embassy in London, for their cryptonyms were found in several wartime NKVD wireless intercepts originating from Boris Krotov, one of Blunt's subsequent handlers. When John Cairncross became the third member of the Cambridge ring to co-operate with MI5, he too corroborated the tale spun by Philby and Blunt. However, as one of MI5's principal molehunters, Peter Wright, later admitted, 'We never identified "Otto" or discovered the reason why the ring were so desperate to conceal his identity so many years later.'[18] The explanation, quite simply, was that at the height of the investigation, Orlov was living in the United States under the protection of the FBI.

Following the release of details from Orlov's personal dossier held by the Russian Intelligence Service in Moscow, it is clear that he had retained a loyalty to Moscow, if not to Stalin. There is also an explanation for why Orlov was sent to England in the first place, given the large number of other competent illegals already there. Maly, for example, had been moved to London in April 1936 under the alias 'Willy Brochart', following a visit in 1935 and another in January 1936, primarily to run John King, the Soviet source in the Foreign Office's communications department. The KGB's successors have identified the illegal *rezident* in London as a certain Ignaty Reif, who, using a stolen Austrian passport issued to

'Max Wolisch', had believed himself to have been compromised. Apparently Reif, who gave his address as 17 Talbot Square, W2, had been called to the Home Office in January 1935 to be interviewed and, dismayed by his frightening experience of British officialdom, had been given three months to leave the country. Reif had arrived in England in April 1934 describing himself as a commercial traveller, and had originally run the London illegal *rezidentura* from Copenhagen. Communication with Moscow had proved difficult, so he had moved to London, but his dependence upon a stolen passport led to his withdrawal and his replacement by Orlov. According to Reif's KGB file, he had been a participant in the recruitment into the NKVD of the ambitious young journalist Kim Philby, and had authorised Edith Tudor Hart to introduce him at a secret rendezvous to OTTO (Arnold Deutsch) in June 1934. The involvement of Edith Tudor Hart, unsuspected by MI5 until Blunt's interrogation, was a further reason for Philby to have muddied the waters in 1963, for she remained in London until her death a decade later.

The revelation of so many illegals deployed in England during the mid-1930s increases the likelihood that the so-called 'great illegals', the cosmopolitan, middle European NKVD recruiters, had been far more active than the Security Service had ever realised, even when, by the middle of the 1960s, it had started to unravel the labyrinthine complexity of the interlocking groups which represented Soviet penetration of the British political, economic and scientific establishment. The ultimate irony, of course, lay in the fact that so many of the puzzles which had perplexed the molehunters could have been solved by an elderly couple living under the FBI's protection in Ann Arbor, Michigan.

6 · Squad 34 v. the Line N Illegal Support Officers

I wish we had a couple like him in Moscow.
Allen W. Dulles, Director of Central Intelligence (DCI), 1953–61[1]

The first significant post-war defection of a Soviet illegal took place in Ottawa when a man calling himself David Soboloff telephoned the headquarters of the RCMP in November 1953 and offered to give himself up. He described himself as a Russian spy, but working on the principle that a controlled agent would be of more use than a prisoner in custody, the RCMP Security Service was far more interested in keeping him in the field. In particular, Soboloff represented proof that the use of illegals by the Soviets had not been a temporary phenomenon limited to the pre-war days, or even an aberration that had ended after the damaging defection of Igor Gouzenko. Accordingly, Soboloff was assigned the codename GIDEON and debriefed.[2]

The son of a senior Soviet employee of Amtorg who had been brought up in New York, the young man had returned to Moscow with his parents at the conclusion of his father's tour of duty, but when he arrived at Halifax in 1953 he was equipped with a false US passport in the name of the son of an American industrialist. When he reached Montreal new papers had been left for him, those of David Soboloff, a member of an immigrant family that had gone back to the Soviet Union during the Depression. Using a genuine birth certificate he had travelled to Vancouver and had obtained an authentic driver's licence. Once established in Montreal, Soboloff had undertaken various preassigned tasks but had failed to obtain a job as a watchmaker, as instructed. Then disaster had struck: he had fallen hopelessly in love with the wife of a Canadian soldier based in Kingston, Ontario, and had sought permission from the KGB to let him live there. This naïve request had prompted an emergency meeting with his contact, later identified as Leonid Abramov of the Soviet Embassy in Ottawa, who had rejected his plea and accepted his offer to open a small photographic studio in Montreal. Soboloff had started his business in the suburb of Verdun but had found his new contact, Abramov's replacement, Vladimir Borodin, rather more demanding as a controller. Borodin proved a hard taskmaster and reprimanded the illegal for failing to acknowledge all the shortwave transmissions that had been broadcast to him. Soboloff blamed poor reception and bad atmospheric conditions, but in reality Soboloff had grown tired of his burden, working for both the Soviets and the RCMP.

Fortunately, Borodin had been replaced soon afterwards by Nikolai Ostrovsky, who had entrusted Soboloff with a mission of more significance, handling the communications of his first agent, a technician at the aircraft assembly plant in Toronto building the Avro Arrow. This operation had gone well, and Ostrovsky had promised Soboloff that he was to be entrusted with an OMEGA, allegedly the KGB's most advanced tape-operated burst transmitter, a technical development more sophisticated than anything then available in the West. Unfortunately, before the illegal could take delivery of this prize and pass it on to the RCMP for inspection, arrangements had been made for what he had been assured would be his temporary, routine visit to Moscow. Although Soboloff understandably was apprehensive that his duplicity might be discovered, he was persuaded by his RCMP case officer, Charles Sweeny, that in the absence of any Canadian facilities abroad, the British would monitor him after his arrival in the Soviet Union, and a scheme was devised for him to signal an SIS officer at the British Embassy. Soboloff made the journey in October 1955 and Terence Tear O'Bryan, the SIS officer who had been stationed in Moscow for the past two years, was alerted to watch at a preagreed time and place for a Russian walking alone and carrying a record album under his arm. If he considered himself to be in any danger, GIDEON had been instructed to blow his nose. However, apart from one sighting, when GIDEON inexplicably deviated from his instructions by showing up at the right place with the gramophone record but accompanied by an unidentified woman, he was never seen again.

Operation KEYSTONE, the codename assigned by the RCMP to the plan to run GIDEON as a double agent, was to be the subject of several post-mortems, and it was concluded, more than a decade later, that Tear O'Bryan had been compromised in London by George Blake before he had even arrived in Moscow, and that GIDEON himself may have been betrayed to Ostrovsky by James Morrison, a Soviet mole in the RCMP. Against Blake and Morrison, both traitors whose duplicity was to go unsuspected for years, GIDEON had never stood a chance. At the time, of course, molehunting was still in its relative infancy and high-level penetration of the West's security agencies seemed an acknowledged, but rarely accomplished, Soviet objective. Even within the closed confines of the British intelligence community Kim Philby had many loyal defenders who believed that his dismissal in 1951, following the defections of Burgess and Maclean, had been unjustified. The puzzle confronting the handful of counter-intelligence personnel indoctrinated into the GIDEON case centred on whether his loss had been bad luck, poor tradecraft or evidence of something altogether more sinister: Soviet penetration.

The mysterious loss of GIDEON was still being debated in Western security circles when, in May 1957, Reino Hayhanen, an alcoholic KGB officer of Finnish origin, presented himself at the American Embassy in Paris and demanded to see the local CIA chief of station. On that particular day Jim Hunt was absent abroad as his son had recently died, but Hayhanen was ushered in to see Charlie Grey, the Embassy's long-time CIA fixer, who had been in Paris since 1944, much of that time having been spent at the famous Travellers' Club. Hayhanen volunteered his co-operation to Grey in return for resettlement and, by way of credentials, offered a hollowed-out Finnish five-mark coin in which could be concealed a tiny photographic negative. While this item did not constitute proof, Hayhanen's initial statement to the CIA was persuasive and he was considered an important catch. Grey gave Hayhanen a room in his palatial home just outside the capital and for three days the Embassy doctor treated his acute alcoholism in order to prepare him for his flight to Washington. Hayhanen's story encapsulated a wealth of knowledge about the recruitment and development of KGB illegals and, after he had been escorted across the Atlantic by the CIA's John Roberts on a TWA flight, the DCI Allen Dulles was on hand to greet him. In particular, Hayhanen was able to make an important disclosure to the FBI about Morton Sobell, betray the spy Roy A. Rhodes, and help identify the KGB's illegal *rezident* in New York, the Briton named William Fisher who became known as Colonel Rudolph Abel.[3]

Hayhanen's story was to be a classic case history of a Soviet illegal. He revealed that he was a professional KGB officer from a village near Leningrad, who had served as an interpreter in the Karelia Peninsula during the Soviet–Finnish War. Later he had been transferred to Estonia, where he had been taught English, and in 1948 he had been sent to Tallin for intensive training as an illegal. A year later he was smuggled into Helsinki by a TASS correspondent and had spent the next two years confirming his 'legend' as Eugene Maki, the son of a naturalised American citizen. This part of the operation was known as *stazhirovka* or 'staging', a process of establishing the credentials and documentation of agents before their deployment on their main mission as illegals. Hayhanen was to be staged through Finland and his cover was to include marriage to a local girl, Hannah Kurikka, despite the fact that he already had a wife and son in Russia.

In 1951, he had turned up at the US Embassy in Helsinki and, upon production of an authentic birth certificate showing him to be Eugene N. Maki, born in Enaville, Idaho, and his signature on a formal statement confirming that he had not served in the Finnish army, or voted in Finnish elections, both constitutional requirements for the retention of US citizenship, he had been issued with a passport. Once his application for a US passport had been accepted, Hayhanen had been recalled to Moscow to hear details of his main assignment: to travel to New York, where he could be joined by Hannah after six months. Using this genuine document he travelled to England the following year and caught the *Queen Mary* in Southampton for a transatlantic voyage to New York, where he acclimatised himself. Soon after the arrival of his wife the Hayhanens rented an apartment in Brooklyn, but in March 1953 they bought a house in Peekskill, New York. Hayhanen asserted that he had operated independently as an illegal, admitting to only one clandestine meeting, on a subway train, with a KGB officer named Mikhail N. Svirin, whom he had encountered previously in Moscow at the very beginning of his mission.

Svirin had been attached to the UN Secretariat in New York since August 1954, but had returned to Moscow in November 1956. Coincidentally, it was not until August 1954 that Hayhanen had met his *resident*, who was clearly a KGB professional of much higher calibre, at a prearranged rendezvous outside a cinema in Flushing. Under the *resident*'s supervision Hayhanen had opened a photographic shop in Newark, New Jersey, as a cover for his activities, but, upon his return from six months' leave in Moscow in late 1955, the *resident* had submitted an adverse report about his subordinate's competence. Hayhanen had been recalled, but had broken his journey in Paris to defect to the CIA in an alcoholic haze. During his five years at liberty as an illegal in the United States, he said that he had sent about thirty messages to Moscow and had received twenty-five. By a remarkable coincidence, his first, concealed in a hollow coin, was already in the possession of the FBI. It had been handed in to the New York police in Brooklyn in the summer of 1953, but the FBI had failed to decrypt the message contained in a tiny microfilm. Hayhanen disclosed his personal code and demonstrated how the five-figure groups had to be substituted by subtracting by four separate key numbers: the numbers represented by the eight letters of the Russian word *Snego-pad*, or 'snowfall'; the date 3 August 1945, which was the end of the war with Japan; the first twenty words of a traditional Russian folksong; and finally his own personal number, thirteen. Once this procedure had been completed, the message in Hayhanen's coin, which evidently had been mislaid by his *rezident*, was transformed into a note of welcome, some instructions regarding financial support for his business cover, a caution that it was premature to take receipt of a GAMMA transmitter and some security advice, dated six weeks after his arrival in the United States:

We congratulate you on a safe arrival. We confirm the receipt of your letter, to the address V repeat V and the reading of the letter no. 1. For organisation, we gave instructions to transmit to you $3,000 in local currency. Consult with us prior to investing it in any kind of business, advising the character of the business. According to your request, we will transmit the formula for the preparation of soft film, together with your mother's letter. It is too early to send you the Gammas. Encipher short letters, but the longer ones make with insertions. All the data about yourself, place of work, address, etc. must not be transmitted in one cipher message. Transmit insertions separately. The package was delivered to your wife personally. Everything is all right with the family. We wish you success. Greetings from the comrades. December 3[4]

Hayhanen's meal-ticket was comprised of three separate items of solid information: enough circumstantial information for the FBI to trace Hayhanen's *rezident* to the Latham Hotel in New York and arrest 'Mark Collins' on 21 June 1957; to disclose sufficient data for the FBI to entrap Master Sergeant Roy A. Rhodes of the US army and convict him as a Soviet spy codenamed QUEBEC; and to reveal details of a dead-drop in the Bear Mountain State Park used to supply financial support to Morton Sobell's wife, Helen. His original assignment had been given to him in Moscow in the summer of 1952 by a person he named as Vitali G. Pavlov, the KGB officer who had played a key role in the Gouzenko case in Canada several years earlier, and who had been posted to Canberra between October 1952 and February 1953. According to Hayhanen, Pavlov had been promoted to deputy chief of the KGB's American section and had supervised his mission, which had been approved by Colonel Aleksandr Korotkov, the long-serving head of what had become known as 'Line N', the Illegals or 'S' Directorate of the KGB's First Chief Directorate (FCD). Korotkov had played a part in running Boris Morros and had also been named by the defectors Ilya Dzhirkvelov and Vladimir Petrov.

Of crucial interest was Hayhanen's evidence concerning the *rezident* illegal. Although he knew the man by sight, he had never learned his cover name, but he recalled that on one occasion he had visited a storeroom in Fulton Street, Brooklyn, used by the illegal. The FBI found the address, which was a fifth-floor studio and storeroom rented to a commercial artist named Emil R. Goldfus, and kept it under surveillance. On 23 May, a man answering the *rezident*'s description, as supplied by Hayhanen, was spotted, but on that occasion the suspect effortlessly shook off the FBI Special Agents attempting to keep him under observation. Three weeks later Goldfus reappeared and was traced to the Latham Hotel in Manhattan, where he was registered under the name 'Mark Collins'.

The FBI's investigation of Collins/Goldfus revealed, from a hotel bill found in his room, that he had recently returned from Daytona Beach, Florida, whence he had fled following Hayhanen's defection. His original entry into the United States had been from Canada in November 1948, and his arrival in Quebec from Cuxhaven aboard the ss *Scythia* in the middle of the month had been accomplished with an authentic US passport identifying him as a naturalised US citizen living in Detroit named Andrew Kayotis. The real Kayotis, who was Lithuanian in origin, had returned in poor health to Kaunas in July 1947, where he had died soon afterwards. Exactly where he had been between his arrival in the United States and the time he appeared in early 1950 to rent a furnished apartment in New York is unknown, but the identity he had used then, that of Goldfus, was also false. The birth certificate he carried was genuine, but it belonged to a child born in Manhattan to a German immigrant family in 1902, who had died just after his first birthday, in October 1903. The identity of Mark

Collins, the name under which he was registered at the Latham Hotel, was entirely false and supported only by a forged birth certificate. A bankbook issued by the East River Savings Bank in June 1950 showed a balance of $1,386, with the most recent entry dated 5 April 1957. A further $15,000 was recovered from a safety deposit box held at the Manufacturers Trust Company in the name of an acquaintance. In his hotel room FBI Special Agents found a coded message written in five-figure groups on a slip of graph paper, and a piece of wood covered with sandpaper was split open to reveal a 250-page one-time pad printed in red and blue, together with a signal schedule. Close examination of an ostensibly ordinary pencil produced eighteen microfilms, some of them containing letters from his wife and daughter in Moscow. Arrested on immigration charges, 'Goldfus' was flown to an immigration holding centre at McAllen, Texas, where the FBI attempted to break the prisoner's silence, apart from a willingness to be deported, by offering him resettlement and a handsome pension in return for his co-operation.

Under interrogation Collins/Goldfus quickly declared himself to be Rudolph I. Abel, supposedly a Russian refugee, who had bought a false US passport in Denmark. He named his parents, claimed that he once had been a teacher of English in Moscow, and accepted that he was eligible for deportation, but denied any involvement with espionage. Nor was there much evidence to implicate him. A detailed forensic analysis of Abel's activities during his eight years in the field failed to disclose any significant espionage. Although there was plenty of incriminating paraphernalia found in his apartment, including a Hallicrafter shortwave wireless receiver, a radio schedule, microdot equipment and large sums of cash, there was no evidence of any significant intelligence-gathering. When translated, a copy of his most recent signal home proved to contain an innocuous message to his mother, details of the chemical composition of a soft film laminate, and an acknowledgment from his wife of some gift packages. Apart from some cryptic messages concerning signals to be used in Mexico City, presumably part of an escape plan, the only secret messages found proved to be seven letters from

Abel's wife Ilya and their newly married daughter Evelyn, containing mainly trivial domestic news about their apartment and dog. Having analysed the information contained in the correspondence, the FBI concluded that Abel had left New York for Moscow on 10 June 1955 and had travelled via Paris and Vienna. Although of minor intelligence value, the letters give some insight into Abel's home circumstances, and a letter dated 20 February 1956 from his daughter suggested that Abel had left Moscow the previous November:

It is almost three months since you went away. Although it's not so much to compare with eternity, still it is a long time and the more so as there is a great quantity of news to tell you. First of all, I am going to marry. Please don't be astounded. I am much surprised myself, and still it is a fact to be taken for granted. My future husband seems to be a good guy. He is thirty-four and a radio engineer. Mother likes him very much. We met at the birthday of our friend who lives in the bungalow. On Feb. 25 we shall celebrate our wedding. I hope you will like him when you get back. I think you will have much to talk about. News number two – we are to get a new flat of two rooms – it is not what we're supposed to get but it is a flat for ourselves and much better than what we have now. News number three – I found a job, engineer referent in aviation, so now I shall be somewhat closer to you. The job seems to be a decent one. They promised to pay me well and my future boss seems to be an intellectual and polite guy. I did some odd jobs there and received a pretty sum of money. My future husband and I are both deeply interested in photography, especially in colour photography. He has an Olympia car and we both enjoy meddling with it. We received both your letters and the key from the suitcase, but the latter is still wandering somewhere. Our childhood friend writes regularly and sends you his and his family's best regards and wishes. All our friends wish you health and happiness and a happy and quick way home. Well, this is all I have to say. Yours, Evelyn.[5]

Abel's wife also experienced difficulty in reconciling herself to her husband's absence and one of his possessions, probably his guitar, is a reminder of his departure. In an undated note she wrote:

After your departure, I certainly was ill. There was a hardening of the arteries of the heart. I sleep poorly and I do not go out on the street. I walk on the balcony. Sometimes I approach your instrument and look at it and want to again hear you play and I become sad. For the remaining money I asked them basically to have them send it all to you. Evelyn has married (in late February) and she, after getting married, always says there are no such men as her papa and therefore she is not too much in love with her husband. You are the best of all for us. And don't frown, everyone says this who knows you. If you look at things with a philosophical point of view, then taking hair from your head doesn't pay. I kiss you firmly and congratulate you. Try to arrange everything so that you do not delay the period of our meeting. Years and age will not wait for us. How are you there? How is your stomach? Take care of yourself – I want to live together with you for ourselves.[6]

A further, undated letter from Evelyn appeared to be birthday greetings, which would suggest it was written shortly before Abel's true birthday, 2 July 1956, a deduction confirmed by the reference to her wedding, which had been scheduled for 25 February:

Many happy returns. Daddy dear, I am missing you so much. You just cannot imagine how much I need you. It is about four months now since I have married and to me it seems like an eternity, so dull it sometimes is. In general, he is a good chap, but he isn't you. I have got a job. My boss . . . is a bit like you though not so broadminded and not a very great erudite. Though very clever. I am in a great hurry now as I have to go to work.[7]

The next in the sequence is from Abel's wife, dated 6 April, in which she indicates that she has not received a reply to her earlier note:

I am writing a second letter – up till now I only heard from you from the trip. I want very much to find out how you are. How is your health? I am gradually beginning to come to myself. I could go for a rest but I am afraid to travel alone, so that I have not yet decided, although I passed the medical board. How necessary you could be to me now. And how good it is that you do not feel the need of being with us. Evelyn works part time and on her free time from her husband and work she took me to the doctor and at the same time she herself had a check-up. Spring here will again be late. Up till now, it has been cold, damp and snow. The winter was simply horrible. And I am worried about my flowers. Evernya says the plum trees froze and it's hard to get the plums. Your father-in-law . . . is awaiting your earliest return, and I, although I know it is silly, I am counting off the days of the known period. I have not received your package yet . . . A childhood friend visited us . . . we talked a lot, reminisced, and most all day-dreamed. Don't let us down. In general, our whole life, constant waiting. That's the way it is, dear. Write as often as possible. The children, there are two now, send greetings. Son is very disturbed what kind of an impression he will make on you. He might not appeal to you at once. I kiss you firmly. I wish you luck, health, and most of all a speedy return.[8]

By 21 June, the date of the next letter from Abel's wife, she has heard from her husband. A reference to Abel gathering the last apple harvest was helpful in pinning down the period he spent in the Soviet Union the previous year, and the comment about a dacha and servant prove he is a privileged member of Soviet society:

At last we received your small package. Everything pleased us very much, and as usual, whatever you do, with care and attention. We were glad to receive a letter from you and to learn that everything is fine with you. It is a pity you have not had letters from us – such a long time. I sent you several. Congratulations on your birthday. We drink a toast to your well-being and your early promised return. We are at the summer place. In many respects our garden has suffered. On the best apple trees, from which last year you culled a plentiful harvest, only now have the leaves started to appear. I am still fighting with the house servant and do not have a new one . . . The television works but I seldom look at it. The dog behaves very well – she too awaits her master, and I also wait. It is desirable to have a husband at home; at the present time I feel your absence more, especially since I have been with you and remember what you promised me before your departure. Our new chef is wonderful, attentive and tactful.[9]

The last letter from Abel's wife, dated 20 August, acknowledges receipt of her husband's gift, which presumably was despatched from the United States either via the diplomatic bag, or perhaps mailed to a third country:

How glad I was to learn you have received one of my letters. We received the package in May. It is a shame the hyacinths travelled long and two of them perished altogether. The rest are planted and already have rooted. This is a live greeting from you. Next year they will bloom. We count every month that passes and you remember this.[10]

The day after her mother had written, Evelyn wrote a third letter to her father, dated 21 August, and evidently in response to one from him:

We liked your presents very much – we planted the hyacinths that survived and by now three of them have sprouted. You say you want more particulars about my husband. I shall try to give you a better picture of him. He is short, green-eyed, rather handsome. He is rather gay and talkative when the conversation considers cars or football. He works as an engineer – he is capable though rather lazy . . . You ask me whether I am happy with him. As one of our greatest poets once said, there is no happiness in life but there is peace and free will. The only thing that troubles me is that I find him boring sometimes. Now about my in-laws. They are awful. I do wish you were with us. Everything would be much easier for us then. I am missing you very much. I thought at first that my husband could substitute you in some respects, but now I see that I was mistaken. Now about my work. I like it fine. I have a splendid boss. He is a very interesting man, clever, talented, tolerant and handsome. We like each other and spend much time talking about various things. He is forty-four, single and rather unhappy. I wish you could see him and talk to him. My health is OK.
PS I have started writing poetry in this language. Next time I shall send you a sample.[11]

Having heard his characteristically northern English accent, his interrogators suspected that Abel had used yet another identity, that of a British businessman called 'Mr Milton' for whom Morris and Lona Cohen were known to have given a dinner party at their East 71st Street home in February 1950, and there was a belief that Morris Cohen, an electrical engineer by trade, might have worked briefly as Abel's wireless operator, but no supporting evidence was found apart from passport photos of the two Cohens recovered from Abel's briefcase, attached to a large quantity of dollar bills. It was this bundle, for which there was no innocent explanation, rather than the recollection of other witnesses who had been interviewed during the FBI's investigation of the Rosenbergs, that represented the most compelling proof of Abel's espionage.

Hayhanen completed a thirty-seven-page confession in May 1957 for the FBI in which he gave an account of the various tasks he had undertaken. He recalled early in 1953 having met a courier in Hoboken, a Finnish seaman code-named ASKO, whom he had paid for the delivery of several messages. He also claimed that Abel had been entrusted with just three tasks, only one of which proved to be of special interest to the FBI. Hayhanen recalled requests from Moscow to trace the whereabouts of three people: a Swedish ship's engineer named Olaf Carlson believed to be living in Boston, a possible recruit in Arleigh, New Jersey, and Master Sergeant Roy Rhodes. Only in the last case had he achieved a degree of success, having traced Rhodes's sister to Salida, Colorado, and elicited from her her brother's current address. The subsequent investigation revealed that Rhodes, who had been posted to the US Embassy in Moscow between 1951 and 1953 as a mechanic and chauffeur, had been black-mailed into co-operating with the KGB. A case summary found at Hayhanen's home in Peekskill, concealed inside a hollow steel bolt, offered damning evidence of what had happened to Rhodes:

Roy A. Rhodes (Codename QUEBEC) Born in 1917 in Oiltown, Okh. A senior sergeant in the War Ministry, former employee of the US military attaché staff in our country. He was a chief of the garage of the US Embassy. He was recruited to our service in January 1952 in our country. He left in June 1953. He was recruited on the basis of compromising materials, but he is tied to us with his receipts and the information he had given in his own handwriting. He had been trained in code work at the ministry before he went to work at the Embassy but as a code worker he was not used by the Embassy. After he left our country he was sent to the School of Communications of the Army CI services at the city of San Luis, Calif. He was to be trained as a mechanic of the coding machines. He fully agreed to cooperate with us in the States or in any other country. It was agreed that he was to have written to our Embassy here special letters but we have received none during the last year. It has been recently learned that he is in Red Bank N.J., where he owns three garages. The garage work is being done by his wife.

His father, Mr W. A. Rhodes, resides in the United States. His brother works as an engineer at an atomic plant in Camp Georgia.[12]

Having been caught in a classic honeytrap just after Christmas 1951, when he was told that he had got a Russian girl pregnant at an encounter following a drunken orgy, Rhodes had returned to the United States in June 1953, having compromised himself further by taking various small sums of money from the KGB and having signed receipts for the payments. In total, Rhodes admitted to having met his Soviet contacts fifteen times in Moscow and to having been paid about $3,000. After six months at a signals base in San Luis Obispo, California, he had been transferred to Fort Monmouth, New Jersey, and lived in a house nearby, at Linden Place, Red Bank. At the time of Abel's signal, Rhodes had been moved back to his unit's permanent base at Fort Huachuca, Arizona, where he received an honourable discharge at the end of his term of service, on 17 November 1955. In January the following year, he had re-enlisted and had been assigned back to Fort Monmouth as a code clerk with access to classified material. However, Rhodes had declined to renew the contact, as he had been instructed, and this failure led to Abel's enquiries to establish his current location. When confronted with Hayhanen's statement in June 1957, Rhodes confessed and appeared as a prosecution witness against Abel. Later, at his own court-martial, he was sentenced to five years' hard labour at Fort Leavenworth. Hayhanen was resettled at Keene, New Hampshire, but was reported to have died of cirrhosis of the liver in 1961.

Even if it appeared that Abel had not achieved much of operational importance, he clearly was valued by the Soviets and, in February 1962, he was freed from a thirty-year prison sentence and swapped for the U-2 pilot Gary Powers, who had been shot down near Sverdlovsk in May the previous year. While in the federal penitentiary Abel improved his very considerable artistic skills and, after his departure for Berlin, left behind several noteworthy pictures which were to become much sought-after collectors' items. According to some of those who knew him upon his return to Moscow,

Abel was never trusted entirely again by the KGB, not because his mission had been a failure, but just because he had spent so long in the West. Abel became something of a celebrity, but his popularity within the KGB suffered when he took up the cause of two former colleagues, both close associates of Beria, who had been imprisoned and purged after Stalin's death. Abel himself died in November 1971, and it was only much later that his much-publicised background was revealed to be as false as the name Abel. His parents were Russian émigrés of German background named Fisher and he was born in Benwell, Newcastle-upon-Tyne, in July 1903. His father, Genrykh M. Fisher, a radical revolutionary and a friend of Lenin's, had emigrated to England two years earlier and had worked in the Armstrong shipyard as an engine fitter. During the Russian revolution of 1905, Genrykh had practised his political agitation on the crews of two Russian ships that had docked in the Tyne for repairs. After the failure of the rising, Genrykh had been implicated in a plot to send arms and subversive literature to Russia. The scheme had failed and various participants were prosecuted for their part in it, but although Genrykh escaped being charged, it apparently jeopardised his chances of obtaining British nationality. During the First World War, he had continued his political activities among visiting Russian crews, but had returned to Russia in 1921, taking his son with him, who had evidently come to share his Bolshevik ideology. According to one report, Genrykh renewed his friendship with Lenin and became his close confidant, being assigned an apartment in the Kremlin. The following year Genrykh adopted the name A. Fisher to publish his memoirs, *In Russia and England: Observations and Recollections of a Petersburg Worker, 1891–1921*. He died in 1935, but there is some evidence that his son later returned to London on his British passport and may have fought in the Spanish Civil War.[13]

Abel was to achieve considerable status in the intelligence world, partly because the KGB chose to publicise his exploits, but more importantly because he was the first KGB officer of his rank, as illegal *rezident*, to be caught by a Western security agency. Whilst his capture was hailed as a

counter-intelligence triumph, it also marked a serious departure from what had hitherto appeared to be a well-established
Soviet policy. Initially illegals had been recruited from political
sympathisers, but when this resource proved too limited,
Soviet personnel were trained for deployment in the West.
The favoured route to a target country, through Canada,
made the exercise difficult to detect. More than a third of
Canada's population were immigrants and the US border controls were, for the detection of well-documented illegals,
wholly inadequate. That Abel had operated in New York since
1948 demonstrated the West's vulnerability to the new-style
illegal. His papers had never been challenged and the FBI's
routine surveillance of diplomatic staff had given no clue to
his existence. Along with the recognition of the threat posed
by the new illegals was an exaggerated worry that Abel had
been but one of many, and perhaps had supervised training
classes of equally talented agents upon his return to Moscow.

Soon after Hayhanen's approach to the CIA station in
Paris, another KGB illegal took the same route. Operating
as a studio photographer on the Seine's *rive droite*, Mikhail
Federov offered to defect but was persuaded to stay in place
by Richard Kovich, the CIA officer from the Soviet Russia
Division who had helped George Kisevalter to run Major
Piotr S. Popov, the GRU walk-in who had volunteered to
spy in Vienna in 1953. Assigned the cryptonym UN/ACUTE,
Federov remained in touch with Kovich for three years, holding secret meetings with him around Europe, before he was
recalled to Moscow in October 1958 and disappeared for
ever. A subsequent CIA analysis of the case concluded that
Fedorov, whose true name was believed to be Alexei Chistov, was probably a deliberate provocation, a plant manipu-
lated by the KGB throughout the operation with the intention
of misleading or entrapping CIA personnel. This concept, of
the despatch of specially briefed agents intended to make
contact with the opposition and sow confusion, was a sophisticated interpretation, which, to this day, remains a matter of
great controversy within the intelligence community. Indeed,
the whole question of the way the West responded to the
issue of illegals is still a matter of heated debate.

The proposition that the KGB had made a substantial investment in illegals was first propagated in 1961 by J. Bernard Hutton, the former Czech writer who first revealed the existence of a sophisticated training area, allegedly located at Gaczyna, a 'hundred miles south-east of Kuibyshev',[14] where illegals supposedly underwent an indoctrination lasting ten years into foreign lifestyles. Hutton claimed to have had four years' first-hand experience of Soviet espionage training techniques and asserted that he had secret contacts within the Soviet intelligence apparatus who had kept him supplied with the latest information. Gaczyna was a 425-square-mile area in which illegals were prepared for their life in the West. Red double-decker buses operated a service in a carefully constructed artificial English environment of 'perfect Anglo-Saxon surroundings', where 'waitresses, shop assistants, bus conductors and people of many other professions'[15] assisted in the training of illegals. Although Hutton's apparently authentic book was widely accepted as genuine, it was a complete fabrication. Nevertheless, some CIA officers were inclined to believe the notion that the KGB had created a mass-production assembly-line of illegals, and one even quoted Hutton as his source in his unclassified account of the KGB's history which perpetuated the myth.

Whatever the influence of Hutton's dubious book, both the CIA's Counterintelligence Staff and the FBI's counter-espionage branch became increasingly preoccupied with the idea that what the KGB was known to call 'the main enemy' was a target for the deployment of illegals. Each time a Soviet intelligence officer defected or, more rarely, was recruited while still in place, the completion of a questionnaire on the subject of illegals became a priority. When the CIA handled Major Popov, codenamed GR/ALLSPICE, he had been asked to learn what he could about illegals. Like the KGB, which exercised elaborate security around the division known as Directorate S, the department responsible for illegals, the GRU's own illegals unit was shrouded in secrecy. Nevertheless, the FBI had acquired a useful source of information about them from another Soviet walk-in, Major Dmitri F. Polyakov, arguably one of the most significant sources ever

exploited by the West. Codenamed TOP HAT by the FBI,
Polyakov was recruited in November 1961, towards the end
of his second tour of duty in the United States. A senior and
experienced GRU officer, Polyakov had spent five years in
New York on the staff of the United Nations, returning to
Moscow in 1956. Shortly before he left, Polyakov had
received an approach from the CIA known as a 'gangplank
pitch', in which a suspected Soviet intelligence officer is supplied with the means of making contact with the CIA in a
third country, just as he is leaving for home. Although the
procedure had not succeeded in recruiting an active source,
it had at least the merit of distracting the KGB's counter-
intelligence personnel, who became inordinately anxious if a
returnee failed to report the CIA's standard attempt to elicit
a defection. The FBI's second approach to Polyakov, made
by John Mabey of the New York Field Office, fortuitously
coincided with his own decision to offer his services for sale
to the Americans. An intermediary introduced Polyakov to
an FBI officer at a diplomatic reception and a rendezvous
was arranged for the following evening. Thus Polyakov
agreed terms for the purchase of his information and
underwent an intensive debriefing, at which he revealed that
prior to his appointment to the Soviet delegation to the UN,
he had served in Berlin with Piotr Popov as an illegal support
officer. Coincidentally, he had been the GRU conducting officer who had escorted Margarita Tairova to Berlin and introduced her to Popov (see page 187). At a series of secret
meetings held before his departure, Polyakov effectively
destroyed the GRU's operations in the United States. Even
after he had left the meetings continued, for Mabey arranged
to sail to Europe on the same ship as Polyakov. Furthermore, he was to continue supplying material of unprecedented
sensitivity for the next twenty years, thereby handing
the FBI and the CIA a fabulous and previously undisclosed
advantage.

Polyakov revealed that as an illegal support officer he was
currently supervising three illegals who had already been
infiltrated into the United States. He also disclosed the full
KGB and GRU order-of-battle in Washington, New York and

San Francisco, thereby compromising every Soviet professional intelligence officer currently active in the States. This data was recorded on MOUSNAT cards, the FBI's abbreviation for 'Movements of Soviet Nationals'. When completed, the cards were shown to Polyakov and another FBI source, codenamed FEDORA, which meant that the FBI could not only investigate specific spies, but also ensure that their limited surveillance facilities were deployed only against hard targets, the KGB 'Line PR' and GRU case officers known to be running agents. Polyakov's co-operation amounted to a complete reversal of the disadvantages under which the FBI had hitherto been obliged to work. Within the thousand-strong New York Field Office the espionage branch, designated Division 5, was organised into separate teams, with Squad 34 producing a weekly *Intelligence Digest* and monitoring the much-feared Line KR counter-intelligence specialists. Sub-units concentrated on other suspects, with Squad 341 working the UN mission and the Line N Illegal Support Officers; 342 watching the UN Secretariat; 343 was assigned Amtorg, *Izvestia* and the other official fronts like the TASS agency; 331 looked at the GRU and 332 kept the Soviet mission to the UN under observation. For particular operations, Squad 344 could deploy more than a hundred Special Agents on physical surveillance duties. A file known as a '105' was opened on each of Polyakov's Soviet colleagues, and a '65' reserved for Americans suspected of espionage. Although Polyakov was never told, some of his information was double-checked with two other, equally sensitive FBI sources, FEDORA and MITRE.

FEDORA was Alexei I. Kulak,[16] an employee of the UN Secretariat, who had literally walked into the FBI's Field Office in Manhattan in early 1962, just a few weeks after his arrival in New York in November 1961, the same month Polyakov had started work for the FBI. Kulak was 'Line X', a radiation specialist working for the KGB's scientific and technical directorate, and although he knew little about individual agents, he was able to give valuable confirmation to the true roles of his colleagues fingered by Polyakov. In addition, there was a further defector, codenamed MITRE, a

'Line PR' KGB officer, also based at the UN, whose details are still highly classified.

The first of Polyakov's illegals was a Finn named Kaarlo R. Tuomi, whom he ran with assistance from Anatoli B. Senkin and Lev V. Sosnovski. Ostensibly a shipyard worker who had been born in the United States but had been taken home to Europe as a child, Tuomi lived in a rented room in a suburban house in Hillyer Street, East Orange, New Jersey. Following Polyakov's tip, he was placed under surveillance by the FBI and had once been seen communicating with two of Polyakov's men, Ivan D. Egerov and Alexei I. Galkin, through dead-letter drops in the Bronx and Queens. He was seized off the street by Jack O'Toole, a highly intuitive counter-intelligence expert based at the New York Field Office, and interviewed continuously for ten days at a safe-house in the wilds of Michigan. Working with Special Agent Joe Diffley, who had been a schoolteacher before he had joined the FBI, O'Toole enjoyed unorthodox solutions to difficult problems; presenting Tuomi with the evidence of his clandestine contacts, he offered him an irresistible deal: immediate arrest and a lengthy term of imprisonment, or full protection if he made a complete confession and agreed to operate as a double agent. Confronted with such a stark choice Tuomi opted to help the FBI and described his life as an illegal. He had been born in the United States in 1917 and had emigrated from Michigan in 1933 with his mother, sister and Finnish stepfather, who was an ardent Communist. During the war he had fought in a Soviet infantry battalion and, in 1950, was recruited for intelligence duties while attending a language school. Like his KGB counterpart Rudolph Abel, Tuomi had been staged through Canada and had undertaken a previous assignment lasting three weeks which had taken him through Copenhagen, Paris, Brussels and finally Finland before returning to Moscow. On his main assignment he had arrived in Montreal in December 1958 by air, after a week in Paris and a further few days in Belgium, using a genuine US passport issued to a Finnish American. Once in Canada, he had switched to the identity of Robert B. White, from Chicago, and had taken the train to New York, checking into the

George Washington Hotel on 3 January 1959. Later he found an apartment in Jackson Heights, before moving to East Orange, New Jersey.[17]

The FBI's control of Tuomi, who was codenamed KAROT, continued until after Polyakov's return to Moscow in 1962, and led directly to the identification of his successor as the GRU's principal illegal support officer in the US, Piotr E. Maslennikov. While the FBI stepped up surveillance on Tuomi and his contacts, two other illegals were placed under observation. The pair were Robert K. Baltch and Joy Ann Garber, who had been living in Greenmount Avenue, Baltimore, since March 1962. He taught French at a Berlitz language school and she was a hairdresser in a local beauty salon, and at the weekends they stayed at a cabin in Dulaney Valley, a forested area north of the city. Soon after the FBI operation began, the Baltches moved to 27th Street NW in Washington DC, where Robert found a job lecturing in French at George Washington University. He also enrolled as a part-time student of German at the University, while his wife continued to work as a hairdresser. The FBI's surveillance of the Baltches was to last two years, during which they were spotted making contact with their GRU case officers. In May 1963, Robert was watched while he conducted a fruitless search for a small container that had been hidden under a railway bridge in Queens by Ivan Egerov, the First Secretary at the Soviet delegation to the UN, who had served previously as a diplomat in Ottawa and New Delhi. On that occasion the connection failed, but a month later Egerov, accompanied by his wife Alexandra, succeeded in using the same site to communicate with Baltch. This particular episode seemed to prompt a change in the Baltches' behaviour, for they sold their car and were seen to make preparations to move home, thus prompting the FBI to raid their apartment on 9 July. A search revealed a mass of espionage paraphernalia, including a pair of forged US passports, a Hallicrafter shortwave receiver, a wireless schedule and a one-time cipher pad. The forged passports, in the names of James O. Jackson and Bertha R. Jackson, were entirely false, although when checked the actual details proved authentic.

The genuine James Jackson, an athletics coach living in Texas, had been issued with a passport bearing the same number on the same date, and he had used it to travel across Eastern Europe in May 1961. Bertha's passport had been issued to a Harry Lee Jackson, an advertising executive from Maryland who had visited Europe in July 1961 and apparently had inadvertently provided the GRU with an opportunity to copy the contents.

From the documentary material recovered from various ingenious hiding-places, the FBI was able to reconstruct some of the Baltches' background. Evidently they had arrived separately in the States on false documentation some time in late 1958. He had rented an apartment in New York on West 48th Street, and she had lived alone at 105 Riverside Drive. In his original job application to the Berlitz branch at the Rockefeller Center, Baltch had claimed that he had been born in the United States but had been brought up and educated in Canada and France. In April 1959, he had married Joy Ann Garber and they had moved to an address in East 139th Street, in the Mott Haven neighbourhood of the Bronx. When they moved to Baltimore, in March 1962, they had stayed temporarily in Mount Royal Terrace while Joy Ann had qualified as a cosmetologist and had received a New York State certificate at that address.

While tracing the Baltches over the past three years proved a straightforward task for the eighty FBI Special Agents assigned to the investigation, who simply followed the paper trail left deliberately by the two illegals in New York while they had created a past for themselves, the question of their true identities was to be rather more complex. For example, the real Robert K. Baltch turned out to be a Catholic priest from Dormont, Pennsylvania, whose parents had been immigrants from Lithuania. They had returned home in 1933, having acquired US citizenship, and had taken their son and daughter with them. After the war, in March 1947, the entire family had travelled back to America, where Robert had been ordained and had even applied for a renewal of his US passport. At the time the impostor was obtaining a marriage licence in lower Manhattan, the real Robert Baltch was serving his congregation in Amsterdam, an industrial town in up-state New York. As for Joy Ann Garber, she also existed, as a married woman in Norwalk, Connecticut. While it was evident how the GRU had obtained details of Robert Baltch's passport, probably in Moscow soon after his father had applied for passports for his family at the US Embassy in Moscow back in 1940, the use of Joy Garber's identity was rather more unusual. In the various official papers she had signed since her arrival in the United States the illegal masquerading as Joy Ann Garber had correctly given her birth details as 16 May 1930, at Springfield, Massachusetts. Curiously, when the FBI checked the original record, it was discovered that Joy Ann's parents had been Ossip and Sonia Garber, her father being the photographer who had been convicted with eight others in a fraudulent passport racket in New York in 1939 (see chapter 1). He had been released from prison in 1940 and had died in 1951.

One item recovered by the FBI from Baltch's apartment was to be the key to his true identity. A name and address in France was found among his belongings, and when the French DST eventually traced the person listed, she instantly recognised the FBI's photograph of Baltch as being that of Alexandre V. Sokolov, a childhood friend. Having established Baltch's true identity, his family background was relatively easy to research, for Alexandre, born in Tiflis on 26 February 1923, had already earned a substantial DST dossier for his political activities in Paris. Under interrogation, 'Robert K. Baltch' admitted that he was really Sokolov, the eldest of four children born to Vincent, a White Russian army officer who had been a liaison officer with the British forces in southern Russia. A skilled interpreter of Far Eastern languages, he had fled to France not long after the revolution. His unit had been disbanded on the Persian front and he had been taken aboard a British ship to Constantinople, where his wife Nadine had been delivered of a second son, Igor. Vincent, who had found work in a German shipping company in Paris run by a Tsarist family, had died of tuberculosis in 1931, causing his children to be split up, with one of Alexandre's younger brothers, Misha, being placed with a guardian in England. At the end of the war Alexandre, a committed Socialist, had persuaded his mother, sister Moura and brother Igor, who had joined the French army and had fought with the resistance during the Nazi occupation, to return to the Soviet Union. Alexandre had met his wife, Lise-Lotte, in the Soviet zone of Germany and, subsequently, both were recruited by the GRU as illegals. Like his brothers and sister, he spoke French and English as well as Russian, and with his ideological zeal, which was not shared by the rest of the family, he must have been a natural for the GRU. He remained in Potsdam for a period and then had been infiltrated into America, where he had pretended to meet and marry Lise-Lotte, the woman who was already his wife. Further details of the Sokolov family background were added by Misha, Alexandre's brother, who had moved to England and had later been educated at HMS *Conway*, and had served in the Royal Navy. The British Security Service traced him without difficulty because he had worked in the Intelligence Division of the Control Commission for Germany after the war. Later, he had trained for Massey-Ferguson, the agricultural machinery manufacturer. His wife, Shiela Grant Duff, whom he had married in 1952, was related to Clementine Churchill and she had headed the BBC's Czech department. Before the war she had travelled widely in Europe as a journalist and had reported on the Spanish Civil War. When the Sokolovs were interviewed at their farm in Stowmarket, Suffolk, they were, not surprisingly, horrified to discover that Alexandre, the brother Misha had not seen since he had bade him farewell in Paris after the war on his journey to the Soviet Union, had been arrested in America as a Soviet illegal. [18]

Almost immediately after the Baltches were arrested, Ivan and Alexandra Egerov were detained at their home in Flushing, Queens, and charged with conspiracy to commit espionage. As an employee of the UN, Egerov was not entitled to diplomatic immunity, despite the protests of the Soviet authorities. Also named on the indictment were Alexei I. Galkin, First Secretary of the Byelorussian delegation to the UN, Piotr E. Maslennikov, First Secretary at the Soviet mission, and 'various others'. Galkin and Maslennikov had returned to Moscow in May, but when pressed by the defence lawyers, the prosecution confirmed that the 'various others' included Anatoli B. Senkin, Lev V. Sosnovski, a certain Dmitri F. Polyakov and a witness named Kaarlo Tuomi.

This was a particularly dangerous development for the FBI because the public disclosure of so many Soviet intelligence personnel indicated the scale of the FBI's penetration. More significantly, if Tuomi was subjected to any cross-examination, it was likely to become clear how and when the FBI had first approached him. Under skilful questioning he might easily unwittingly betray information that would suggest to the Soviet observers present that the FBI might have relied upon another method, other than routine surveillance on the Egerovs, to tip them off to the existence of the Baltches. On the assumption that Tuomi had switched sides, which, intentionally, was the clear implication of the indictment, the Soviets would have been keen to learn exactly when he had defected so that the appropriate precautions could be implemented. Since Egerov had serviced dead-drops for both Tuomi and Baltch, it was a reasonable assumption for the Soviets to make that either Egerov had been the victim of Tuomi's treachery or, less likely, that the FBI had been led to Tuomi by routine, random surveillance on the UN official. What the FBI feared, of course, was the leakage of any information that might suggest the existence of a mole in the GRU's apparatus in New York and, thereby, jeopardise Polyakov. Naming him in the indictment had been something of a risk of course, but one that had been judged acceptable and, in the circumstances, justifiable. Those circumstances were to change dramatically when the State Department, without knowing of the complex background to the case, or of Polyakov's role, which was a secret held by a handful of individuals, unexpectedly released the Egerovs on 12 October 1963 and swapped them for two Americans held in Soviet labour camps. In the absence of the Egerovs, the prosecution's case against the Baltches relied almost entirely upon Tuomi and this held grave implications for the safety of Polyakov, who was by then back in Moscow and out of touch. Accordingly, when the trial opened almost a year later, in

October 1964, the government attorneys offered no evidence and the case was dismissed. Their excuse was the Brooklyn federal court's ruling which accepted the defence's inconvenient demand for the public disclosure of the addresses of every prosecution witness. The prosecution asserted that the court order would endanger Tuomi's life and pretended that there was no choice but to protect its witness by dropping the case. As the jubilant Baltches congratulated themselves on this surprising development, they were arrested by agents of the Immigration Service and deported, at their request, to Prague. Alexandre, the idealist who was to become disenchanted with Communism after his return to the Soviet Union, died of a heart attack on a station platform in Moscow in 1973; his widow, Lise-Lotte, continues to live and work in Nizhni-Novgorod (formerly Gorky), not far from the foreign languages institute where her sister-in-law Moura teaches English and French.

In order to protect Polyakov, the FBI later took elaborate steps to provide journalists with a sanitised version of how Tuomi and the Sokolovs had been apprehended. For example, when the respected *Reader's Digest* journalist John Barron wrote *KGB: The Secret Work of Soviet Secret Agents* in 1974, he was told that Tuomi had been a KGB illegal and had been approached by the FBI in Milwaukee on 9 March 1959, with the intention of conveying to Barron's Soviet readership the misleading impression that Tuomi had switched sides a clear two-and-a-half years before he really had defected, and at a time when Polyakov was in Moscow. Barron also reported that Tuomi had finally broken contact with the KGB in July 1963, soon after he had delivered to his contact details of US missile sites in the Midwest. The proposition that the FBI had run Tuomi as a double agent for more than four years had been calculated to cause much confusion in Moscow for the KGB's counter-intelligence analysts, who undoubtedly would have to backtrack over every one of Tuomi's messages home in an attempt to ascertain what information was bogus and what was authentic. Similarly, for his treatment of the Sokolovs, the author David Wise was given the false impression for his book, *The Espion-*

age Establishment, that they had come under the FBI's scrutiny as a direct result of Tuomi's defection. In reality, of course, both authors had been duped into protecting the FBI's most valuable source ever in what was unquestionably a very successful exercise in disinformation.

Although the FBI regretted the loss of a conviction against the two authentic GRU illegals who had been flown to Czechoslovakia, Polyakov's original list of Soviet agents operating in the United States gave the New York Field Office plenty of work. In addition to Tuomi, who was resettled with a protected identity, and the Sokolovs, Polyakov was responsible for tipping the FBI off to the existence of two other important GRU sources: Yeoman Nelson C. Drummond and Sergeant Jack F. Dunlap. A black sailor from a poor background, Drummond had been supplying the GRU with classified information from the US naval base at Newport, Rhode Island, since his original recruitment in London in 1957. While under the FBI's surveillance Drummond was seen to fill dead-drops in New York which were emptied by Evgenni M. Prokhorov and Ivan Y. Vyrodov, both diplomats at the Soviet delegation to the UN. In September 1962, all three were arrested together at a rendezvous, a roadside diner in Larchmont, Connecticut. The two Soviets, both GRU officers, were declared *persona non grata* (PNG), while Drummond was tried and sentenced to life imprisonment. Under interrogation he made a detailed confession and identified four other Soviet case officers to whom he had sold secrets.

Sergeant Dunlap, a driver at the NSA with expensive tastes that he could not support on his salary, committed suicide in July 1963 before he could be interrogated. In both cases the FBI leaked false stories to the media to protect its prize source, Polyakov. According to TOP HAT, Dunlap had been selling the NSA's secrets to the GRU since 1958, when he was working at the US Embassy in Moscow, and accordingly he had been placed under surveillance by the FBI as soon as he was identified. In March 1963, four months after the tip, Dunlap applied to leave the army and transfer to a civilian job in the NSA. At this stage he probably realised that he had come under suspicion, for he was subjected to polygraph tests and, when told that he had failed, lost his security clearance. However, at no time during the investigation was Dunlap ever seen to communicate with his GRU controllers, so his suicide took place before any evidence had been found that could be used against him. Indeed, a charade was played out after his death in which it was suggested that Dunlap's expensive tastes had attracted attention, and that classified documents had been found by his widow a month after his death. This fabricated scenario, which stressed Dunlap's ownership of a speedboat, a Jaguar and two Cadillacs, was first published in an anthology of intelligence literature, *Great True Spy Stories*, [19] edited by Allen Dulles, the DCI who retired in November 1961, the very month Polyakov had held his first meeting with the FBI. If this fable was meant for Soviet consumption, it left the definite impression that Dunlap had only been investigated as a spy after his death, thereby reassuring the KGB that its source had not been the victim of a betrayal. In a similar account of the case provided by Professor David Kahn in 1966, it was suggested that Dunlap had probably started betraying secrets 'in mid-1960', [20] another obfuscation intended to give the KGB confirmation that Dunlap's exposure had not been brought about by a breach of the GRU's security.

In Drummond's case, a similar disinformation exercise was undertaken, with journalists informed that the FBI had been alerted to his high-spending 'towards the beginning of 1960', when in fact the FBI had not placed him under surveillance for another year, and had not found any evidence against the sailor until August 1962, when Drummond unwisely called at the New York apartment of Vadim V. Sorokin.

Polyakov's information was not limited to the GRU. He identified Fedor D. Kudashkin, a relatively junior Third Secretary at the UN mission, as a senior Line N KGB officer in New York running an important source. Because Kudashkin proved to be an unusually cautious professional, constantly taking counter-surveillance measures, the FBI watchers were obliged to adopt a novel form of observation to trace his movements. A time-elapse camera was secretly mounted under the bonnet of his car overnight, when he was suspected of meeting his agent, and the film was developed the following morning. By using the photographs to reconstruct his route, the FBI agents were able to retrace Kudashkin's journey to Long Island and were, therefore, able to prepare a series of observation points in the area where he had spent most time parked by the side of the road. It was noted that on the occasions that Kudashkin ventured out of Manhattan he was accompanied by Yuri Lysov, a Line KR counter-intelligence expert, and Herman Levakov, a UN Secretariat employee who was flagged by TOP HAT as Line N. In addition, Levakov's wife invariably cruised the area in her car to detect hostile surveillance.

On 11 June 1963, Kudashkin was spotted in Lynbrook, Long Island, with a man who was later identified as Robert G. Thompson, a veteran of air-force intelligence who had started an oil delivery business in the locality. When Thompson was interviewed by Special Agent Paul Tompkins in August 1964, after more than a year of surveillance, he began to deny any contact with the Soviets. However, after some twenty-five interviews, he confessed to having spied for the KGB since he had approached them in East Berlin in 1955. Since that date, when Thompson had worked with classified material in a branch of the Air Force Office of Special Investigation, he had given everything to the KGB. Armed with a comprehensive confession extracted from Thompson, Kudashkin was expelled, and in May 1965 Thompson was sentenced to thirty years' imprisonment. When the episode received publicity, the FBI pretended that Thompson had been watched constantly since January 1958, when the airman had been transferred from Berlin to Malmstrom Air Force Base, Montana. Once again, the intention was to deceive the GRU about exactly when the FBI had started its investigation and divert attention away from Polyakov, and perhaps implicate Oleg Penkovsky, the GRU colonel who had been convicted of espionage and executed in May 1963. In fact, Thompson had only been spotted when Kudashkin was seen meeting him on Long Island in June 1963. Because Thompson had identified Boris V. Karpovich as a Soviet who had made contact with him in Great Falls, Montana, it was also suggested that the Second Secretary from the UN mission in New York had been spotted by the FBI in 1958, and on this excuse he too was expelled, the implication being that Thompson had been compromised much earlier than had actually been the case.[21]

After Polyakov's return to Moscow in 1962, he was promoted to the rank of colonel and in late 1965 was appointed to Rangoon as military attaché for a tour of duty lasting four years, during which the CIA re-established contact with him. In 1973, he was sent to New Delhi, and was back in Moscow in 1976. Each time he went abroad he signalled his arrival and the CIA assigned a case officer to meet him. His duplicity went unsuspected by the KGB, and when he returned to India in 1979, he had achieved the rank of general-lieutenant. He was finally arrested by the KGB in July 1985 and executed after a brief trial three years later, in March 1988. His KGB counterpart, Alexei Kulak, completed his two-year tour in New York in 1963 and was later posted back to the United States in 1966 and in 1975 as a scientific attaché to the UN. After his return to Moscow in 1977, he was seen several times by CIA officers anxious about his safety, and he is reported to have died of natural causes.

During the two decades Polyakov and Kulak sold information to the CIA, they were responsible for alerting their American contacts to several important espionage cases, including those of Lieutenant-Colonel William H. Whalen, who was arrested in July 1966, and Staff Sergeant Herbert W. Boeckenhaupt, arrested in October the same year, both as a result of a tip from Polyakov to the CIA in Rangoon. TOP HAT denounced Whalen, who was then working for the Chiefs of Staff in the Pentagon, as a source originally recruited in 1955 in Washington DC by Mikhail M. Shumaev, who had later passed the case on to his GRU colleague Colonel Sergei A. Edenski. Whalen was convicted and sentenced to fifteen years' imprisonment with the minimum of publicity. Boeckenhaupt, a German-born communications technician specialising in the repair of cryptographic equipment, was based at March Air Force Base in California at the time of his arrest and had been in touch with the GRU since October 1962, when, posted to the USAF communications facility at Sidi Slimane, Morocco, he had volunteered to sell classified information to the Soviet Embassy in Rabat. His GRU case officer, Aleksei R. Malinin, from the Soviet military mission in Washington DC, was expelled on the spurious claim that he had been seen meeting Boeckenhaupt twice, an assertion designed to suggest that Malinin had been under routine surveillance when he had met his agent. In reality, TOP HAT had been responsible for tipping off the FBI, which secured the airman's conviction and a thirty-year sentence.

In his confession Boeckenhaupt revealed his method of communicating with the GRU, via an accommodation address in England, which prompted a flurry of activity from the British Security Service. The custodian of the postbox turned out to be Cecil W. Mulvena, a shipping forwarder based in Southend-on-Sea, who was raided. Mulvena admitted having carried out various minor tasks for two members of the Soviet Trade Delegation over a period of five years, but only one amounted to an offence under the Official Secrets Act. In June 1965, he had applied for a British passport in the name of John H. D. Foreman, a man who was alive at the time, but had subsequently died. This passport had been handed over to his Soviet contact, named Petchenko, and presumably had been used by an illegal. Mulvena pleaded guilty to making the fraudulent application and was sentenced to four years' imprisonment.

Together Polyakov, Kulak and the source codenamed MITRE allowed the FBI to acquire a wealth of knowledge about illegals, but that was not always enough to find and exploit them. A woman visited by the FBI in the Bronx as a probable illegal committed suicide as soon as the Special Agents left her apartment. The FBI also followed up numerous other leads in pursuit of illegals believed, on the evidence of TOP HAT, FEDORA and MITRE, to have been infiltrated into the United States. The NSA undertook a massive exercise to isolate clandestine wireless signals and Squad 34 moved into several hotels on Manhattan's Westside with specially designed equipment tuned to frequencies recommended by the NSA, at certain times, in the hope of entrapping an illegal while he transmitted. One operation which lasted several years was a covert examination of letters mailed in Manhattan without return addresses. The FBI learned through experience that illegals often communicated with their case officers via the regular mail and, characteristically, wrote the envelope address in the Russian box-like form, whereas Westerners tended to slope their addresses, but the scheme was eventually abandoned for lack of productivity.

As the Sokolovs had demonstrated their zeal for accumulating incidental pieces of documentation to support their bogus credentials, the FBI followed another interesting line of enquiry. A couple of illegals had applied to the New York Public Library for readers' cards, a useful if innocuous item that established the holder's name and address. The FBI began a trawl through all the recent applications for library cards and found one written in poorly disguised Cyrillic script. This clue also put them on the trail of an illegal.

While the final arrangements were being negotiated for Abel's return, which was completed on 8 February 1962, and the FBI was processing the debriefings of Polyakov, Kulak and MITRE, the CIA was preoccupied with the debriefing of Anatoli M. Golitsyn, one of the most influential and well-informed defectors of the post-war era. Calling himself Anatoli Klimov, Golitsyn had turned up on the doorstep of Frank Friberg, the CIA station chief in Helsinki, in December 1961 and had demanded asylum in the United States for himself, his wife and daughter. His request was granted, and Golitsyn had proceeded to give the CIA in Washington a detailed account of his career in the KGB's FCD. He explained that he had fallen foul of his local *rezident*, Colonel Zhenikhov, but nevertheless he presented his defection as politically motivated. He offered a wealth of information about KGB operations, but his participation in one particular illegal exercise had, unknown to him, already been disclosed to the CIA. It was to be a unique example of a KGB illegal operation in which both participants, the illegal and his support officer, approached the CIA.

Yuri N. Loginov was intended to be one of the new breed of illegals, a professional who had undergone intensive training in anticipation of his deployment in the West. One part of the preparation was a preliminary trip to Italy, routed through Helsinki in May 1961. While in Finland, and equipped with a US passport in the name of Ronald W. Dean, he had attended a routine rendezvous organised by Nikolai A. Frolov, the local illegal support officer based at the Soviet Embassy. Also present on that occasion had been Golitsyn, who had accompanied his colleague to the meeting with Loginov, never realising that Loginov had already established contact with the CIA and, in a gesture of good faith, had compromised Golitsyn, who already had been flagged only as a suspected intelligence officer. After Golitsyn's defection his bona fides were confirmed by Piotr S. Deriabin, the KGB defector who had switched sides in Vienna in February 1954 and had originally identified Golitsyn as a KGB colleague.

Coincidentally, Loginov had also tried to defect to Frank Friberg but Richard Kovich, who flew in specially from Vienna, persuaded the illegal to continue his work for the KGB. Loginov agreed and gave Kovich a biographical sketch of his background, describing his father as a senior Party apparatchik and a deputy of the Supreme Soviet. Having studied foreign languages Yuri had joined the Institute of Foreign Relations in Moscow, but had been recruited by Boris A. Skoridov of the KGB, who was later to serve a tour under diplomatic cover in London for three years from 1962 with third secretary rank, using the cover name Boris A. Zhiltsov. Under Skoridov's supervision, he was taught clandestine wireless techniques by a radio operator, who, incidentally, had been compromised by another defector, Nikolai E. Khokhlov, and given a course in illegal tradecraft by a KGB veteran, Ishak A. Akhmerov, who was married to Elena Ivanovna, the niece of Earl Browder, Secretary-General of the CPUSA. At Kovich's prompting Loginov recalled the various KGB personalities he had met while training with the Illegals Directorate, which had previously been headed by Vitali G. Pavlov until he was posted to Vienna under the name Nikolai G. Kedrov. His successor was Mikhail S.

Tsymbal, who had been the KGB *rezident* in Paris until 1959, using the name Mikhail S. Rogov, and who was subsequently promoted in 1966 to Deputy Chief of the FCD. Another of those to have operated as an illegal and named by Loginov was Vasili V. Grigoriev, who had been based in West Berlin in 1955. His training virtually over, Loginov had been sent to Prague with a false identity and had lived there under operational conditions in preparation for his main assignment.

Kovich assigned the cryptonym AE/GUSTO to Loginov and made arrangements for an exchange of signals so that they could meet again when the occasion arose. Although the CIA had assumed, based on its limited previous experience of illegals, that Loginov would now be despatched to the United States, he instead received a series of short-duration missions, to Paris in 1962 and to Brussels two years later. This third trip to the West, on which Loginov used a Canadian passport, took in Austria, Germany, Beirut and Cairo, but to the surprise of his CIA contacts, there was still no sign of his ultimate mission, an inexplicable delay that suggested to Jack Fieldhouse of the CIA's Counterintelligence Staff that Loginov's true intention was to deceive the CIA. After all, it was a fact that after years of groping in the dark, the FBI and CIA inexplicably had been the beneficiaries of a steady flow of line-crossers. As well as Loginov and Golitsyn, and the three sources run by the FBI in New York, there had been the controversial defection of Yuri I. Nosenko in Geneva in February 1964. In the latter's case the CIA had detected some flaws in his story, and he had been incarcerated in the hope of finally obtaining proof of a KGB plant, but the evidence had been ambiguous. Nevertheless, the sheer volume of apparently disaffected officers seeking to betray the KGB gave rise to a suspicion that was reflected in the way Loginov was handled. Finally, in January 1967, when patience at Langley was beginning to wear thin, Loginov turned up in Antwerp, destined for South Africa and equipped with a Canadian passport in the name of Edmund Trinka. A check in Canada revealed that the real Trinka had been born in Fort Whyte, Manitoba, but had died in Lithuania.

In May 1967, after Loginov had established himself in

Johannesburg for five months, he held a rendezvous with the CIA in Nairobi, but evidently the meeting did nothing to allay the fear that he was no more than a KGB plant. Although circumstantial in nature, the evidence against Loginov was, in counter-intelligence terms, quite compelling. For example, he had often told his CIA handlers that his main mission to the United States was imminent, but it had never seemed to materialise. Unlike illegal support officers, who gained a knowledge of other espionage cases, Loginov had not given any clue to the identity of Soviet spies. Indeed, some of his replies to very specific questions which had already been answered by FEDORA and TOP HAT tended to contradict them. His motivation also seemed shallow and was certainly not inspired by any hatred of the KGB or the Soviet political system, and for all his long visits to the West, he had not really achieved anything of substance. Why had the KGB invested so much in an illegal who had done so little? Was he to be accepted, and the word of FEDORA and MITRE disbelieved? If that scenario was followed to its logical conclusion, a major conspiracy of labyrinthine complexity was the only explanation. Such an interpretation would also cast doubt on the meal-tickets, the numerous Soviet spies that had been identified from information supplied by the suspect sources. As the CIA had not found the answers to any of these conundrums, a dramatic solution was found: the betrayal of Loginov to the South African security police, who arrested him and subjected him to a lengthy hostile interrogation.

This extraordinary development occurred after a long debate at Langley about how Loginov should be developed. As he was suspected of having become a triple agent for the KGB, the final verdict was in favour of tipping off the South Africans, who, no doubt, would have their own methods of extracting the truth. Loginov's apartment in Johannesburg was raided in July 1967 by the director of the Security Police, General Henryk van den Bergh, and in the following September a statement was released in which it was announced that Loginov had admitted to espionage and had signed a confession in which he had named numerous KGB officers masquerading under diplomatic cover in Europe. In fact, Loginov had been astonished by the action of the South Africans and had conceded his clandestine role as a double agent for the CIA, no doubt on the mistaken assumption that he could rely on the Agency's intervention and protection. As for the list of compromised KGB personnel, it had been fabricated by the CIA with the express intention of persuading Loginov to be entirely candid with his interrogators. To eliminate any doubt about the depth of Loginov's supposed confession, a local journalist was offered the opportunity to write his biography and was provided with what were presented as details of his background supposedly supplied by him. What Barbara Carr was not told was that the data she received about Loginov was from the CIA, and not the South African police.

Barbara Carr's *Loginov: Spy in the Sun*[22] was not the first biography of a Soviet illegal – Abel's lawyer, James B. Donovan, had written *Strangers on a Bridge* about his client in 1964 – but it was the first detailed case history of an illegal, albeit with the omission of Loginov's role as a double agent for the CIA. Publication must have amounted to a death sentence in the Soviet Union for Loginov, but nevertheless in July 1969 he was deported to Frankfurt and exchanged at the Herleshausen border checkpoint for eleven BND agents captured in the East. Loginov's few supporters in the CIA were appalled by this ruthless treatment, certain that he would face a firing-squad upon his return, but the counter-intelligence specialists who had been persuaded of his duplicity were confident that the illegal would be given a hero's welcome. Whatever the truth, which remains highly debatable, Loginov now lives in honourable retirement in the Russian Federation, apparently untroubled by the recriminations that almost paralysed the CIA's Counterintelligence Staff.

7 · The Illegals from Germany

The loss of a spy is a blow to an intelligence service only if, upon losing that man, it simultaneously loses a significant and talkative person who happens to be privy to secrets.

Rupert Sigl in *In the Claws of the KGB*[1]

That the KGB had adopted a new policy regarding the recruitment of illegals had first become evident when the defector Vladimir Petrov revealed to the Australian Security and Intelligence Organisation (ASIO) and the Royal Commission on Espionage the numerous official documents that he had removed from the Soviet Embassy in Canberra. The need for illegal networks that could remain in place in times of international tension when diplomatic relations might be cut was well recognised by Moscow, but the bitter experiences of the disclosures made by Bentley, Gouzenko and Gold had illustrated the need to build illegal organisations in isolation from the local Party apparatus. In June 1952, while he had still been the KGB's legal *rezident* in Canberra, Petrov had received a directive, circulated to all *rezidents*, that had placed a new and special emphasis on the development of illegal rings:

The aggravation of the international situation and the pressing necessity for the timely exposure and prevention of cunning designs of the enemy, call imperatively for a radical reorganisation of all our intelligence work and the urgent operation of an illegal apparatus in Australia which could function uninterruptedly and effectively under any conditions.[2]

While Moscow's requirement in Australia was for the construction of an illegal apparatus which could work on a contingency basis, other *rezidentzia* had more compelling preoccupations. In a divided Germany, for example, the Cold War had given an added incentive to the KGB to develop and deploy illegals. The West's knowledge of the KGB's use of illegals in Germany emanated principally from two defectors, Nikolai E. Khokhlov, who had switched sides in Frankfurt in February 1954, and Bogdan Stashinsky, who surrendered to the German authorities in Berlin in December 1961. Whereas previous illegals had been trained to gather intelligence about 'the main enemy', this pair had been trained as assassins and had been despatched on missions into the Federal Republic to murder leading members of the émigré community, but neither Khokhlov nor Stashinsky had completed their assignment.

'Liquidation', of course, had long been a feature of Soviet intelligence operations and the term was recognised by the Eastern Bloc professionals as a transparent euphemism for cold-blooded, state-sanctioned murder. It had been an occupational hazard under Stalin and there had been numerous examples during the 1920s and 1930s of assassination as a policy to silence the Kremlin's opponents. Among the more notorious examples in Paris had been the murder of the Ukrainian general, Simon Petlura, in May 1926; the seizure of the White Russian general, Aleksandr P. Kutepov, off a Paris street in January 1930; and the disappearance of General Eugene Miller in September 1937. Nor had the abductions and shootings been limited to exiled anti-Bolsheviks. In 1937 alone, more than forty *rezidents* had been recalled to Moscow to disappear and in subsequent years even Stalin's most ruthless henchmen, like General Jan Berzin, who had faithfully served the cause, suffered the same fate. What made Khokhlov's testimony so shocking was the fact that he had been trained as an illegal for this single homicidal purpose.

Khokhlov, who had been a KGB killer since he had operated as a partisan behind German lines during the war and
had played a key role in the assassination of Wilhelm Kube,
the Nazi gauleiter of Minsk, had married Yania Timashkevits
in 1952 and, thereafter, had fallen under her influence. She
came from a Uniat Christian family and she secretly converted
her husband to Orthodox Christianity. Accordingly, when
assigned to kill Georgi S. Okolovich, the leader of the exiled
NTS (Ukrainian) nationalists headquartered in Frankfurt-am-
Main, Khokhlov had called at his apartment on 18 February
1954 and given himself up to his intended victim. Okolovich's
organisation, financed jointly by the CIA and SIS, was an
important target for the KGB because it distributed subversive literature across the Ukraine and supplied the CIA with
volunteers willing to be dropped into their homeland as agents
and guerrillas. Since Okolovich enjoyed close ties with all the
Allied intelligence agencies, and was actually the director of
the NTS's covert operations branch, he asked Khokhlov
which service he wished to defect to. 'Not the British,' he
had replied. 'My impression is that in the name of the British
Empire they would cheat us or even betray us. As to the
French, I don't know whether they could handle it.'[3]

Having chosen the Americans, Okolovich had promptly put
Khokhlov in the hands of the big CIA station in Frankfurt,
and a debriefing session had been held over the following
weekend at a safe-house where Khokhlov had described his
mission to an astonished audience of two Russian-speaking
CIA officers and a representative from the local SIS station.
The defector identified himself as a captain in the Soviet
intelligence service, who had spent four years in Romania
perfecting his illegal cover, and asked for resettlement in the
West for himself and for his wife and young son Alushka. His
story was so extraordinary that Leslie Humphreys, an SIS
officer who was under consular cover and affected a bow-tie,
at first refused to believe that Khokhlov was anything more
than an embittered émigré suffering from delusions, and
became increasingly hostile to the Russian. However, as the
defector described his background and demonstrated the
depth of his knowledge about his target, the CIA officers

were gradually convinced of his authenticity and transferred him to Camp King, the CIA's refugee screening centre located in the old Luftwaffe barracks seven kilometres north of the city. Michael Burke, one of the CIA officers who was present at the time, recalled that the KGB officer 'had arrived in Germany . . . brilliantly briefed':

Khokhlov was a slight, blond, scholarly appearing young man of thirty-two. He wore rimless glasses and spoke gravely. He expressed himself well, answered questions adroitly, and pleaded that his wife Yania . . . be brought out of Moscow as quickly as possible. It was Yania, he said, who had convinced him to defect rather than to become an assassin. He claimed that he would have sealed his own death warrant had he refused the assignment. Now he begged the Americans to save Yania and the child.[4]

During a further interrogation conducted by specialists who flew in from Washington DC, Khokhlov established his credentials by his identification of WOLF, the KGB's mole in the NTS organisation who had supplied much of the data he held on Okolovich, such as a detailed schedule of his movements, the registration number of his Mercedes, and a floor plan of his apartment and of his office in Bad Homburg. This information was so accurate that it was obvious the NTS had suffered penetration at a high level. The candidate denounced by Khokhlov, Nikita Khorunsky, had been an instructor at the NTS training facility at Bad Homburg and was, therefore, well placed to compromise NTS agents and plans. Having accepted Khokhlov as genuine, it was decided by Tracy Barnes of the CIA that the defector should attempt to persuade his two Moscow-trained co-conspirators, Kurt Weber and Hans Kurkovich, to defect as well. According to Khokhlov, both were committed Communists, but they were disillusioned with recent events following the death of Stalin in March 1953 and the arrest of Lavrenti Beria. He said that the chief of their department, Lieutenant-General Pavel A. Sudoplatov, had been 'sacrificed to the machine' and the Soviet intelligence apparatus was undergoing a debilitating purge which was sapping the morale of the illegals, the elite that expected better treatment.

The majority of both legal and illegal residencies were recalled to Moscow for consultation. Temporarily, at least, there could be no question of the creation of new illegal residencies. The whole country was holding its breath and waiting. The strategy pursued by the post-Stalin government was to remove from itself the stigma of the dead dictator. The 'collective leadership' adopted ingratiating tactics towards people . . . A series of official statements 'exposed' the crimes of the former MGB–MVD [KGB] leadership, and declared that such evils would not recur. A purge of the 'organs of State Security' was instigated, and hundreds of dismissed employees began to wander through other institutions seeking work. No matter by what methods Stalin's heirs were trying to earn popularity for themselves, all were equally haunted by the fearful ghost of a people's revolution. They were astute enough to realize that this ghost could not be laid by promises of butter and consumer goods, nor by dressing the MVD wolf in sheep's clothing. At this same time Soviet intelligence was being reorganised. In the new structure more emphasis was placed on the struggle against anti-Soviet organisations, both within the USSR and abroad.[5]

Whereas, Khokhlov explained, some months earlier it had been intended that 'Sudoplatov's service should create an illegal centre for co-ordinating the work of all combat groups in Western Europe. Organised in a neutral country, this centre should be isolated from all other intelligence networks,'[6] the new management had abandoned the project. Once likely to have gained considerable status within the KGB, Khokhlov and his fellow illegals, who regarded themselves as rather more than mere thugs, had been sidelined in the hierarchy.

A veteran of the Spanish Civil War, Weber was a lifelong Communist who had joined the French resistance and found a talent for forgery and the procurement of weapons. He had even run an underground printing press for the Maquis. In contrast, Kurkovich was an adventurer who had specialised in the elimination of Nazi collaborators. He too had fought with the French and once had been rescued from the Gestapo by Weber, who had made some bogus papers requiring his release from a prison hospital. At the end of the war both had trekked home, where Kurkovich settled down with a young widow in Potsdam and Weber found a job as a clerk in a police station in Kopenik. According to Khokhlov, they were skilled and dangerous illegals, but they were also a little disenchanted. Escorted by the CIA to the prearranged rendezvous in Augsburg, where they were to collect some special weapons for the murder from a cache hidden by an Austrian businessman, Khokhlov met Weber and Kurkovich and offered them political asylum in the West. Both men agreed, and all three were accommodated in the CIA's compound at Oberursel, where they were interviewed by American, British and French intelligence personnel. Together they gave damning accounts of the training they had undergone at Kuchino prior to their deployment for what they termed 'wet affairs' in the West. When their stories were later made public, the CIA released photographs of the ingeniously lethal weaponry with which they had been equipped by the KGB, including a silenced pistol and a miniature gun capable of firing three potassium-cyanide-tipped dum-dum bullets from inside a container disguised as an ordinary cigarette case.

Despite the defections, for the following fortnight the KGB continued to believe that the three illegals were still at liberty in the West and, under the CIA's supervision, an operation was mounted in Vienna to entrap Khokhlov's handler, Lieutenant-Colonel Oleg Okun. This scheme had been made possible because Nikita Khorunsky, the KGB's mole in the NTS, had defected to the French in January, so the KGB had not been surprised at his disappearance. A former prisoner of war held by the British, Khorunsky had infiltrated the NTS and had used his wife and brother-in-law to act as couriers and smuggle messages hidden in chocolate bars to the KGB in the Russian zone. The fact that Khorunsky's original confession had been less than complete, and had omitted much of the detail subsequently supplied by Khokhlov, ensured him a prison sentence in the Federal Republic before he was exchanged in a spy-swap with the East. However, for the time being the KGB evidently had failed to notice that Khokhlov and his two companions had suddenly dropped from view, and this had provided the CIA with the opportunity to make a pitch for Okun. The proposal was to corner Okun, break the news to him that his entire network had come under the

CIA's control, and offer him and his family resettlement as an alternative to enduring the KGB's wrath at what it would regard as his criminal incompetence. As well as losing Khorunsky, Khokhlov, Weber and Kurkovich, he would also be told that his only other source inside the NTS, a Russian émigré named Shmelyov, had been compromised. The *coup de grâce* was to be delivered by the Austrian who had smuggled Khokhlov's exotic weapons into Germany concealed inside a car battery. Khokhlov had identified him to the CIA and assured his new handlers that the wealthy former Communist was ripe for recruitment as a double agent. However, when the businessman was approached in April, soon after his return from a visit to Switzerland, he declined to co-operate and warned Okun, who was promptly recalled to Moscow. Khokhlov was almost suicidal at the failure of the operation as he believed that the KGB would now be bound to realise that he had defected, but in fact Okun had attributed his betrayal to the coincidental defection in Vienna of his close colleague Piotr Deriabin. Having abandoned any chance of ever seeing his wife and child again, Khokhlov was persuaded to make a public statement at a press conference in Bonn on 22 April about his mission to kill the NTS leadership, in the vain hope that his notoriety might help save his family in Moscow. In June, when he learned that his wife and child had been arrested, Khokhlov abandoned his plan of resettlement in America sponsored by the CIA and took up residence under a new identity in Switzerland.

To the CIA's dismay, the subsequent investigation prompted by the various leads provided by Khokhlov had revealed his Austrian passport to be authentic, and to have been issued to 'Josef Hofbauer' at the request of the Soviet occupation authorities, a development that suggested other Soviet illegals might also be equipped with genuine documentation from the same source, thereby making the task of Western security agencies all the more difficult. The CIA was equally appalled to learn from Khokhlov that his mission, codenamed Operation RHINE, had been personally authorised by the new head of the KGB's FCD, Aleksandr S. Panyushkin, who had been appointed in June 1953. The defector recounted how he had been introduced to Panyushkin, 'a tall, lean man in a grey suit'. His face

was deeply lined beyond his age. Pale to the point of greyness, his expression spoke of extremely poor health. It was a complexion such as miners or workers in lead plants have. The impression of ill-health was also created by his stooped manner of walking, as though he had no strength to carry himself straight. When he spoke, his voice sounded soft and hoarse.[7]

Incredibly, Panyushkin, who had previously been the Soviet Ambassador in Washington DC between 1947 and 1952, and had also served as a diplomat in China, allegedly had personally supervised the development at the KGB's Kuchino workshops of the project to perfect Khokhlov's assassination tools. Another of Khokhlov's unlikely assertions, that Panyushkin had been the legal *rezident* in America in 1949 and 1950 while simultaneously fulfilling his ambassadorial duties, was also to be confirmed soon afterwards by no fewer than four other defectors who were to cross the lines in the coming weeks: the Petrovs in Australia, Deriabin in Vienna and Yuri A. Rastvorov in Tokyo. This evidence amounted to undeniable proof, if any was still needed, that assassination and the deployment of illegals were effectively official Soviet policies, endorsed at the very highest level in the Kremlin. Nor, as subsequent events demonstrated, was this some temporary aberration.

The defection of Bogdan Stashinsky seven years later was prompted not by his revulsion at the murder of the Ukrainian politician, Stefan Bandera, whom he killed with an ingenious cyanide gas-gun in October 1959, but by his love for Inge Pohl, a young German hairdresser, who had married him and, later, had persuaded him to surrender to the Federal authorities. Originally a KGB informer around Lvov where he had been brought up, Stashinsky had operated as a low-level penetration agent targeted against local nationalists and, in particular, the OUN resistance movement. His cover had survived until early in 1952, when the murderers of the Ukrainian writer, Yaroslav Galan, were arrested on his tip. Regarded as a traitor by the nationalists, Galan had been assassinated by members of the OUN cell Stashinsky had cultivated, which effectively terminated his future in Lvov.

As a consequence of the Galan murder Stashinsky had been sent to Kiev to learn German and, subsequently, had gone to Karlshorst for training as an illegal. There he adopted the authentic identity of Josef Lehrmann, a German born in Lukowek, Poland, and until January 1956, when he was entrusted with minor tasks in the West, such as mailing letters, he built up his legend as a metalworker in Zwickau. On his first assignment he travelled to Munich to service a KGB penetration agent, an émigré journalist on the Ukrainian anti-Communist paper, *Ukrainski Samostinik*. He was to hold four further meetings with the agent, supplying him with money and messages from his wife who was still in the Ukraine, until the strain became too much for the agent and he was repatriated in the late autumn of 1956. Stashinsky replaced this source by recruiting another on the same newspaper, using a combination of bribery and blackmail, for the agent both received cash for his information and was left in no doubt that his wife and family in the Ukraine were vulnerable to reprisals.

In the spring of 1957, Stashinsky was given a new identity, that of Siegfried Drager, from Rehbrucke near Potsdam, and, armed with his authentic identity card, was sent to Munich to watch Lev Rebet, the exiled Ukrainian nationalist leader. Stashinsky kept his quarry under almost continuous surveillance from April until 12 October, when, armed with a specially designed weapon, he encountered Rebet outside his apartment and sprayed prussic acid into his face. By the time Stashinsky had returned to Karlshorst, his victim's body had been found and the cause of death declared to be a heart attack.

While preparing for his second assassination, that of the OUN leader Stefan Bandera, and under the influence of his German fiancée, Stashinsky had begun to lose his commitment to the cause; nevertheless, he fired a second, double-barrelled gas-gun directly into Bandera's face outside his home in Munich on 15 October 1959. Like Rebet, Bandera inhaled a lethal dose of prussic acid and died. Once again

Stashinsky returned by train and air to Karlshorst and reported the success of the operation to his KGB handler. The following month he was summoned to Moscow, where he was decorated with the Order of the Red Banner by Aleksandr N. Shelepin, the Chairman of the KGB. He was also granted permission to marry Inge Pohl, which he did in Berlin in April 1960. Their baby son was born a year later, but died in August, prompting Inge and Bogdan to evade their KGB escort and, on the day before the Wall was erected, to flee to West Berlin, where they surrendered to the German authorities.

At his subsequent trial at Karlsruhe in October 1962, Stashinsky confessed to the murders of Rebet and Bandera, and received a sentence of eight years' imprisonment, but he was to be released after less than four and resettled in the United States.[8]

Khokhlov and Stashinsky were both KGB illegals and, accordingly, they were unable to shed much light on the GRU's activities, which, in the mid-1950s, were known to be considerable. The German Federal authorities were dealing with literally thousands of espionage cases, and in May 1960 the Interior Ministry reported officially that over the previous eight years 18,300 suspected Soviet agents had been arrested. As illegals were acknowledged to be virtually impossible to detect after their deployment in the West, the CIA and FBI routinely had sought advance notice from defectors and other sources of information regarding illegal operations. One exceptionally useful windfall occurred in 1955, when Major Piotr S. Popov, a current CIA source in the GRU, was transferred to the GRU's illegal support section in Schwerin, Berlin. While Khokhlov had given a very comprehensive account of the KGB's extensive facilities for illegals at its high-security compound in the Karlshorst district of Berlin, relatively little was known about the GRU's activities.

Popov, who had been recruited as a walk-in volunteer in Vienna in 1953, had already alleged that some 370 GRU illegals were operating in the West and had supplied many of their official cryptonyms, which he had succeeded in extracting from the files undetected. He was able to do this because he was on especially good terms with the GRU illegals support officer in Vienna, Colonel Alexei Kriatov, who had relied upon a well-placed civil servant recruited from within the Austrian bureaucracy by Popov to supply genuine Austrian identity documents. Of those 370 illegals, according to MI5's Peter Wright, who made a study of Soviet illegals, about forty were positively identified in Germany and Austria, and thereby neutralised.

Popov revealed that the GRU had transferred several important departments from Moscow to Schwerin, and that the GRU's deputy chief, General Feodor Fedorov, had been given the assignment of expanding the GRU's base in Karlshorst. In addition to the GRU's efforts, it was clear that the KGB also intended to develop its illegal operations, for Popov reported that in the aftermath of Khokhlov's defection, General Aleksandr M. Korotkov had been appointed chief of liaison in Berlin. In October 1957, Popov had achieved enough access to accomplish what hitherto had been considered an impossible dream by the CIA: he was also able to compromise an illegal operation *before it had even started*. Popov told his Russian-speaking CIA case officer, George Kisevalter, about an illegal named Igor A. Tairov, who had already completed a mission in England and had been infiltrated into the United States. He was now to be joined there by his wife, Margarita N. Tairova, an experienced GRU officer, who had adopted the identity of an American of Polish extraction and had already acclimatised herself to the role in Vienna. As Popov had been designated her conducting officer while she passed through Berlin, he had been able to supply Kisevalter with all Tairova's details, including the two names she intended to use to travel to New York; these were duly passed to the FBI, which kept her under surveillance from the moment her flight arrived at Idlewild. 'Mary Grodnik' was trailed to a hotel in Manhattan, where her luggage was searched surreptitiously; her room was bugged and she was watched when, soon afterwards, she made contact with her husband in a Yonkers cinema. According to Popov, the intention had been that they would pretend to meet for the first time and then undergo a marriage ceremony in New York to cement their documentation.

Margarita's meeting with her husband had led the FBI to investigate 'Walter A. Soja', ostensibly a book-keeper at a wholesaler of women's accessories who lived alone in a dingy apartment in Manhattan's upper west side. He too had been placed under surveillance, but the pair continued to act normally until mid-March 1958, when, with no warning, they both vanished. Subsequently the FBI denied that either had shown any sign of having spotted the surveillance, but when Popov reported their return to the CIA in Berlin, he disclosed that Margarita had claimed that she had been kept under observation from the moment she had arrived at Tempelhof to catch her flight to New York the previous December. The KGB had taken her complaint seriously and had initiated an intensive post-mortem, but although Popov had been obliged to undergo an uncomfortable interrogation, he appeared to have avoided suspicion. Nevertheless, the inter-agency recriminations between the CIA and FBI over the handling of the Tairovs were to last for years. Although on this occasion Popov had experienced a narrow escape, he was eventually to be arrested by the KGB in a Moscow bus in October 1959, in the act of passing a message to his CIA contact, and executed.[9]

Piotr Popov was not the only GRU officer to feed the CIA information about illegals. Not long after GR/ALLSPICE had dried up, another GRU source unexpectedly came on stream. Colonel Oleg V. Penkovsky made several, initially fruitless approaches to Western intelligence agencies before he started co-operating with SIS and the CIA on a joint basis in April 1961, when he volunteered a quantity of cryptonyms which he said had been allocated to GRU personnel in the West, including some illegals. While the CIA accepted the data at face value, and it was processed and distributed under the codename classification RUPEE, not a single operational GRU illegal was to be identified in the exercise, which had the effect merely of whetting the CIA's appetite for yet more details. One of the more tantalising items betrayed by Penkovsky was the text of a lecture given by Lieutenant-Colonel

I. E. Prikhodko, a GRU officer who had been attached to the United Nations in New York between 1952 and 1955. Entitled *Characteristics of Agent Communications and of Agent Handling in the United States of America*,[10] Prikhodko had produced a tradecraft manual which documented methods of running illegal networks and of arranging their communications. Also described were counter-surveillance techniques and numerous tips about the preparation and use of cut-outs and dead-drops. If all Prikhodko's tips were followed, the illegal theoretically could successfully avoid detection by the FBI. While much of his advice was somewhat naïve and rather basic, such as a warning to avoid holding illicit meetings near the FBI building at 201 East 69th Street and the FBI's permanent observation posts around the UN building, some of it was quite sophisticated, and this passage in relation to illegals underlined the GRU's continuing interest in the development of illegal rings in the United States:

The operating conditions of a *rezidentsia* will, of course, change in time of war. As is known, the *rezidentsia* under cover will cease to exist the moment the official Soviet installations shut down. Therefore, one of the most important tasks of the *rezidentsia* under cover is to train during peace-time agents and agent nets to conduct independent communications with the Centre so that they can operate in time of war. This training is rather complex and includes the following basic features: training the agent to operate radio sets; supplying him with a radio set; setting up a reserve radio set in case the agent's radio goes out of commission and preparing for this eventuality by securing an independent power supply; providing for secure long-term storage of all radio equipment; acquisition of safe apartments for operational radio communications; conducting trial-runs of radio communications in peace-time for the purpose of keeping radio operators in reserve and of systematically checking the combat readiness of the equipment.[11]

Not surprisingly, by the mid-1960s, the CIA Counterintelligence Staff's obsession with illegal penetration came to match its paranoia about the infiltration of its own ranks by skilful moles. Khokhlov had demonstrated the KGB's continued long-term commitment to illegal methodology, and both Popov and Penkovsky had indicated the scale of GRU illegal operations in the West. One vital question to be answered was, what were they all doing? Had traitors been cultivated within the CIA, and were they serviced by unsuspected illegals? It was a proposition that was to gain considerable currency, as did the fear of direct penetration of Western agencies by illegals. This new dimension, of illegals despatched to infiltrate specific targets, was of particular concern to the British and American intelligence services, which, to a large extent, relied upon émigrés and foreign nationals for low-echelon activities, but also for the footsoldiers who were trained to return home and foment resistance. The ease with which the CIA's very large presence in West Germany could be undermined became clear in August 1960, when Vladimir Sloboda disappeared from his unit and surfaced in an embarrassing blaze of publicity in East Berlin.

Of indeterminate Ukrainian origin, Sloboda had been one of thousands of Polish refugees to undergo a routine security screening at various displaced persons' camps in 1953. He was given work with the US army in Brement and, well qualified by his fluency in Russian, was quickly assigned to an intelligence detachment training paramilitaries for the CIA. Sloboda was transferred to Fort Bragg, North Carolina, for a US Special Forces sabotage course and remained there until 1958, when he acquired American citizenship. Upon his return to Germany with his wife and three children, he was posted to the 513th Reconnaissance Group, based at Oberursel, near Munich, where, with the rank of senior NCO, he participated in the CIA's recruitment and training programme for émigrés destined to be dropped back into Soviet territory as guerrillas. These operations experienced a tragically high failure rate, not least because many of the identities of individual volunteers had been betrayed long in advance of their missions starting. When interviews with Sloboda were published in *Izvestia* and *Pravda*, in which he detailed the CIA's clandestine operations and identified his former commander as Colonel Franz H. Ross, it was clear that he had made a considerable contribution to the disaster.

With growing evidence, not only from Penkovsky, that dozens if not hundreds of illegals like Sloboda were at liberty in the West, a concentrated effort was made by the British, American and Canadian authorities to track them down. The challenge, of course, was immense and daunting. However great the records of a security agency, how can it even begin to trace an individual who has adopted the identity of a person entitled to full citizenship? Several schemes involving documentation checks were initiated, such as the random examination of applications for birth certificates and drivers' licences, and the study of immigration records, but these trawls proved highly demanding in manpower, with no obvious benefit. As the Soviets had taken the precaution of insulating the GRU and KGB illegal organisations from each other, and from the local diplomatic missions, surveillance on suspect intelligence personnel operating from embassies and consulates held virtually no prospect of exposing illegals. Nevertheless, communications remained a potential weakness, for almost every one of the illegals caught in the West had been equipped with shortwave receivers. It had also been noted that in his lecture Colonel Prikhodko had laid a special emphasis on the importance of independent radio channels, and his dissertation had obviously reflected the official view. Abel, for example, had possessed a Hallicrafter radio and it was evident from the cipher paraphernalia seized from his apartment, which included a cipher grid and a radio schedule, that he had relied upon one-way Morse signals broadcast from Moscow at specific times for messages. The advantage of this arrangement, which had required Abel to send messages home on microfilm collected by couriers from dead-letter drops, meant that unless the drop itself had been compromised, there was no likelihood of entrapping the illegal through the interception of his signals. Clearly the Soviets had learned from the bitter experience of the wartime *Rote Kapelle* in Belgium and the *Rote Drei* in Switzerland, both of which had been caught following the deployment of direction-finding equipment, and had taken the precaution of modifying their standard tradecraft. Doubtless the Soviets believed that by eliminating the return radio traffic, their illegals would remain immune from hostile interception.

The confidence the Soviets placed in the integrity of their

communications was misplaced, for a technical breakthrough in the mid-1950s had led to the development in 1958 of an apparatus of unprecedented sensitivity which could register the minute radiation, known as the IF value, emanating from wireless receivers. The discovery had been made in London, where MI5's technicians, led by Tony Sale, had attempted to prove that the KGB *rezidentura* in the Soviet Embassy in Kensington Palace Gardens had been monitoring the signals of MI5's Watcher Service. A radio engineer formerly with Marconi, who had been recruited into MI5's scientific section by his old colleague and mentor, Peter Wright, Sale was the genius who had first realised the potential of the IF receivers.

For reasons that then could not be easily explained, it had seemed certain that targets selected for surveillance by the renowned watchers had experienced very little difficulty in detecting their presence. Accordingly, an elaborate experiment had been conducted to determine whether the radio equipment known to be installed in the Embassy had been tuned to channels reserved for MI5's mobile communications. A special receiver was adapted to detect and amplify the radiation originating from the oscillators integral in all wireless sets, and the prototype had been placed in a nondescript van parked close to the Embassy building. The exercise had accomplished what it had set out to achieve, for during the trial a watcher vehicle close by had accidentally transmitted a signal to its base. The strength had been sufficiently powerful for MI5's detection equipment in the van to produce an audible reaction, positive proof to MI5's operators, Peter Wright and Tony Sale, that the Embassy was operating a receiver tuned to the same frequency. It therefore seemed likely that if similar equipment was to be located near to the site of all known Soviet shortwave equipment, much would be revealed about Soviet listening habits.

A refined version of this apparatus was developed by GCHQ and codenamed RAFTER in the expectation that continuous monitoring would not only reveal the times that the Soviets were listening to shortwave broadcasts, but even isolate the exact frequencies. On the basis that the specialist KGB and GRU illegal support officers would be bound to check Moscow's signals, there was an attractive prospect of reconstructing an illegal's radio schedule. MI5's belief that support officers listened to Moscow's signals stemmed from a comment attributed to the bully Vladimir Bourdine by his agent GIDEON and passed on to London by the RCMP. When GIDEON had used poor atmospheric conditions as an excuse for his laziness, Bourdine had reprimanded him and had been able to quote the exact transmissions that GIDEON had skipped. Either Bourdine had been sent this data from Moscow, which seemed implausible, or he had drawn up the list himself, having compared the broadcasts he had heard with GIDEON's acknowledgments. Whichever the explanation, there was a strong chance that support officers around the globe conformed to the same procedure and routinely double-checked that their agents could hear the signals intended for them. There was also another possible advantage to RAFTER: by correlating the movements of Embassy staff with the times when broadcasts had been received, there was also some potential for learning the identities of the professional intelligence personnel mingling among the diplomats.

Soon after its inception in London, RAFTER provided scientific proof that certain Embassy personnel, all suspected intelligence officers, were regularly switching on their shortwave receivers at particular times and monitoring Morse from Moscow. Whilst this certainly appeared to be circumstantial evidence of the existence of undetected illegals in England, it failed to take MI5 any closer to actually finding one of them. However, APPLE CIDER in Canada promised to offer an ideal opportunity to test RAFTER with an identified illegal.[12]

APPLE CIDER had begun in 1959 with a tip from the Swiss Bundespolizei, which had intercepted a letter postmarked in Vancouver addressed to an espionage suspect in Lausanne. The recipient had been under investigation as a possible 'post box' employed by an identified GRU officer, and the correspondence, secretly opened and photographed by the Swiss, indicated that 'John Weitz' had successfully opened a business in Vancouver. The Bundespolizei had sent a copy to the CIA, which, having failed to find any person named Weitz in Vancouver, had handed it over to the RCMP as possible evidence of an illegal. Using the handwriting in the letter as a sample, the RCMP undertook a lengthy search of the records of the 100,000 or so immigrants who had entered Canada in the past year to find their quarry, the illegal they codenamed FUZZY. When that expedient failed, the RCMP turned to the records of those that had similar backgrounds to Abel's: a single, middle-aged male with a solitary occupation and a European family background, equipped with some German documentation that had been difficult to verify, and perhaps some evidence of the individual having been staged through a third country. Working with this profile the RCMP had isolated several candidates, and upon further investigation had eliminated all except Rudolph Kneschke. In many respects Kneschke manifested a similar profile to Abel, for he was single, middle-aged and claimed to be of German origin. His story was that his family had left Russia soon after the revolution and moved to Harbin in China, where he had lived until 1953, when he had settled in Sao Paulo. After five years in Brazil, working as a clerk in a clothes shop, Kneschke had applied for an immigrant visa and had supplied the necessary two referees. Upon his arrival in Vancouver he had not opened a business, as had been suggested by the Swiss letter, but had enrolled in a training course to study television repairs. When the RCMP attempted to verify the overseas part of Kneschke's story, SIS had confirmed that debriefed refugees from Harbin had recalled the Kneschke family, but the CIA had reported that his two visa referees in Brazil were regarded as suspect, being listed in their indices as having had contact with the local Soviet Embassy. Accordingly, Kneschke was placed under surveillance, and it was established that the loner had virtually no friends but owned a shortwave radio and had festooned the bedroom in his lodgings with an antenna.

When Kneschke completed his study of television, he rented premises for a small television repair shop selling second-hand radios and electrical goods, and one of his first customers was an RCMP investigator who obtained a sample of his handwriting, which was found to match that of the Swiss letter. Furthermore, although Kneschke was supposedly a poverty-stricken immigrant, with a business that could scarcely support him, his bank account was found to contain $50,000, a sum which was subsequently transferred to the wife of another recent migrant. The RCMP became increasingly convinced that Kneschke was the elusive FUZZY, an authentic illegal, and deployed RAFTER to prove that he was listening in to weekly coded broadcasts from Moscow. Combined with a bug planted in his bedroom, RAFTER twice provided the proof that Kneschke had set his alarm for the middle of the night and had tuned in to Morse signals transmitted from the Soviet Union. Indeed, on a third occasion the assiduous Kneschke was heard to mutter curses when he overslept and missed a broadcast. As the RCMP stepped up its surveillance, Kneschke unexpectedly put his stock into storage, bought an airline ticket to Holland and closed his shop. Because the RCMP had only limited facilities abroad, the CIA agreed to keep him under observation in Europe, but, having successfully picked him up in Amsterdam, lost him in Rome. Soon afterwards the storage company in Vancouver received a letter postmarked in Switzerland from Kneschke instructing them to ship his goods to a forwarding agency in Helsinki. After that, there was no further news of Kneschke, who had simply disappeared.[13]

The RCMP's investigators were disappointed at the loss of FUZZY and uncertain as to the cause of Operation APPLE CIDER's premature termination. Had Kneschke spotted the RCMP's intensive surveillance, or had the operation been betrayed from within? The conundrum would remain unsolved.

Further information about KGB illegals reached the West from Evgenny E. Runge, who defected in Berlin in October 1967. His background was that of a Ukrainian born of German parents, who had undergone three years of preparatory training in Moscow before working first in East Germany and then in Munich. His cover was that of the proprietor of a dry-cleaning business, which he ran with his East German 'wife'. When this enterprise failed, Runge moved to Frankfurt, where he operated rather more successfully as a salesman peddling automatic vending machines. Runge's illegal network included Heinz Sutterlin, who had cultivated and then married Leonore Heinz, a secretary in the Federal Republic's Foreign Ministry. Under her husband's influence Leonore had provided the KGB with a wealth of classified data from her office, but some suspicion must have arisen in Moscow for Runge was recalled unexpectedly for an extended interrogation. At its conclusion he was told to return to his duties in Frankfurt, but without his wife. Runge had appealed against the decision to leave his wife behind to the KGB's Chairman, Yuri Andropov, who had sympathised and had rescinded the order. The Runges travelled back to the Federal Republic, but, fearful of what they perceived as their bleak future as distrusted illegals, surrendered to the CIA at the first opportunity. In return for betraying the Sutterlins and some other minor figures, including a source in the French Embassy in Bonn, Runge was given the full defector treatment and resettled. Heinz Sutterlin was arrested by the Federal authorities, but his wife, filled with remorse, committed suicide.

It was not until the defection of Rupert Sigl in Berlin in April 1969 that the CIA obtained the full co-operation of a Soviet illegal and learned, first hand, of a complete case history. An Austrian from Ybbs, near St Poelten in what had been the Soviet-occupied sector, Sigl was a carpenter who had served as a Wehrmacht officer during the war and had been wounded in the arm. His initial recruitment by the KGB had been as an informer in 1950, but his enrolment as a KGB officer had taken place in 1952 following a period of training in Moscow. Far from attending any school for illegals, he had been taught his tradecraft at a dacha at Malachovka, a small village twenty kilometres from the capital. Of particular interest to Sigl's CIA debriefers was the identity of his principal case officer, Yuri V. Novikov, who had been expelled from Washington DC in January 1953, following a lengthy double-agent operation run by the FBI over the previous two years, and was therefore well known to Western security agencies. Holding second secretary rank at the Soviet Embassy, Novikov had been declared *persona non grata*, along with his wife Helen, when one of his American sources, ostensibly a military intelligence clerk, had turned out to be an FBI informant. Novikov had been flown back to Moscow with a KGB escort, but evidently this episode had not ruined his career. Sigl reported that Novikov had spent almost eight years in East Germany, returning to Moscow in 1964. He also asserted that he had been one of the KGB officers selected to investigate the defection of Bogdan Stashinsky, and that he, Sigl, had helped interrogate Stashinsky's parents-in-law.

Sigl claimed that he had never been ideologically suited to his KGB work but had collaborated as a means of getting himself to the West. He had undertaken various assignments in the Federal Republic and could name several of his recruits. His initial approaches to Western intelligence agencies, through intermediaries, had been incorrectly interpreted as provocations and had been rebuffed, but eventually he managed to make contact with the CIA late in 1968 and operated for a period as an agent so as to establish his bona fides.

Sigl's story was not dissimilar to that of Khokhlov and Abel. He had received specialist training in the Soviet intelligence compound at Karlshorst in Berlin shortly before his first mission, under an elaborate false identity, to Leipzig. There Sigl had found work as a carpenter, but from November 1953 onwards he had ventured into the West, running minor errands for the KGB. These had ranged from contacting German ex-prisoners who had been talent-spotted by the KGB during their captivity in Soviet prison camps, to reconnaissance trips made to targets in the American zone, and mailing letters and money to addresses in the West. He had participated in the recruitment of other agents and later named a well-known East German television journalist, Fritz Moellendorf, as an important KGB asset. Late in 1954 Novikov had been appointed his handler and, thereafter, Sigl had been entrusted with more significant assignments, but he had retained detailed notes of all the operations he had participated in so as to develop a worthwhile meal-ticket for his future defection. Of particular interest to the CIA was his denunciation of Dr Alfred Lomnitz, a German-born chemist who had been imprisoned at the concentration camps of Sachsenhausen and Dachau before the war, and had later become a naturalised American citizen and changed his surname to Laurence.

Laurence's story was an extraordinary one.[14] Having studied law at Breslau, he had graduated as a chemical engineer from Tours in France in 1936 and had worked subsequently in Hamburg in a petroleum laboratory. Although not formally a member of the KDP, he had been arrested by the Gestapo as a Communist sympathiser and imprisoned. His release from Dachau in October 1937 had been negotiated by an English friend, an author with whom he had stayed while perfecting the language in 1934. Armed with a visa for India he had moved to Bombay to work for Burma Shell, until he was interned as an enemy alien. In 1941, he had travelled by ship to Philadelphia and in 1943 had joined the US Army's Quartermaster Corps. After landing in France in June 1944, he was commissioned and transferred to intelligence duties. As a war crimes investigator he had participated in the trials at Dachau, and upon his discharge in 1946 had returned to the USA, where he had worked for Shell in San Francisco. In 1952, he had come back to London to work for Rudy Sternberg's (later Lord Plurenden) Sterling Group. This had lasted only two years, and Laurence moved back to the States to join the Minnesota Mining Company in St Paul, a post he kept until 1962 when he took up consultancy work which gave him some contact with the CIA.

Sigl described how he had 'recruited' Laurence as a spy in East Berlin in September 1963, when the 'industrial expert' was living in England, shortly before he had been due to take up an appointment with the United Nations. Once he had made what he described as a successful pitch, Sigl had handed the 'agent' over to Novikov's successor, Eugene, who allegedly had expressed his satisfaction with Laurence. As soon as this news reached the Security Service in London, early in April 1969, Dr Laurence was investigated. He was then living in Higher Drive, Purley, but was on holiday in Majorca when his home was searched. His second address, a weekend cottage at St Lawrence in the Isle of Wight, was also raided and upon his return to England Laurence was interrogated by Special Branch detectives. Although he admitted having met Sigl and a KGB officer named Kruglov in East Berlin in September 1963, and at three clandestine meetings around London, Laurence denied ever having passed secrets to them and, in the absence of any incriminating confession, the British authorities released him.

Laurence later became a visiting professor of sociology at the University of Utah at Salt Lake City and now lives in retirement in the Isle of Wight. He insists that he was never a spy, but is good-humoured about his experience as an espionage suspect. 'I was the spy who never was,' he says. 'That's what the newspapers called me.'

8 · LAST ACT and SHAH

Every Illegal rezident must train a radio operator and then properly legalise him, must get the latest radio equipment (from the Centre) and check its operation. This must be done now, in peace-time.

Lieutenant-Colonel I. E. Prikhodko[1]

The excitement that had swept through the British Security Service's counter-espionage branch on that Saturday morning, 9 July 1960, was quite unlike anything its Director, Martin Furnival Jones, or his small staff had previously experienced. This was not entirely surprising, for to date their research had been largely academic, limited to reading and rereading David Dallin's standard text on the subject, *Soviet Espionage*,[2] listening to lectures from ex-officers with pre-war experience, and patiently trying to deduce items of significance from the monitored comings and goings at the Soviet Embassy in Kensington Palace Gardens, the nearby Consulate, and the homes of suspected KGB and GRU intelligence personnel. Now, for the first time, a man positively identified as a spy had been spotted meeting his contact, an individual who had not returned in his unostentatious Standard Companion car, as expected, to the safety of Soviet diplomatic premises, but to a small hotel off the Bayswater Road.

To put the moment into its proper context, one should

consider the relative dearth of cases handled by MI5 since the end of the Second World War. Much work had been devoted to the clues provided by defectors, and the successful conviction of Allan Nunn May in May 1946 had been the direct consequence of references to him in documents supplied to the RCMP by Igor Gouzenko. The arrest of Klaus Fuchs had followed in February 1950, not from a tip-off from a defector, but from the detailed analysis of the highly secret VENONA cryptographic material extracted from Soviet diplomatic wireless intercepts.[3] Under interrogation Fuchs had implicated Ursula Kuczynski as a Soviet illegal, but the evidence had come too late for MI5. She had already been interviewed as a suspected GRU agent and had fled to East Germany before her true role had been realised. There had only been one other case of any significance for D Branch, and that had been the entirely fortuitous identification of William Marshall, a Diplomatic Wireless Service radio operator, as a source run by Pavel S. Kuznetsov. Marshall had been imprisoned in 1952, and Kuznetsov had been recalled to Moscow.

Since then D Branch had concentrated its efforts on the most basic building-blocks of counter-intelligence, the construction of an order-of-battle for the GRU and KGB legal *rezidentzia*. Help from Australia, where Evdokia and Vladimir Petrov had annotated a copy of the current 'blue book' of accredited diplomatic staff, and had studied MI5's album of photographs snatched of Soviet personnel, had identified those whom they believed to be the current KGB *rezident* and his deputy. Sergei Tikhvinsky, who had supervised the Marshall business, had been recalled when the Petrovs had defected, and had been replaced temporarily by the urbane Press Attaché, Yuri Modin. His appointment had proved short-lived and, in 1956, Nikolai B. Korovin, who had previously spent five years in London after the war, had taken up the post of first secretary. However, despite intensive surveillance, neither Korovin nor the man supposed to be his deputy, Nikolai P. Karpekov, had appeared to be particularly active in the field. There were, of course, other explanations. Perhaps both men were sufficiently skilled to have detected the surveillance and had taken the appropriate counter-measures, or perhaps these people were mere decoys to draw MI5's attention away from the genuine articles. Later, another more unpalatable possibility was given serious consideration: that MI5's elite Watcher Service had itself sprung a leak.

One strong explanation for Korovin's studied inactivity was the existence of an illegal counterpart for him, and the discovery of an illegal contact that Saturday morning had lent weight to the theory. The trail that had led to him had started with the CIA, which had alerted MI5 earlier in the year to two KGB spies referred to as LAMBDA 1 and LAMBDA 2. The first was supposedly a source inside British Intelligence, and this individual was eventually identified as George Blake. The second, with access to the secrets of the Royal Navy, apparently had been recruited in the early 1950s in Warsaw. Without disclosing its source, who was actually a well-placed Polish intelligence officer intending to defect to America, the CIA had given MI5 enough data about the spy in March for its tiny investigative staff to identify him. Howard Roman was the CIA officer in Vienna who had received the anonymous tip, and this had been passed to the FBI in Washington DC and to Frank Wisner, the CIA chief of station in London. As Wisner was on leave, the news was conveyed from Washington by the head of the CIA's British desk, Cleveland Cram, to Wisner's deputy, John F. Caswell. He reported that the CIA knew, for example, the circumstances of the spy's recruitment when he had been stationed in the office of Captain Nigel Austen, the Naval Attaché at the British Embassy in Warsaw. They also had a rough idea of his name, something like 'Horton', and that he had become a valued conduit for classified information about submarines. All these clues had led to Harry Houghton, a civilian who had been disciplined in Warsaw for trading on the black market while on a secondment in a clerical capacity to the Embassy for a period of fifteen months between July 1951 and October 1952.

After Houghton had left the Royal Navy in 1945 with an honourable discharge and a small pension after twenty-four years' service, and having achieved the non-commissioned rank of Master-at-Arms, he was found a civilian post in the naval dockyards at Gosport. Before the war he had married a widow in his home town of Lincoln, but their childless marriage had ended in divorce in 1958 after twenty-three years. He lived in a small, four-roomed cottage at 8 Meadow View Road, Broadwey, just outside Weymouth, and, since his return from Warsaw, had worked as a clerk at what had then been the Underwater Detection Establishment at Port-land in Dorset. This site was of considerable sensitivity and, thereby, of strategic importance to the Soviets, because much of NATO's acoustic research and experimental work into anti-submarine systems was undertaken at the base. Trials of new equipment, including the highly secret strings of SOSUS sensors which were laid on the seabed to record Warsaw Pact submarines, the passive arrays towed behind surface vessels, and the 'dunking' sonar deployed by heli-copters, were all conducted in the sea off Portland. The Soviets would have been especially anxious to penetrate the base's security, and no doubt were disappointed when, in January 1957, Houghton was transferred to the Port Auxiliary Repair Unit at the same base, which had been renamed the Admiralty Underwater Weapons Establishment.

According to his confidential personnel file, Houghton had been denounced as a spy by his embittered wife Peggy at about the time of their divorce, but neither this, nor the later suggestion that his free-spending habits had drawn attention to his espionage, had been responsible for tipping off MI5. The vital information had come from the CIA, and at that stage even the Agency had little idea as to its own informant's true identity whom MI5 referred to gratefully as LAVINIA. He had been supplying them with high-grade material anony-mously, using the codename '*stutzstaffel*' ('sniper' in German) to conceal his true identity. He was finally to reveal himself late in December 1960 as a senior officer in the Polish intelli-gence bureau, UB, (and part-time KGB informant) named Michal Goleniewski, and to request political asylum for him-self and his German girlfriend.

Once the fifty-six-year-old Houghton had been confirmed as the most likely candidate for the spy, he had been placed under surveillance. MI5 watchers moved into Broadwey, close to Houghton's home, but no attempt was made to isolate him from classified papers at the Portland base as, theoretically, his job in the repair unit gave him no access to secrets. Nevertheless, when he travelled to London by train on Saturday, 9 July, he had been observed exchanging envelopes with a stocky, middle-aged man who had carried a shopping bag. While some of the watchers had stuck to Houghton and trailed him back to Dorset, another group had peeled off and kept their contact under observation as he made his way to his hotel in Bayswater.

Discreet enquiries at the hotel revealed Houghton's link to be a Canadian guest, a bachelor named Gordon A. Lonsdale, who had only recently moved in. This information seemed proof that Lonsdale was either an intermediary between Houghton and his Soviet controller, perhaps designed to operate as a cut-out so as to protect the Soviet from direct involvement, or that Lonsdale was himself the Soviet illegal *rezident*. Further surveillance and an overheard conversation produced a pattern of meetings between Houghton and Lonsdale, usually on the first Saturday of the month, as happened the following 6 August. At the first meeting, which had taken place in a small public park opposite the Old Vic theatre near Waterloo station and had lasted an hour, Houghton had been accompanied by Ethel Gee, a colleague from Portland with whom he spent the weekend at the Cumberland Hotel, Marble Arch. Both had driven up to London in Houghton's new car, an inexpensive Renault Dauphine, and later had attended a performance of the Bolshoi Ballet at the Royal Albert Hall with tickets supplied by Lonsdale. Whereas Houghton's job did not give him access to secrets, Gee's position in an adjoining building which housed the Drawing Office records section most certainly did. She had worked at the base since October 1950 and had moved from the stores department in 1955, two years before she had been accepted as an established civil servant. Although she spent much of her spare time with Houghton, Gee, who was known as Bunty, lived with her elderly mother, uncle and disabled aunt in a small terraced house at 23 Hambro Road, Portland. She too was placed under surveillance, as was Lonsdale, who drove away from the rendezvous in a Vauxhall Vanguard saloon. At the second meeting, on 6 August, two MI5 watchers kept Houghton and Lonsdale under observation as they met outside the Old Vic, and later sat so close to them in Steve's Restaurant, Lower Marsh, that they were able to eavesdrop on some of their conversation, which had centred on a newspaper report of the recent defection of two American NSA analysts.[4]

MI5's watchers learned that Lonsdale, who was referred to within the Security Service by his codename LAST ACT, ran an amusement machine and jukebox leasing business from a small office at 19 Wardour Street, so a permanent observation post was established in The Falcon, a public house directly opposite Lonsdale's building. On Friday 26 August, the watchers followed Lonsdale to his branch of the Midland Bank in Great Portland Street, where he had held an account since April 1957, and where he was seen to deposit a tin box and an attaché case. On the following Sunday he flew to the Continent, having told friends that he was visiting Canada. When the case was removed from the bank and examined by the Security Service over the next weekend, it was found to contain a roll of film for a miniature Minox camera, an apparently innocuous Ronson table lighter, and a zip bag for developing film with a Praktina camera inside fitted with a special lens and attachment for photographing documents. There was also a single sheet of paper, on which was typed a list of London street names, followed by some meaningless figures. Under X-ray examination the lighter could be seen to contain a small hollow, and when MI5's technicians unscrewed the mechanism they found a one-time pad and a tiny radio schedule which indicated a signal watch on the first and third Sunday of the month. If any further evidence was needed, this was positive proof that MI5 had at last found a genuine illegal. All the paraphernalia was replaced in the case and returned to the bank, but towards the end of the month the operation was repeated with the intention of copying the coding material. In the meantime, MI5's technicians had developed a method of taking the 250 pages of the one-time

pad apart, photographing them and then reassembling the
sheets so that it could not be spotted that they had been
disturbed. The plan worked perfectly and a complete replica
of Lonsdale's one-time pad was passed to cryptographers
at GCHQ, who thereafter intercepted and decrypted all of
Moscow's bi-monthly shortwave traffic destined for Lonsdale. When the Minox film was copied and printed, it was
discovered to be a series of holiday snaps of Lonsdale and a
good-looking woman, probably taken in Prague. From correspondence recovered much later, it was deduced that the
subject had been his wife.

On 24 October 1960, Lonsdale returned to the bank for
his briefcase and, having been alerted by an obliging bank
manager, MI5's watchers followed him to his office in Soho
and then, by tube from Piccadilly, to Ruislip Manor station,
west London, where he disappeared from view. However,
after a meeting with Houghton at The Maypole public house
in Ditton Road, Surbiton, on the evening of 5 November,
Lonsdale led MI5's watchers, in his new car, a distinctive
white American Studebaker Farina, to Willow Gardens, Ruislip, and once again dropped from sight. The following morning
he was spotted emerging from a nearby house, at 45 Cranley
Drive. This address was to lead to the identification of two
further KGB illegals, 'Helen and Peter Kroger', and to provide strong evidence that Lonsdale had not realised that the
contents of his case had been examined, as he later claimed
in his autobiography. If his version had been true, and he
really had discovered himself to have been under surveillance
at that early stage, he would hardly have compromised the
other members of his clandestine cell.

Lonsdale's destination that Saturday evening had been a
bungalow at the end of a cul-de-sac, a location which posed
special problems for the watchers. Fortunately, they had
been able to establish an observation post in a nearby house,
at the corner of Courtfield Gardens, with a view from the
rear of the front of the suspect property. Research into the
occupants showed them to be an apparently respectable
middle-aged couple, who for three years had run an antiquarian book business from premises in the Strand, almost

directly opposite the law courts. They had been in the country since December 1954, when they had rented a furnished house at 18 Penderry Rise in Catford, south-east London, and a second-hand bookshop nearby, at 190 The Drive. Their neighbours had been told that they had just arrived from Canada, but this was almost certainly untrue.

The surveillance on 24 October was to be of critical importance and reassured MI5 that its quarry had not given it the slip, a thought that certainly had occurred when Houghton had made no effort to meet Lonsdale on what MI5 supposed ought to have been the scheduled dates in September and October. As well as leading MI5 to the occupants of the bungalow in Cranley Drive, who now fell under suspicion for the first time, Lonsdale inadvertently revealed his address in London, a ninth-floor, one-bedroomed flat in the White House, an apartment block in Albany Street, just north of Regent's Park. This too became the subject of technical surveillance, from the neighbouring flat, number 634, where Arthur Spencer from GCHQ and his monitoring equipment were secretly installed, and from the one directly above Lonsdale's. According to the building's management, Lonsdale had been accepted as a tenant with written references from two officials of the Royal Overseas League, a club in Park Place, just off St James's Street, catering for foreign visitors to London. Apparently, this was where Lonsdale had stayed soon after he had first arrived in London, between March and April 1955, before moving in May 1955 to the White House, where he remained until June 1958. After moving elsewhere briefly, he later returned to the White House. His flat contained few furnishings, but there was a single possession of significance: a large Bush radiogram capable of tuning in to Moscow's shortwave broadcasts.

Elaborate arrangements were made to conceal the combined MI5 and GCHQ project launched next door to Lonsdale. A woman MI5 officer pretended to be a new tenant and went off to work every morning, apparently leaving her flat empty. In reality, Spencer remained there for two months, moving about silently and never going out of doors. In addition, a listening device was placed through the wall which was linked by a secure landline to equipment at MI5's head-quarters, where every gasp of Lonsdale's very active love life was recorded. Spencer monitored the RAFTER apparatus, which determined the exact frequency of Lonsdale's wireless signals, and wore an earpiece connected to Lonsdale's radio-gram, which alerted him every time the illegal listened in to Moscow.[5] Although the first attempt to decrypt one of his messages was unsuccessful, because GCHQ had failed to spot the correct starting-point in the one-time pad, a further illicit inspection of the contents of the Ronson lighter was made and the relevant page identified. Thereafter, every message received by Lonsdale from 'the Centre' was inter-cepted and read in full. To the surprise of MI5, none con-tained any clue to the existence of any other agent, apart from SHAH, the Soviet cryptonym for Houghton, who evidently was Lonsdale's sole preoccupation.

Continued surveillance on Lonsdale over the following fort-night brought Lonsdale to a rendezvous with Houghton and Gee on the first Saturday in December, held outside the Old Vic. On the following afternoon Lonsdale led MI5's watchers back to Ruislip, where they had linked up with their col-leagues who had established a static observation post close to Cranley Drive. For legal reasons the Security Service was later to pretend that little had been known about the Krogers until after their arrest, but in fact a good deal of research had been undertaken already, and several issues worthy of further investigation had become apparent. Kroger was regarded as something of a novice in the book trade, for he often paid substantially over the odds to build his stock of titles, and his knowledge of the business was noticeably superficial.[6] Nevertheless, he was popular among his trade rivals and had experienced no difficulty in being elected to the trade's two associations.

MI5 discovered that the couple had entered the United Kingdom on New Zealand passports, but they both spoke with American accents, hers being a particularly strong Bronx twang. However, according to the New Zealand Security Ser-vice, their passports were authentic and had been issued in Paris by the New Zealand Consulate, on an application accompanied by the required birth and marriage certificates, which had been mailed from what was subsequently discovered to be an accommodation address in Vienna. There was nothing especially irregular about any of this transaction, for the genuine Peter Kroger had indeed been born in Gisborne, New Zealand, but he had not married 'Helen Hale' in New York in 1943; he was in fact dead. By coincidence the official in the Consulate responsible for authorising the application issuing the passports had been Paddy Costello, a Russian-speaking academic with a long history of Leftist politics, who was later to be appointed Professor of Russian at Manchester University. When interviewed, he denied any personal knowledge of the Krogers and, as no direct link between them could be proved, no action was taken against him.[7]

As for where the Krogers had been since their precipitate departure from Manhattan, there was very little certainty. One possibility was that they had fled to Australia before making their way to Europe, and the evidence of American Express travellers cheques purchased in Vienna and redeemed in Paris on 8 February, in Hong Kong on 18 February and then in Tokyo, suggested that the couple had taken a roundabout route to Geneva and Zurich, where bank accounts were opened in their names, and eventually to London.

Confident that it had acquired more than enough evidence to convict Houghton, Gee and Lonsdale, the Security Service was anxious to stem the haemorrhage of secrets from Portland, but the watchers were obliged simply to observe Houghton, Gee, Lonsdale and the Krogers. The problem facing MI5 was twofold: firstly, no hasty action could be taken which might compromise the CIA's valuable source, LAVINIA, who was then still at liberty; and secondly, there seemed a strong possibility that the urbane and cosmopolitan Lonsdale could be running rather more than a single source, however important Houghton was considered by the KGB. However, there was no firm evidence that Lonsdale was involved with others, even though MI5's investigators were convinced that the KGB would not have made a significant investment in Lonsdale and his legend merely to service a single source.

Indeed, Lonsdale was later to claim that he had run several other agents, but had warned them in December 1960 to escape abroad.

The opportunity to arrest the network occurred on the first Saturday of January 1961, when Houghton and Lonsdale (accompanied by Gee) held their regular rendezvous close to Waterloo station, and when the CIA announced that its Polish UB source, '*stutzstaffel*', had escaped to West Berlin. While the Security Service was ready to close in as the three met, there was a danger that the KGB might have realised that '*stutzstaffel*'s defection had placed SHAH, and therefore Lonsdale, in jeopardy, and tip off the illegal. In anticipation of such an eventuality a special watch was kept on Lonsdale and his radio traffic early on Saturday morning, just in case he was ordered to flee. However, Lonsdale received and decrypted his message without demur, leaving intact the original plan to arrest the trio together. Before leaving his flat, Lonsdale wrote a letter to his wife, in which he omitted to mention the girl who had spent the previous night with him, and emphasised his feeling of isolation by quoting a line from a melancholy Russian poem:

For the last twenty minutes I have been pacing my room and I simply cannot continue the letter. This is literally a case of 'I am weary, I am sad, and there is no one to shake hands with'. I am not complaining. But even you cannot imagine how saddened I feel in general and especially at this moment. . . . I celebrated New Year's with a fellow baptized and punctually at midnight Moscow time we drank Stolichnaya to all friends in the Union. We drank separate toasts to you and the children. I personally felt very sad this was the 8th New Year since 1954 which I celebrated without you. Some wise man said in the long ago 'such is life' . . . I'll be thirty-nine shortly. . . . Is there much left?[8]

Throughout their journey, by car to Salisbury and then by train to London, Houghton and Gee were monitored by MI5 watchers operating from a series of inconspicuous vehicles, and from a small aircraft equipped with receivers tuned to a homing device surreptitiously fitted to Houghton's Renault. Ethel Gee had chosen to accompany Houghton so as to do some shopping in London and was present when Houghton met Lonsdale in Waterloo Road. Led by Superintendent George Smith, Special Branch detectives closed in as the pair greeted the Russian, and when Lonsdale was searched he was found to be carrying two sealed brown envelopes, one containing £125, the other fifteen $20 bills. In Gee's straw shopping bag were four Admiralty files and a sealed tin containing a roll of undeveloped film. When processed, the film was found to have 310 exposures, all from a classified book, and forty-two negatives of drawings relating to the construction of the submarine HMS *Dreadnought*.

Synchronised raids were mounted on the Krogers in Ruislip and the homes of Houghton and Gee in Dorset. When confronted later the same evening by Superintendent Smith and Detective Chief Inspector Ferguson Smith of Special Branch, the Krogers innocently denied any knowledge of Lonsdale, the man who habitually had stayed with them overnight on the first Saturday of each month. However, a search of Mrs Kroger's handbag, snatched by an alert policewoman, revealed a white envelope containing a six-page letter, handwritten in Russian, a glass slide holding three microdots and a sheet of paper bearing a typed list of London street names. This latter item was recognised by Smith as the same piece of paper that he had seen in Lonsdale's bank deposit. The Krogers were taken into custody and a longer, more intensive search of the bungalow yielded five passports, including two British passport blanks, and two New Zealand passports hidden behind a bookcase. Four cameras, including Lonsdale's Praktina, and various large sums in cash and travellers cheques were also recovered from the loft, which was festooned with a seventy-four-foot radio antenna connected to a specially adapted radiogram and tape-recorder. The full inventory was even more impressive than the espionage paraphernalia found in Abel's apartment in New York. In fact, the property turned out to be a veritable treasure trove. Among the Krogers' possessions were glass slides and a microscope for handling microdots, handwritten signal plans referring to dates in November and December 1960, and an Olympia typewriter with a print face matching notes found in Lonsdale's flat. Almost nothing in the house was exactly what it seemed. Beside Kroger's bed was a hip flask containing whisky, and three hidden compartments, one of which was full of a black powder, magnetic iron oxide, a substance used for making Morse symbols recorded on magnetic tape easy to read; a family bible had sheets of light-sensitive cellophane paper treated with silver bromide in-between its leaves; a torch had hollow batteries; a tin of talcum powder had an ingenious microdot reader and a set of radio callsigns inside; and a Ronson table lighter bore two sets of one-time pads and signal plans printed on to a tiny photographic negative. The pads were typical KGB, printed on highly inflammable cellulose nitrate, impregnated with zinc oxide, making them easy to destroy.

The search continued for nine days, at the end of which a large cavity was discovered in the foundations under the kitchen floorboards and there, below a heavy concrete slab, was a sophisticated high-speed shortwave transmitter complete with a tape-keying apparatus, control charts and various other accessories. Eventually the investigation was concluded, but some years later a second transmitter was accidentally uncovered in the garden by the new owners. Nor was that quite the end of the story, for two further items were found by a nominee acting for Lonsdale who was given access to the house: two forged Canadian passports, allegedly issued in June 1956 to James T. Wilson and Jane M. Smith, complete with exit stamps from Holland and Belgium, sewn into a leather writing case; and a pair of wooden bookends with $4,500 sealed inside.

At Houghton's cottage detectives found hidden in a radiogram three Admiralty files that had been removed by Gee from Portland the previous day. In the bedroom was an Exakta camera and three Admiralty charts in a suitcase; in addition there was a plan of the naval base with HMS *Osprey*, the Royal Navy's school of submarine warfare, where the very newest Sonar technology was tested, highlighted in pencil. A Swan Vesta matchbox produced coded instructions for a rendezvous in London and the garden shed yielded an old paint tin containing £650. At Gee's home her bedroom provided a handwritten, twelve-point questionnaire on the subject of the latest developments in British anti-submarine detection equipment. Recovered from three separate handbags were: a list of eighteen Admiralty files; a piece of paper bearing the serial number of a classified file concerning Sonar; and another list detailing the four files handed to Lonsdale by Houghton, and the three files found at his home.

In custody Houghton and Gee quickly confessed, while Lonsdale and the Krogers stubbornly refused all cooperation. When the police eventually obtained the Krogers' fingerprints, and discovered their previous career from Charles Bates, the FBI's Legal Attaché in London, they were incriminated further. Peter and Helen Kroger were revealed by Bates to be Morris and Lona Cohen from New York, both known to the FBI as suspects in the Rosenberg case, who had vanished in 1950. Since then the only trace of them had been in the form of their passport photographs, found with a quantity of cash in an envelope belonging to Rudolph Abel. According to the FBI, Morris Cohen, who had a long history of Communist activism and had served in the Spanish Civil War with the Abraham Lincoln Battalion, had probably acted as Abel's radio operator in New York in 1950. There was also some doubt about their true identities and origins. Both claimed to have been born in the United States, but the remote possibility existed that they had entered as illegals and subsequently had adopted their identities. Certainly Morris, whose immigrant parents had run a grocery store in the Bronx, and who had won an athletics scholarship to Mississippi State College to play football and graduated from the University of Illinois in social studies, had returned to New York in September 1938 from Spain on a false passport, in the name of Israel Altman. Upon his return he had trained to become a teacher and in 1941 had married Leontina (Lona) Petka, the daughter of immigrant parents from Austria, in Norwich, Connecticut. Born in Adams, Massachusetts, Lona had been first a governess for a wealthy family in Park Avenue, New York City, and then a trade-union official in an aircraft factory. After working as a substitute teacher, Morris had taken a temporary job at the Soviet pavilion of the 1939 World's Fair held in New York, and had moved from there to

Amtorg, before having been drafted into the Quartermaster Corps of the US army in 1942, where he served for two years as a cook. At the end of hostilities he had trained to become a teacher in New York and had been assigned to a secondary school in Manhattan. Following their sudden disappearance in August 1950, supposedly to take a job as a scriptwriter in Hollywood, the cashing of a $1,000 savings bond and the closure of their bank account, Morris's father had told friends that his son and daughter-in-law had left the States for ever.

Recently new evidence has emerged in Moscow to suggest that Morris was rather more than a talented illegal who had been recruited by the NKVD in 1938 while recuperating in Barcelona from a leg injury sustained during the Spanish Civil War. According to Anatoli Yatskov, his controller in New York until December 1946, Cohen had been responsible for the recruitment of a nuclear physicist, codenamed PERSEUS, who had agreed to infiltrate the Manhattan Project and reveal its secrets. As well as enrolling PERSEUS as a spy, Morris arranged for his wife to act as his courier, and she met him on at least one occasion in Albuquerque to receive his report. As PERSEUS escaped detection, and apparently continued to supply his Soviet contacts with classified material, there was an obvious incentive for the KGB to remove both Cohens from New York, and the FBI's grasp, as quickly as possible when they fell under suspicion.

None of this background data emerged during the eight-day trial in London, during which Houghton admitted his guilt, Gee pretended that she had been an innocent dupe, Lonsdale took the blame upon himself, and the Cohens, who were charged as 'Kroger', maintained their complete innocence. No doubt the Krogers had hoped that the FBI had lost track of them, but it was only after the jury had convicted them that the prosecution revealed the depth of its knowledge regarding the two Americans. Nevertheless, at no time did the authorities disclose the extent of the surveillance that had been conducted by MI5 on Lonsdale before his arrest. Lonsdale received the longest sentence of twenty-five years, with the Krogers getting twenty. Houghton and Gee got fifteen each, but, because the other three defendants were eventually exchanged, ended up serving the longest term.

Under interrogation Houghton admitted that he had been selling secrets from Portland since 1953, when he had met a Soviet known to him only as 'Nikki' outside the Dulwich Art Gallery. From MI5 photographs, Houghton identified 'Nikki' as Nikolai Korovin, the current legal *rezident* at the Embassy, who promptly returned to Moscow accompanied by an attaché, one of his subordinates, Vassilli A. Dozhdalev. After his trial, at which he had alleged that he had been coerced into co-operation by threats against his family and his girlfriend in Warsaw, Houghton made a more candid statement in which he identified Dozhdalev as the case officer who had succeeded 'Nikki'. In a rare breach of tradecraft for a highly experienced professional, who was soon afterwards to be named by George Blake as his principal contact, Dozhdalev had given Houghton his home address in London, 16 Lancaster Road, W11, in case of emergencies. Dozhdalev was a known KGB officer, who had undertaken a short tour of duty in London in 1952, which had coincided with the end of Korovin's first visit, and who had returned with the rank of second secretary in 1959.

As for Lonsdale, it was clear that his identity had been fabricated with considerable care, although his birth certificate, issued in Ontario on 7 December 1954 in respect of a birth registered at Cobalt, Temiskaming, on 7 August 1924, was genuine, as was his passport issued on 21 January 1955. However, when the RCMP traced the two referees who had acted as sponsors for the application, neither had heard of Lonsdale, and both disowned what had purported to be their signatures. The RCMP's research showed that the earliest trace of the 'Lonsdale' under arrest in London was at lodging houses in Picksmill Street, and later Pendrell Street, Vancouver, in November 1954. According to US records, he had crossed the Canadian border by train at Niagara Falls on 22 February 1955. British immigration records indicated that he had arrived in England at Southampton from New York aboard the liner *America* on 3 March 1955.

The other stamps in his passport showed that since his

arrival Lonsdale had been abroad, sometimes for up to ten weeks at a time. Indeed, just four months after his arrival in London he had visited Scandinavia for a fortnight with a coach party of tourists, and at its conclusion a fortnight later had joined a similar group for a two-week tour of Italy. There were other trips abroad in 1957, 1959 and finally August 1960. However, it was to be the FBI which finally established the truth. Enquiries made later in Canada revealed the father of the real Gordon Lonsdale to be Jack E. Lonsdale, a lumber-jack of mixed race who had been separated from his Finnish wife, Alga Bousu, a year after his son's birth at their home in Lang Street in the remote gold-mining settlement of Kirkland Lake, fifty-five miles north-east of Cobalt. He explained that his wife, whom he had married in January 1924, had left him for a Finn named Hjalmar Philaja. When her son enrolled in the local infants school, he did so under the name Arnold Philaja. Alga and Hjalmar had remained in Canada until 1932, when they had returned together to Karelia, Finland, with the eight-year-old child. It was only when his mother attempted to obtain a passport for Gordon in September 1931 that she registered his birth, six years late. Not long after their arrival, probably in about 1934, Gordon had died. This would have made 'Lonsdale' thirty-seven at the time of his arrest, yet in his letter to his wife he let slip that he was approaching his thirty-ninth birthday, a discrepancy of two years.

The physician who had treated the Lonsdale family, Dr W. E. Mitchell, and who had also delivered Gordon, was traced to Toronto and when he checked his medical records he confirmed that the young Gordon had been circumcised within a few days of his birth. The man claiming to be 'Gordon Lonsdale' in custody in London demonstrably had not. However, the illegal had obviously spent much time in North America, for his accent was certainly authentic, as was testi-fied to by the two British intelligence officers who had unwit-tingly spent a considerable period with Lonsdale. Charles Elwell had attended the same full-time Chinese course at London University's School of African and Oriental Studies in October 1955, and his wife, Ann Glass, who was also a skilled MI5 officer, had been photographed with Lonsdale at a party held by a Canadian diplomat, a student in the same year, in July 1956. Neither had ever suspected 'Lonsdale', who had left the course in June 1957, of being a Soviet illegal. Indeed, Lonsdale was later to remark that the hardest part of his mission had been his pretence to be a novice and learn the Chinese language. In fact, he spoke it well and had co-authored the standard Russian-Chinese textbook before his departure to the West. That Lonsdale, coincidentally, had been a social acquaintance of the Elwells was later to be a source of some amusement to the illegal, and some embarrassment to the MI5 officer. When Elwell, still using the cover name 'Elton', was assigned to interrogate Lonsdale at Wormwood Scrubs, following his conviction, the Russian thought that their previous encounter had been 'clearly a painful episode in his official life'. As Elwell had said to him, 'Of course, I was asked to explain how it came about that my photograph was found in your flat.'[9]

The search of Lonsdale's flat at the White House had produced a Royal typewriter with a print face that exactly matched some of the coded items found in Ruislip and, of course, the Ronson table lighter first seen at the Midland Bank, which had later been the subject of a clandestine inspection. Inside a decorative Chinese scroll hanging on the wall were three bundles of dollar bills, and more US currency was found in a leather money-belt. Some of the material was similar to that found at Ruislip: close inspection of a tin of Yardley's talcum powder in the bathroom showed it to be a microdot reader with an adjustable magnifying lens, together with a small aperture in which was concealed a signal plan for dates in 1960 and 1961; and ostensibly ordinary torch batteries had been hollowed out as hiding-places, but they were empty. Also of interest were two sales receipts from Selfridges in Oxford Street, which showed that the Krogers had been shopping with Lonsdale on the morning of their arrest.

When the six-page handwritten letter found in Helen Kroger's handbag was translated, it turned out to be from Lonsdale and addressed to his wife in Moscow. The three microdots proved to be correspondence to him from his mother, three letters from his wife Galyusha and one from their daughter Liza, dated 9 December 1960, and from his five-year-old son Trofim, who was clearly missing his father: 'When is Daddy coming, and why has he gone away, and what a *stupid* job Daddy has got,' he observed.

Aged twelve, Liza was reported by her mother to be doing badly at school, particularly in geometry, algebra, English and 'Party training', and occasionally she played truant. Her brother had recently been trapped in the lift between the sixth and seventh floors in their apartment block, and Galyusha remarked that the children's nurse had been of little help in his rescue. From Lonsdale's private family correspondence MI5 deduced that, despite his many girlfriends in London, he had suffered from loneliness. His wife, whom he later said in his memoirs was a Pole named Halina Panfilowska, was thought probably to be of Czech origin, and she was chairman of her community's Party Cultural Commission, which looked after the welfare of the residents. She sang at social gatherings and in her letter pressed Lonsdale for more money and

a white brocade dress, a tight-fitting one, and white shoes. I beg you to forgive me but I would like to meet the New Year well. By the way, I'll be singing in two places. I beg you to carry out my request, my first and last one. I hope that you will not be angry, but I must sing and I would very much like to rise to the occasion.[10]

Although evidently Lonsdale had been able to send Christmas presents to his children, a model car to his son and a teddy bear to Liza, he explained that the dress was quite impossible. 'In respect of a white brocade dress – a very difficult matter. In other countries brocade is not worn. It may be assumed it could be made on order, but to pass it on to you? And when? You must understand that a dress and shoes cannot be put in a pocket.' However, extra cash was possible, he promised, and would be supplied by 'V.M.', presumably his KGB controller. The reference in his final letter to the New Year of 1954 stated that he had not been able to celebrate the holiday with his family for the past seven years, which fitted in with what MI5 had learned about his movements. He acknowledged his wife's complaint that he had missed 'seven Octobers and six May Day celebrations', thereby inadvertently confirming that he had left Moscow some time between May and October 1954. In one rather moving passage, Lonsdale wrote:

I hope you don't think I am an entirely hard-hearted man who gives no thought to anybody. All I am going to say is I myself have only one life, a not entirely easy one at that. I want to spend my life so that later on there is no shame to look back on, if possible, whatever may be said. I do know what loneliness is. From the age of ten, during the past 29 years, I have spent only ten years with my own people. I did not wish it and I did not seek it, but so it turned out to be. I have thought very much about it – why all this? The answer is it all started as far back as 1932 when Mother decided to dispatch me to the nether regions [see page 222]. At that time she could not imagine, of course, all the consequences of this step and I do not blame her. [11]

Lonsdale's mail from his family, never released at his trial, proved that even after his return to the Soviet Union, his account of his activities, or of even very fundamental biographical data, could not be relied upon. For example, in one of the letters from his wife, Galyusha reported that his mother was unwell but his sister was unaware of the crisis:

At your Zubovsky Boulevard home all is well with the exception of mother who complains that she is not feeling well . . . she is afraid of death. But of this fear she only spoke to me, as she is afraid of upsetting Natasha . . . You must hasten home – after all one has but one mother in the world. [12]

This short extract contains evidence that Lonsdale's mother and sister were alive, and that Lonsdale had a home in the Zubovsky Boulevard, yet he was later to assert that his mother had been killed in Poland during the war, when he was aged fifteen.

Despite the overwhelming evidence against Lonsdale and the Krogers, they admitted nothing to their interrogators and they acted in an entirely professional manner, accepting their conviction and long prison sentences with impressive equanimity. None agreed to co-operate with the Security Service, leaving the D Branch investigators to ponder some of the inconsistencies in what had been learned. Unsolved was the amount of trouble taken by the KGB to establish Lonsdale in London, with an apparent lack of any real return on its investment. His cover was, apart from one minor medical detail, faultless, and he had fulfilled his role as a well-heeled man-about-town who had moved from Canada with his savings without difficulty. He had operated almost entirely independently of the Embassy *rezident* and presumably had been briefed during the lengthy periods he had travelled abroad. All of this indicated an illegal of some stature, yet there were contradictions in his performance, quite apart from his supposed servicing of only a single source. His business, for example, was not the success he pretended it to be. Even upon his return to Moscow, after he had been swapped in April 1964 for the SIS courier, Greville Wynne, Lonsdale declined to reveal his true identity and persisted in the pretence that he was truly Gordon Lonsdale, born in Cobalt, Ontario. His subsequent memoirs, the only account of an illegal's activities ever published with the KGB's consent, were studied with interest by MI5, but they made no admission as to his true identity, which was only discovered by SIS a year after the trial, following some discreet research in Moscow.

In reality, Lonsdale was Konon Trofimovich Molody, the son of a Ukrainian, a well-known editor of scientific journals, and had been born in Moscow on 17 January 1922. His mother Evdokia was a physician in Moscow and his paternal grandmother had come from Kamchatka, from whom Molody evidently had inherited his distinctive Mongolian features, which 'Lonsdale' had plausibly described to Western friends as his 'Red Indian blood'. Having been duped by Lonsdale once, Charles Elwell took some satisfaction from researching every detail of the illegal's true family background in Russia, starting with Molody's father who had been sent into Siberian exile in the 1880s:

Trofim left Siberia in 1908 and studied physics at the Universities of St Petersburg and Moscow, where in due course he became one of the Lecturers in Physics. As a teacher and as a research worker, T. K. Molody was distinguished but it was in the field of scientific journalism that he achieved a certain modest fame. His wife, whom he married in 1914, practised for many years as a doctor of medicine in Moscow, where her two children were born, one in 1917 and Konon, the future Russian Intelligence Officer, five years later.[13]

After Molody's father died of a brain haemorrhage in October 1929, his mother entrusted him to the care of her ballerina sister, Tatiana, who had obtained a US visa for him in November 1933 by pretending that he was her son. Thus Molody entered America illegally for the first time, not yet aged twelve, and went to California with his aunt, where he attended a school at Berkeley. Four years later he decided, against Tatiana's wishes, to return home, and in the spring of 1938 he travelled to England. In France he was met by his other aunt, Anastasia, and together with some English friends drove across Europe to Tartu in Estonia where his third aunt, Serafima, lived. A year after he was reunited with his mother, Molody was drafted into the Red Army, and it is likely that at some stage he served in China, where he had became proficient in Mandarin. According to his memoirs, he had also operated as a partisan behind German lines.[14]

SIS discovered that Molody's mother, Madame Molodaya, was still listed in the telephone directory at 16/20 Zubovsky Boulevard. Apartments rarely change hands in Moscow, and Konon's sister was still living in the same flat in 1991. Molody may have suspected that a discrepancy would be noticed, or perhaps he was anxious to make his cover story approximate as closely as possible to the truth, but whatever his motive, he explained where he had lived while undergoing the special training required to become an illegal. When he had lived in Moscow during the war he had 'moved into a big block of flats near Zubovsky Boulevard. My landlady was a member of the intelligence service, and I posed as her nephew on leave. She had no children of her own and took a great liking to me. Eventually she started calling me "son" and I called her "mother".'[15]

Here, quite clearly, Molody used part of the truth, including his mother's real home address and the fact that he had been largely brought up by his aunt, to build his cover story. This is typical illegal tradecraft, but Molody had not always been so meticulous. It was noted that one of his enterprises, the Automatic Merchandising Company Limited, had run into financial difficulty and had been put into liquidation by the official receiver in 1959 with liabilities of £30,000. Started in 1955 in Broadstairs by one Peter Ayres, the company had been based in the seaside resort and had been intended to sell bubble-gum vending machines. After reading a newspaper advertisement Molody had backed the company by buying 500 £1 shares and had become a director. Oleg Gordievsky, a senior KGB officer who trained as an illegal and defected to London in 1985, was to assert that 'not merely did his espionage activities rapidly become self-financing: despite the large sums paid to his agents, he also produced a substantial profit for the KGB'.[16] In an interview published in a Russian magazine, Molody echoed this with the claim that 'the working capital and profits from my four companies (millions of pounds sterling) . . . were increasing year by year',[17] whilst the exact reverse was really true. Although at the time of his arrest Lonsdale had several large deposits in his name with the Royal Bank of Canada, both the companies with which he was associated experienced cash problems. The Master Switch Company Limited of Coplestone Road, Peckham, which was one of his enterprises, possessed only one product, the Allo Switch, a motor immobiliser for cars which was exhibited in Brussels in 1960 and had won a gold medal for its inventors, but it was never a commercial success. In February 1960, Lonsdale had become a director of the company but it had fared little better than his other investment. Whether the Soviets ever knew of the financial difficulties his business ventures experienced is doubtful. Certainly his involvement with a bankrupt company was entirely contrary to the well-established principles of *conspiratsia* and would have been vetoed by his superiors, if they had known.

That Molody had worked in London in isolation from the legal *rezidentura* had been established by MI5 when the tapes of the technical surveillance of Nikolai Korovin's home were analysed. On the night of Lonsdale's arrest Korovin had been watching television with his deputy, Nikolai Karpekov, yet neither had made any comment when the announcement was broadcast on the news. Nor did they attempt to move to more secure premises, perhaps at the Embassy, to discuss what ought to have been a crisis for the KGB. It was obvious to those who had listened in to the inconsequential conversation that had passed between the two senior intelligence officers that neither at that stage had any inkling of Lonsdale's significance to their organisation. Considering the watertight compartmentation between the illegals department and the remainder of the KGB, this was only to be expected.

The Lonsdale case is probably the single, most documented example of an illegal and the investigation that was conducted into his background. Uniquely, after his return to Moscow, Lonsdale wrote his memoirs, *Spy*, which are believed by some to have been ghosted in part by Kim Philby. Whether he was responsible or not, there is strong internal evidence to suggest that the book was completed by at least two authors, with little co-ordination. For example, Lonsdale initially refers to his Polish wife, Halina, as 'a source of great happiness ever since' their marriage: 'My wife has been a true friend and comrade and a wonderful mother. Her loyalty can be gauged by the fact that, despite long and painful separations, she has never once questioned the nature of my work.'[18] Whilst this description hardly accords with the contents of her letters, Lonsdale later in the same book, without explanation, refers to 'my wife Galyusha'. In fact, Molody had enough relatives in the West for the FBI and MI5 to trace and determine that he had only been married once, to Galyusha, leading the investigators to the inevitable conclusion that so much of his memoirs had been invented that even the contributors had become confused.

On the British side, Peter Wright has described his involvement in his notorious autobiography, *Spycatcher*, and Charles Elwell, using the familiar cover name 'Elton', has also published an account from MI5's perspective in the *Police Journal*. In addition, Detective Superintendent George Smith, the Special Branch officer who arrested Houghton, has also written a book,[19] as has Houghton himself.[20] Thus there are no fewer than five separate versions of the episode in the public domain. Despite all this material, what remains unresolved is the exact nature of Lonsdale's mission. Had it really been necessary to involve three illegals and nine cameras to run SHAH? Lonsdale himself insisted that he had handled other sources and, somewhat unconvincingly, asserted that all his outbound communications had been routed through another transmitter. At the moment he was taken into custody, Lonsdale claimed that he had reviewed

my activities during the recent past, wondering who else might have been caught up in the dragnet. The result of this review was, on the whole, heartening. My wireless operator was safely out of the country. So were several others, who might have been severely compromised by my arrest. [21]

Whether Lonsdale can be believed on this point is doubtful, for in his book, which was published in 1965, he was still maintaining the fiction that he had been born in Canada and that the Krogers, who were not swapped for the imprisoned British lecturer Gerald Brooke until 1970, were completely innocent of any involvement in espionage. To emphasise this patently false proposition, Lonsdale reiterated the claim of another, separate line of communication to Moscow:

Of course, I needed radio communications for service messages on operational matters, and for this purpose I had a highly-qualified signal-man operating his own transmitter. He reached the UK a few months after I did. In December 1960, I gave him orders to clear out of the country double-quick. He did. [22]

One of Lonsdale's more plausible claims is that he had teamed up with a Soviet intelligence officer whom he referred to only by his codename, 'Alec', during partisan operations in Byelorussia in September 1943. He alleged that he had first encountered Alec, who was later to become his partner and for whom he was to work as a radio operator, while in German captivity. Alec 'was in fact a Russian intelligence officer who had penetrated the Abwehr' and had secured Lonsdale's freedom. Later he described meeting Alec 'at the end of 1950' in New York's Central Park, a wholly likely scenario, and suggests that his 'duties as Alec's Communications

Officer kept me in New York for most of my time in the
United States', where he supposedly remained until the summer of 1954 when Alec despatched him to Canada, en route
to London. Certainly Lonsdale's description of Alec coincides
with the opinions held by others who met Abel and were,
without exception, impressed by him. When his IQ was
tested at the federal penitentiary in Georgia, he was shown
to have a near genius-level intellect. Lonsdale remarked that
he was

one of the most remarkable men I have ever met in my life, who
is also indeed one of the most astute intelligence officers of all time.
My association with him was to be long and fruitful, and range
over many countries . . . He always seemed to me an exceptionally
interesting and in many ways a really remarkable person. This quiet,
unhurried and somewhat elderly man never attracted attention by
his appearance and easily lost himself in any crowd. At a party he
never attracted undue attention while at the same time impressing
everyone by his attentiveness and courtesy. His intelligence and
penetrating gaze never stopped for long on any particular object
but always noticed everything of real interest. His self-control and
tenacity always impressed me and I am sure he would be as cool
as an iceberg sitting on a powder keg with a smouldering slow match
in it. He would probably crack a joke at such a tense moment and
discover a way of preventing the explosion![23]

That Lonsdale should have been trained by Abel, and that
they should have worked together during the war, was not
surprising. Both were resourceful, if lonely professionals
who politely but firmly declined all temptations placed in their
path by their adversaries. The accuracy of the remainder of
Lonsdale's story is a matter of speculation. He says that at
the end of the Second World War, which found him with
the Soviet occupation forces in Berlin, he was offered the
opportunity to go to university, to study international law,
and then to join Alec as an illegal. His first mission was to
Frankfurt to track down ex-Nazis working for Reinhard
Gehlen's federal intelligence service, the BND; he was then
sent to the United States in 1950 to join Alec in New York.
Details of his assignment are deliberately sketchy, as the
author readily concedes:

I do not propose to describe in any detail my experiences in the United States. Any reader will understand my reason for this; some may even sympathise with it. I have very good reason to know that Mr J. Edgar Hoover is interested in me, and I have no desire to satisfy his curiosity. I hope that many FBI man-hours will be wasted in search of the identity I used in the United States.[24]

Molody may have had good operational reasons to fictionalise his background and conceal the details of his mission in the United States; there is no explanation of how and when he learned his Mandarin, one of the few verifiable facts known about K. T. Molody, apart from the much publicised circumstances of his death, while picking mushrooms in October 1970. The Soviet press understandably omitted to mention that Molody had died a chronic alcoholic and a man bitterly disappointed by his reception in Moscow after his release from Wakefield prison. Evidently, his KGB colleagues could not believe that anyone who had spent so long in the West could still be trustworthy.

At the conclusion of the Molody case, there remained several unanswered questions, three of which remain highly relevant today. Two concern the locations in London where Lonsdale and the Cohens chose to live. The White House was an interesting property for him to select, for at the time of his arrival in 1955 it accommodated CIA personnel who worked at the huge transcription centre in Cumberland Terrace, a short distance across Regent's Park. Ostensibly an anonymous government office, the building processed tapes of intercepted telephone and teleprinter circuits flown in daily from Berlin.[25] At least one CIA officer recalls meeting Lonsdale and having a drink with him in the White House's bar, and there remains speculation that Lonsdale may have been steered deliberately towards the district by the KGB so that he could conveniently service dead-drops in the park filled by agents planted in the joint CIA–SIS facility. Similarly, the fact that the Cohens moved to Ruislip, so very short a distance from GCHQ's secret headquarters at Lime Grove, Eastcote, caused some comment. Might they have been assigned to handle a KGB asset inside GCHQ?[26]

The third unresolved issue relates to Molody's claim to

have alerted other members of his network to his imminent arrest, thereby allowing them to escape. Today Vassilli Dozhdalev says that Molody ran other agents, apart from Houghton and Gee, and the Security Service certainly took the suggestion seriously at the time, pursuing in particular another possible source of a leak in the Admiralty, but that case was shelved for what are believed to be political reasons.[27] Quite simply, the then Director-General of MI5, Sir Roger Hollis, was not willing to risk yet another security scandal and had called off the investigation.

9 · Double Agents and Dangles

For the FBI, the search for an illegal is the ultimate goal in counterintelligence.

William R. Corson in *Widows*[1]

With the help of Dmitri Polyakov, still a rising star in the GRU, and the other Soviet sources, the West's security agencies took the offensive in the mid-1960s in dealing with the threat from illegals. The next stage in an imaginative but highly risky scheme to expose both the remaining illegals and their agents was the development of an ambitious operation that had become known in intelligence jargon as a 'dangle'. The usual objective of such a scheme is to place an attractive candidate for espionage in the path of an active recruiter in the hope that the professional will be unable to resist the temptation to make his pitch for the prospect and thereby compromise himself. At this point in the development of the conventional dangle, the local security agency steps in and arrests the intelligence officer red-handed and, pointing out that his chosen career is about to be rudely terminated, suggests that in his own interests he switches sides. The victim is then recruited, albeit reluctantly, and is in a position to supply information that will compromise others. Often practised rather crudely by the Soviets to justify tit-for-tat reprisal expulsions, Western agencies have used the system very occasionally. In the case of Captain Nikolai Lulakov in 1955,

MI5 had caught the Assistant Naval Attaché in the act of paying a double agent in his car parked on Hampstead Heath, and he had been advised to leave the country, a procedure known as a 'silent PNG' because no public expulsion was announced.[2] By this expedient a troublesome opponent is eliminated from the scene with the minimum of fuss. Lulakov was allowed to slip out of the country quietly, but in the case of Ivan F. Skripov, who was expelled from Australia in February 1963, the background was more complex.

Skripov had arrived in London in 1953 as an attaché and had stayed until 1958, by which time he had been promoted to the rank of second secretary and had been positively identified by the British Security Service as a KGB officer. In June the following year, he was sent as first secretary, accompanied by his wife and son, to reopen the Soviet Embassy in Canberra, which had been closed since the defection of Vladimir and Evdokia Petrov in 1954. Soon after the restoration of diplomatic relations, Skripov recruited a young woman, actually the wife of a serving MI5 officer, who had been sent to Australia for the specific purpose of being dangled before the KGB officer. She had pretended to be a lonely immigrant with a dull job in the passport office while the convivial Skripov, who cultivated a reputation as a gregarious figure on the diplomatic social scene, took the bait, never realising that all his meetings were being taped by a miniature recorder hidden in her purse. He entertained her at expensive restaurants, gave her small gifts and, over a period of two years, cash totalling £425. Skripov was also filmed by ASIO while he emptied dead-letter drops in Sydney's Botanical Gardens and Taronga Park Zoo, and although he never handed his agent over to an illegal, he did arrange for her to act as a cut-out between himself and an illegal supposedly based in Adelaide. After a series of exercises, in which she practised secret writing and recovered a metal canister from a dead-drop in a park near Sydney Harbour Bridge, Skripov instructed her to collect two items left in a drop at a cemetery and to deliver them to him: a single photo and a genuine Canadian passport that had been issued in September 1960 in the name of Andrew Huha. ASIO examined and photographed both before they were passed on to Skripov. Later, after the agent who was being used as bait had apparently gained his trust, Skripov produced a high-speed transmitter concealed inside a hairdryer and told her to take it to a contact who would meet her at a rendezvous in Adelaide. Unfortunately, although an elaborate trap had been prepared, Skripov's elusive illegal failed to materialise and consequently the KGB officer demanded the return of the radio. This placed ASIO in a dilemma as it was unwilling to give back the valuable transmitter, and was equally reluctant to sever the promising link between its double agent and Skripov. Eventually, ASIO was obliged to abandon the case and settle for Skripov's much-publicised formal expulsion. ASIO rightly regarded the confiscation of the transmitter as a very worthwhile consolation prize, for there was immense interest in the ways illegals signalled Moscow and a high value was placed on their methodology and equipment.

Interception of illegal communications was generally regarded by the experts as the West's best hope of catching spies, and any item of equipment of the kind seized from Skripov would be examined carefully to determine whether the KGB's engineers had produced any refinements. Naturally, following the introduction of RAFTER, the apparatus which detected illicit Soviet wireless traffic, it was imperative to study Soviet developments in case the technique had been discovered, an eventuality that might either indicate a leak in the West's security, or might make illegals even harder to detect.

Having lost Skripov, and thereby having alerted the KGB to ASIO's continued vigilance, attention was turned on the Canadian passport and the photograph. The Canadian authorities confirmed that the real Andrew Huha, who had been born in Czechoslovakia in 1903, looked nothing like the man whose photo appeared in the passport, and ASIO drew the conclusion from the two items that Skripov had been undertaking the duties of an illegal support officer to supply documentation to a pair of KGB agents being staged through Australia. In any event, despite a lengthy search, neither person was ever found.[3] As for the KGB's transmitter, it turned out to be the same model as the one found in the home of the Krogers in London in January 1961, without any improvements.

The Skripov dangle was a classic of its kind, but a variation employed in the United States was intended to exploit the possibility that a Soviet professional, having fulfilled his role as a talent-spotter and recruiter, might turn the neophyte over to an illegal for permanent handling. This had become the standard KGB practice where an agent had to be serviced in hostile territory. Rather than risk the deployment of a case officer operating under diplomatic cover, who was likely to attract surveillance, and thereby compromise both the agent and his handler during a clandestine meeting, the KGB had in the past shown a preference for using dead-letter drops and illegals. One objective of mounting a dangle operation is to encourage the original recruiter to pass control of the dangled double agent over to an illegal. Invariably, in operations of this kind, a positively identified opposition intelligence officer like Lulakov or Skripov is the target, and a well-briefed intermediary is the person who is prepared for the initial approach. Nine times out of ten the plan collapses when the intended victim fails to make his move, or he suspects a deliberate provocation, but occasionally the ploy works. Since a large proportion of the most significant spies, for both East and West, have been walk-ins, the risk of compromise is regarded as an acceptable occupational hazard. Professional intelligence officers acknowledge that in accepting a walk-in they are themselves in danger of being contaminated, but when presented with a really promising candidate, the risk has to be taken.

Since the FBI was convinced that there were many Soviet illegals operating in the United States, and conventional methods of detection had failed to find them, the recommended solution had been to identify them through the use of double agents. The proposal called for a double agent to be dangled in front of the KGB for recruitment in the hope that after he had been accepted he would be transferred to an illegal for permanent handling. The logic behind this suggested remedy was compelling. Evidence from the defector Reino Hayhanen suggested that one of the principal roles played by an illegal is that of a cut-out between an active source, such as Sergeant Nelson Drummond, and his controller, who operates from the legal *rezidentura*. The use of an illegal to service dead-letter drops effectively insulates the legals from direct contamination, and there were plenty of examples where the Soviets had demonstrated a preference for complicated tradecraft involving dead-drops and signs so as to avoid the embarrassment of an incident in which a KGB officer under diplomatic cover might be caught red-handed in very undiplomatic conduct. In addition, the FBI had noted that non-commissioned personnel had proved of exceptional value to the Soviets. The most recent rash of cases had followed a discernible pattern of low-echelon staff betraying important secrets. John W. Butenko, an electronics engineer with an ITT subsidiary, had been arrested in October 1963 in New Jersey, in the act of passing Strategic Air Command communications data to two Soviet diplomats from the UN mission, Gleb A. Pavlov and Yuri A. Romashin, and an Amtorg chauffeur, Igor A. Ivanov, who had all been arrested. In his defence Butenko claimed that he had supplied the information in the hope of learning about relatives living behind the Iron Curtain. There had been other examples too. Robert G. Thompson, the former USAF sergeant, had been charged by the FBI in January 1963 after months of surveillance and interrogations, following a tip from Polyakov. James A. Mitkenbaugh, a former army sergeant caught in November 1965, was yet another similar case, and in the same month Sergeant Glen R. Rohrer, who had joined the Counterintelligence Corps in 1949, defected to Prague, ostensibly on ideological grounds. Even as the FBI conducted its survey of potential dangles, in October 1966, Sergeant Herbert W. Boeckenhaupt, the US air-force communications technician serving with the 33rd Communications Squadron, was taken into custody at March Air Force Base, California, charged with having betrayed details of Strategic Air Command's cipher systems to Aleksei R. Malinin of the Soviet military mission in Washington DC. In each of these separate cases the Soviets had obtained important secrets from NCOs, and inevitably had become accustomed to the scenario of a disaffected NCO seeking to betray his country for cash. In its preparations for mounting a dangle, the FBI recognised that the use of a suitably plausible NCO would have the greatest chance of being accepted by the KGB.

The issue of rank had been exploited with considerable skill by the various Soviet handlers who had played upon thwarted ambition, low self-esteem and simple greed to extract highly classified material from relatively junior military ranks. As had happened with Sergeant Jack Dunlap, the NSA driver, lack of seniority had not been a reliable guide in terms of access to secrets. As a clerk-messenger, Dunlap had carried some of the Agency's most secret documents to and from its headquarters. He had also copied them en route and sold them to his Soviet contact. Thus a very minor cog in the most secret part of the US government machine had inflicted untold damage. Indeed, couriers, chauffeurs and technicians often handled a greater volume of classified data than their superiors. In November 1965, an army deserter, Sergeant Robert L. Johnson, volunteered a confession to the FBI in Reno in which he admitted having spied for the KGB since 1953. His case was almost a model for the FBI's planned dangle, for Johnson described how he had tried to defect to the Russians in Berlin in 1953, but had been persuaded to return to his unit and spy for the KGB. When in March 1961 Johnson had been posted to the US Armed Forces Courier Station at Orly airport, he had taken the unpopular weekend duties which had allowed him to work unsupervised. During his hours alone in the top-security document storage bunker, he had arranged for the copying of thousands of highly secret papers which were routinely exchanged between the Pentagon and NATO headquarters, carried by official escorts. Until his transfer to Washington DC in May 1964, Johnson had been a star agent for the KGB and had recruited his old friend from G-2 (US military intelligence), James Mitkenbaugh, with whom he had served in Germany, to help handle the volume of papers copied for the Soviets. Together they had succeeded in photographing the kind of material that a lowly army sergeant might not normally be expected to have access to. In reality, of course, senior officers often left sensitive data to be handled by their subordinates.

Soviet recognition of this fact had manifested itself unexpectedly during the FBI's investigation of Sergeant Roy Rhodes in 1957, and had surfaced again in 1962 when the defector, Anatoli Golitsyn, disclosed that Viktor M. Kovshuk of the Second Chief Directorate had made an illicit visit to America in 1957 to meet a top Soviet spy. Golitsyn had assumed that an officer of such seniority would never risk travelling to the States unless he was in contact with an exceptionally important source, most probably a mole inside the CIA. In fact, as Yuri Nosenko later confirmed, Kovshuk had been involved in the recruitment of Rhodes in Moscow, where penetration of the US Embassy was one of the responsibilities of his particular Chief Directorate. Accordingly, Kovshuk had been one of those who had attempted to reactivate Rhodes as a spy after his return to the US. While Golitsyn's analysis had not been entirely correct, the defector had at least been right about Rhodes's status within the KGB, as described by Nosenko, who, unlike Golitsyn, had served in the Second Chief Directorate prior to his defection and therefore had been in a position to know. The fact that Rhodes had only held the rank of sergeant had not diminished his standing in the eyes of the KGB, as was evident from the fact that Kovshuk himself had handled the case personally.

The study of the most damaging espionage cases over the past decade, and particularly over the previous five years, conducted by the FBI in 1965, proved the Soviet appetite for the recruitment of low-level employees. Nor was this a phenomenon which occurred only in America. Two separate breaches of security in England, involving Harry Houghton and John Vassall, had centred on minor clerical functionaries who had betrayed valuable secrets. As we have seen, Houghton, who had sold *Dreadnought* atomic submarine data, had been run by a legal, Vassilli Dozhdalev, and then by an illegal, Konon Molody. John Vassall, the Admiralty clerk who had been arrested in September 1962, twenty months after Houghton, had been handled by Nikolai Karpekov, a member of the legal *rezidentura* in London.[4]

It was the FBI's plan to turn this structural but unavoidable weakness in the West's system of command to its advantage by drawing up the profile of a disenchanted NCO entrusted with valuable secrets who appeared to conform to the pattern that, over the previous decade, had been so well established. To give the scheme a greater chance of success, the FBI borrowed another characteristic of recent Soviet recruitments: the concentration of effort on émigrés and those with families still living in the Eastern Bloc. The FBI's chosen candidate, Sergeant Ralph Sigler, was selected as a possible dangle in 1966 after its counter-intelligence branch had undertaken a trawl of potentially suitable US service personnel. Sigler was, in effect, a carefully manufactured composite traitor to be used as bait to catch an illegal. If anything, he was almost too perfect, for as well as having family in a Soviet satellite country, he could speak Czech, German and some Russian.

A radio repairman based at Fort Bliss, El Paso, Texas, Sigler conformed to the FBI's profile. Born in Czechoslovakia in May 1928 with the name Rudolph Ciglar, he had emigrated as a child to Pennsylvania with his father. In 1946 he had enlisted in the US army and been posted to Germany. In September 1955, having married a girl from Stuttgart, he became an American citizen and changed his name to Ralph Sigler.[5] Although he had not been in touch with her since a brief visit in 1946, his estranged mother was still living at his birthplace, Hertnik. Furthermore, he was still an NCO after more than twenty years in the military, he worked at a sensitive military base, and his job gave him routine access to the kind of technical information that could be of interest to the Soviets. As for the site of the dangle, the FBI and CIA had agreed that Mexico City held altogether more promise than Washington DC, New York or San Francisco, the three US cities where the Soviets possessed sizable legal *rezidenturas*, but were rather obviously handicapped by the FBI's hostile surveillance. Testimony from defectors, the most recent being Yuri Nosenko, confirmed that Mexico City had become an important *rezidentura*, headed for some years by the Consul, Pavel Yatskov, and staffed with ambitious and highly competent FCD officers, who were always seeking to run operations against 'the main adversary' to the north. Apart from Havana, the Soviet complement in Mexico City of fifty personnel was the largest in Latin America and contrasted sharply with the strength of the Mexican Embassy in Moscow, which boasted just five diplomats. Of those fifty Soviets, the CIA calculated that twenty-five were KGB and ten GRU professionals, operating from separate *referenturas* on the third floor of the ornate Embassy, where the windows of the Victorian villa had been sealed with a layer of concrete.

Whilst the CIA station in Mexico City, with a strength of twenty officers, headed since 1956 by a former FBI Special Agent, Dr Winston M. Scott, attempted to maintain technical coverage of the Soviet Embassy compound on the Calzada de Tacubaya, the surveillance was far from comprehensive and the Mexican authorities posed no threat whatever to the KGB personnel. The CIA station's largest sub-section, consisting of four case officers, three assistants and a secretary, operated two permanent observation posts on the front of the building and one at the rear with a view over the garden. Every person going in and out was photographed and their names added to a comprehensive index of personalities. If individual faces were obscured, the cameras focused on car licence plates and the numbers were later checked and identified with the Mexican police. Continuous observation and a programme of movements analysis had helped the CIA verify Yatskov as the KGB *rezident* and, in the autumn of 1966, confirm his successor as Boris P. Kolomyakov. Another aid to the identification of the legal *rezidentura* had been a couple of limited double-agent operations. One centred on the owner of a grocery store near the Embassy who was in the pay of both sides, and the other was a young American from Philadelphia codenamed LI/COZY, who had been recruited in Mexico City while a student and who had subsequently reported the contact to the FBI.[6] Neither case looked as promising as Sigler's because they could not offer classified information to their handlers.

The objective was to accomplish Sigler's recruitment by the legal *rezidentura* in Mexico, where the Sergeant could visit with relative ease from his base across the border in Texas, and then manipulate the case in the hope of gently persuading the Soviets to entrust his communications to a hitherto unidentified illegal. In practical terms this meant telling his contacts in Mexico City that he had been transferred to a part of the country which would make it difficult for him to travel abroad. The ability of the legal Soviets to travel within the United States was limited, and the key lay in keeping Sigler away from the three big conurbations where they could operate without restriction. Thus if the soldier was posted to somewhere remote from San Francisco, New York and Washington DC, the KGB might be obliged to handle him via an illegal whose movements were unrestricted. If everything went according to schedule, the FBI hoped that at the very least an illegal would be uncovered, and at best an illegal of the calibre of Rudolph Abel or Kaarlo Tuomi might be turned. If, on the other hand, the Soviets proved reluctant to risk an illegal, there was always the chance that they might entrust Sigler with an alternative prize, perhaps a sophisticated transmitter of the kind that was difficult to intercept. Another attractive possibility was that he might be assigned tasks that had a bearing on illegals. For example, James Mitkenbaugh, the ex-army sergeant arrested in 1964, had revealed under interrogation that as well as reporting on missile sites in the Midwest, he had been despatched to Canada to apply for birth certificates in the names of people known to have died. The intention, clearly, had been to acquire documentation for use by illegals, and this was another task that might be given to Sigler if he was accepted by the KGB. Whatever the outcome, the potential downside was judged to be minimal, for even if the dangle was ultimately rejected, the CIA would benefit from information Sigler could give about the *rezidentura* personalities he encountered, which would be added to the CIA's collection of its opponents' biographical data.

Exactly how much of this background was imparted to Sigler is unknown, but at the end of 1966 he agreed to an

FBI proposal that he travel to Mexico City and pose as a disenchanted soldier willing to sell military secrets to the KGB. He was briefed to stick as closely to the truth as possible, particularly when answering the KGB's anticipated probing questions about his experience and background. Codenamed GRAPHIC IMAGE by the US army, Sigler presented himself at the Soviet Embassy as an authentic walk-in and was interviewed by a diplomat who was later identified by the CIA as a confirmed GRU officer. At the end of the meeting Sigler was smuggled out of the Embassy compound in the back of a car and driven to a safe-house for further discussions, during which he complained that after twenty years in the US army he had been passed over for promotion and was short of money. The embittered Sergeant's purported motivation must have struck exactly the right note with his KGB recruiter, for Sigler was promised plenty of cash if he returned a month later with items from a very broad list of requirements concerning electronic equipment and missile-guidance systems.

Over the next decade Sigler was to be paid a total of some $400,000 at regular monthly meetings, in return for what was presented as classified information. In reality, much of the material had been carefully selected for the KGB's consumption by the FBI, working in conjunction with US army intelligence. For the first two years Sigler made monthly visits to Mexico City to deliver secrets and be paid, and he was ordered to buy a shortwave radio and receive instructions by Morse. Whilst this was not quite the same as communicating via an illegal, it did give the FBI an opportunity to study the latest KGB one-time pad and to confirm that the clandestine signals which contained his messages were transmitted from a station located in Cuba. This latter discovery had a chilling effect on the FBI and the NSA, which had monitored the transmitter's prodigious output. If even part of the traffic was authentic, and not streams of dummy texts, the sheer volume suggested that the KGB was in contact with dozens of other spies like Sigler.

In late 1968, Sigler was posted by the army to Nuremberg and, as instructed, he maintained contact with the KGB at meetings in Switzerland. When the two-year tour ended, he went back to El Paso, Texas, and resumed the monthly meetings in Mexico, but again no illegal was introduced into the operation by the Soviets. In July 1972, Sigler was posted overseas for the second time, to a remote army outpost in Korea, where, because of the lack of a KGB *rezidentura* in Seoul, it was hoped that he would be contacted by an illegal, but no meeting took place. Instead, he was instructed to attend a rendezvous in Tokyo early in November 1972. There he was given an address in Austria and directions on how to mail an innocuous postcard to Vienna as a sign that he would be in Chapultepec Park in Mexico City on a particular date. Sigler complied when he returned to Texas in September 1973, and also travelled to Vienna in July the following year for a special meeting which was held in a safe-house over the border in Czechoslovakia. At no time did the KGB express any dissatisfaction with his performance, but nor was there any mention of an illegal. Instead, Sigler was given forged Canadian identity cards for his wife and daughter, apparently for use in an emergency. To improve his radio technique, he attended a course in Morse at the White Sands missile range, but as the NSA was monitoring his traffic, and as the FBI was giving him accurate decrypts of every transmission, his communications with the KGB continued uninterrupted.

Sigler's temporary assignment to White Sands unexpectedly prompted his Soviet controllers to issue new instructions. Henceforth he was to use two dead-drops, located near the missile range. The chosen sites had been prepared beside an oil pipeline and under a child's tomb in a local cemetery. The FBI hoped that these drops would be serviced by a hitherto unidentified illegal and consequently both were covered by discreet surveillance. When the KGB's nominee eventually turned up to empty the drop and leave some money for Sigler, the contact was followed. He was subsequently identified as Rudolf Hermann, a photographer from Hartsdale, New York, who, according to immigration records, had entered the United States as a naturalised Canadian citizen early in 1968, accompanied by his wife Inga and his son Peter. Research in Canada revealed that Hermann and his wife had arrived in Montreal from Frankfurt in February 1962 and had lived in Toronto, where they had run a small delicatessen. Their second son Michael had been born in December 1963 and soon afterwards Hermann had given up the delicatessen and found a job as a cameraman for the Canadian Broadcasting Corporation, before opening his own film production business. Together with his wife and elder son he had become a Canadian citizen in February 1967, declaring himself in his naturalisation documents to be of Sudeten German origin, born in April 1925. Having traced Hermann's antecedents, and having noted how they correlated with a now well-established pattern of illegals, the FBI was satisfied that it had found a live and active illegal and, accordingly, placed him under intensive, but unobtrusive, surveillance.

Early in May 1977, nearly two years after the FBI had first identified Hermann as an illegal, he was confronted by the FBI and offered the usual choice: full co-operation with protection, or arrest and a federal prosecution. Already somewhat disillusioned with his work, Hermann opted for the former choice and identified himself as Colonel Ludek Zemenek, until recently the KGB's illegal *rezident* in the US. The real Rudolf Hermann had died in a Soviet labour camp in 1943, and Zemenek had adopted his identity in 1956 at the conclusion of his training as an illegal. His wife, Inga Juergen, was from a family of East German Communists and had become Ingalore Moerke, a German who had been killed as a teenager in an air-raid on Stettin in 1944. After Peter was born in October 1957, the family had been installed in Stuttgart in the Federal Republic and then in Heilbronn, where Zemenek had opened a camera shop, to build up his credentials in anticipation of moving to Canada. It was a classic illegal 'legend' but what was of critical importance to the FBI was Zemenek's meal-ticket. He had been recalled to Moscow in 1965 to be appointed *rezident* and, on his return, had indoctrinated his son Peter, who was to study architecture at McGill University and who had also become a KGB illegal.[7] As well as his son, he was also able to identify for his FBI debriefers a long-term KGB agent in Canada, whom he named as

Professor Hugh Hambleton of Laval University in Quebec, and to give a full account of the various tasks he had been assigned by the KGB.

Among Zemenek's duties had been to locate the home in Arlington, Virginia, of Yuri Nosenko, the KGB defector, and make contact with a former Soviet naval officer, Captain Nikolai F. Artamonov. Zemenek had been unable to find Nosenko in 1969, but four years later he had traced Artamonov, who called himself Nicholas Shadrin and worked for the Defence Intelligence Agency (DIA). Artamonov had defected to Sweden in 1959 and had been resettled with his Polish girlfriend, whom he married, in McLean, Virginia. Although Zemenek was not to know it, Artamonov had been recruited as a double agent by the FBI. The CIA had been keen to cultivate an FCD officer named Igor R. Kozlov, codenamed KITTY HAWK, who had been assigned the task of finding the defector Artamonov. However, Kozlov had already approached the CIA and offered his services as a spy. Although Kozlov had been considered a good catch, his status within the KGB, and thereby his value as a CIA mole, would be greatly enhanced if he succeeded in tracing and recruiting the naval officer as an agent, particularly as Artamonov now worked as a DIA analyst. The CIA and FBI were anxious to help Kozlov, and although Artamonov had not been indoctrinated into every aspect of the scheme, he had agreed to play along with Kozlov and report his every move. Thus, with the CIA's assistance, KITTY HAWK had accomplished Artamonov's 'recruitment' and had later handed him on to another legal, Aleksandr Solokov, and then to Oleg A. Kozlov. This had enabled the FBI to identify Solokov and Oleg Kozlov as KGB officers, and had the further merit of boosting KITTY HAWK's career.

As a KGB officer Oleg Kozlov was regarded by the CIA as a particularly effective professional, specialising in the coercion of émigrés through threats to their families left at home in Eastern Europe. Artamonov, who had abandoned his first wife and son in Kaliningrad, had informed the FBI of Igor Kozlov's pitch, and had been urged to co-operate in a bid to gain him a promotion and maybe compromise Solokov or his namesake successor, Oleg. However, the second Kozlov had been too shrewd to maintain the direct contact and had handed the naval officer to a hitherto unknown illegal. Indeed, Artamonov had told the FBI about a single call from a woman, an apparently innocuous telephone call in the form of an unsolicited invitation to have his portrait taken at a photographic studio. In reality, the coded conversation had alerted Artamonov to an imminent meeting with Kozlov, and on this evidence the FBI had become aware of the existence of at least one previously undetected Soviet illegal operating in the US during 1963. According to Zemenek, his wife had been the woman who had made the call to Artamonov, and this confirmation had served to verify one of the few parts of Zemenek's story that could be checked and verified. It showed that Zemenek was an important illegal and also demonstrated that the FBI deception centred on Artamonov had fooled the KGB.[8]

Once Zemenek's credentials had been accepted by the FBI, he was run as a double agent for more than two years. The RCMP Security Service was also invited to meet him at a lakeside safe-house in Maryland and, in May 1978, three RCMP officers flew to Baltimore for a dramatic encounter. The RCMP counter-intelligence experts were persuaded, during a three-hour videotaped meeting, of the identity of Zemenek's main source in Canada. As a result of Zemenek's compelling statement, his principal meal-ticket, Professor Hugh G. Hambleton, was placed under covert surveillance, which was to last eighteen months. Whenever Hambleton travelled abroad, as he did soon afterwards, the RCMP followed, assisted by the local security agency. Much later, on 4 November 1979, two months after Zemenek's switch in loyalty had been disclosed publicly and he and his family had been resettled, a raid was mounted on the home of the much-respected academic who was an expert on Latin America.[9]

The son of a wealthy and politically prominent Ottawa family, and known to his friends as Hugo, Hambleton had been an active agent for the KGB over the past decade, having been recruited originally in Ottawa in 1949 by Vladimir Borodin, the suave young Cultural Attaché who was one of the legal *rezidentura* which had handled RCMP's ill-fated double agent codenamed GIDEON. An intelligence liaison officer with the Free French forces in North Africa at the end of the war, Hambleton had made only limited admissions concerning his espionage to the RCMP in 1979, but early in 1980, after thirteen sessions with RCMP interrogators, he agreed to co-operate and make a full confession in return for a formal immunity from prosecution signed by the Canadian Solicitor-General. His later statement to British detectives, which was to run to 264 pages, centred on his work in NATO as an economist, a post he had been appointed to in 1955 after he had graduated from the Sorbonne. However, Hambleton admitted that his first act of espionage had been the theft of a secret paper on the subject of submarine detection systems from his father-in-law, a senior French-Canadian civil servant named Beaulieu, who, at the time of Hambleton's marriage to his daughter Therese in 1948, had held an important post at the Department of Defence. Hambleton explained that he had first met Borodin at one of the regular social gatherings organised by his Marxist-leaning mother, Bessie Hambleton, a well-known Ottawa hostess who often entertained middle-ranking European and Eastern Bloc diplomats at her sumptuous home on Ruskin Avenue. Borodin had become the student's case officer, and had encouraged him to leave his job at the National Film Board of Canada and take up an academic career, which had started after his release from military service at Ottawa University and was to continue through studies in Mexico City and the Sorbonne. Four years later in Paris, towards the conclusion of his course, Hambleton recalled that he had unexpectedly encountered Borodin, who had turned up in March 1955 at his home in the suburbs, accompanied by a colleague, Pavel P. Lukyanov, who was actually a senior FCD officer based at the Paris *rezidentura* and working under a trade delegation cover. Having graduated from the Sorbonne, Hambleton had intended to use a scholarship he had won to gain his PhD at the London School of Economics, but Borodin and Lukyanov persuaded him to delay his departure to London and to seek a job with NATO instead. In November 1956, his application was successful and, during the five years he spent with NATO's International Secretariat in Paris, Hambleton confirmed that he had given hundreds of photographs of classified documents to Lukyanov and estimated that between 1957 and 1958 he had taken 750 pictures of secret papers, an average that he had continued to maintain. Hambleton was later to concede that one of the papers he had removed in late 1958 had contained references to Western intelligence sources in Estonia and Lithuania, and may have endangered the lives of agents.

Significantly, Lukyanov had not merely instructed his agent to copy everything he could, but had directed Hambleton to specific dossiers, to the extent of giving him lists of particular files, each with its correct NATO registry number. There was no doubt that Hambleton was not the only Soviet asset to have penetrated NATO's headquarters, as was later to become clear when Anatoli Golitsyn disclosed enough information to the CIA for the French DST to identify and arrest Georges Paques, the deputy head of NATO's press department. He was eventually caught in August 1963 as he handed over a bundle of secret documents to a KGB legal, Vassilli Vlassov, and was subsequently sentenced to twenty years' imprisonment. According to Golitsyn, much of the NATO information that had reached Moscow had been channelled through General Ivan Agayants, who had operated in Paris under the name of Ivan I. Avalov. What Golitsyn had not realised was that the KGB had been running more than one source in the heart of NATO.

Hambleton was by now an experienced spy, receiving coded signals every week at eight on Thursday evenings on a shortwave radio and using one-time pads to decipher the texts, but he was anxious to return to academic life. In 1961, after a rendezvous with the KGB in Vienna, Hambleton had resigned from NATO and had moved to England, with his second wife, to study for his doctorate at the London School of Economics. Nevertheless, the KGB remained in touch and Borodin, who was later attached to the Soviet Embassy in The Hague, visited Hambleton at the academic's holiday villa in Spain. Four years later, having obtained his PhD,

Hambleton accepted an appointment at Laval University in Quebec. It was not until April 1967 that Zemenek, acting for the KGB and declaring himself to be a movie producer, re-established contact with Hambleton and arranged for him to attend a meeting with two KGB officers in Ottawa who had given him details of dead-letter drops so that he could continue to communicate. Having indicated his willingness to work for the KGB, he was given an assignment, to meet Lukyanov in Vienna in preparation for a mission to Tel Aviv. The objective was a survey, conducted under the cover of historical research into the siege of Rhodes in 1480, of the economic prospects for Russian immigrants to Israel, with the underlying purpose of discovering how illegals could be infiltrated into the country and be established in business. Hambleton's ten-page report was handed to Lukyanov at a second rendezvous held in Vienna in July 1970, and the academic later recalled that he had also mentioned a side trip he had made to Beersheba, the town nearest the secret Israeli atomic weapons facility located at Dimona in the Negev Desert.

Upon his return to Quebec Hambleton, who had cultivated a reputation as an expert on the Caribbean and Latin America, based on his student days in Mexico and a visit to Cuba in 1961, obtained an invitation to take a year's leave from Laval and act as an adviser to the Canadian International Development Agency (CIDA). In this capacity he was seconded to Lima in 1972 as economic adviser to General Velasco Alvarado, the Left-leaning, anti-American leader of the military junta that had taken control of Peru. Hambleton returned briefly to Quebec in 1972, but in September the following year he was posted to Port-au-Prince on behalf of CIDA to supervise an agrarian reform project. This assignment lasted until 1975, following which he made an extensive tour of Europe, accompanied not by his second wife, but by his newly acquired twenty-two-year-old Haitian girlfriend.

At the end of his appointment in Haiti Hambleton returned to Paris and, missing a prearranged rendezvous with Lukyanov in Vienna, flew to Tel Aviv in July and spent three weeks undertaking academic research at the Hebrew University in

Jerusalem. Since he had last visited Israel more than 160,000 Soviet Jews had settled as immigrants, among whom the KGB had concealed an unknown number of illegals. While the Israeli security agency, Shin Beth, routinely screened all the new arrivals and had uncovered several putative illegals who had intended to travel on to Canada and the United States, an undetermined group had almost certainly slipped through undiscovered. One of Hambleton's tasks in Israel had been to discover a more effective method of protecting illegals from the ubiquitous Shin Beth, but as he believed that he himself had come under its scrutiny, he had not undertaken any clandestine activities. Early in August, he flew to Athens and then caught a train to Vienna, stopping to stay overnight in Belgrade with Lili Galeva, a young Yugoslav girlfriend with whom he had shared a compartment. During this short interlude Hambleton had been unnerved by an interview with officers from KOS, the Yugoslav security agency, who indicated that they knew of his KGB connections. He reported this to Lukyanov the following day when they met in Vienna, and arrangements were made for Hambleton to be driven to Bratislava in a Soviet diplomat's car, whence he caught a military flight to Moscow. For the next six days Hambleton was fêted by the KGB and introduced to its Chairman, Yuri Andropov. He was also trained in the use of a new communications device, an ingenious gadget that when placed next to his Grundig radio would convert shortwave signals and display them as numbers on an illuminated panel. A few months after Hambleton's return to Quebec, he was sent a letter in secret writing from Berlin which instructed him to collect one of these conversion units from an unidentified intermediary, who met him in the underground garage of a shopping centre in Montreal.

As we have seen, Hambleton had come under surveillance by the RCMP immediately after Zemenek had denounced him in May 1978, and later in the summer he was investigated by the British Security Service when he had taken a leave of absence from Laval and had moved to London, where he had borrowed a friend's flat in the Barbican estate. On most days he had visited the British Museum, where he had worked on an analysis of the oil industry in the Persian Gulf, and in October he had travelled to Vienna for a meeting with Luky-anov, at which the Soviet had warned him that Zemenek, whom Hambleton had known as the movie producer 'Rudolf Hermann', could no longer be regarded as reliable, and that Hambleton should consider urgent defection. Hambleton had rejected the offer and instead had spent the rest of his sabbatical criss-crossing the Continent, visiting his girlfriend in Belgrade. When the university term started in September 1979, Hambleton was back at Laval, teaching his students and occasionally emptying dead-drops, apparently unaware that he was under the continuous gaze of the RCMP. At one point, after his return from London, Hambleton was observed to insert surreptitiously a note into a book on a shelf in a bookshop on Elgin Street, which had been retrieved moments later by a Soviet diplomat.

When Hambleton accepted his immunity from the Canadian authorities, he was warned that he should not contemplate travel to Britain or to the United States, where he would certainly face arrest, but in June 1982, aged sixty, he flew to London with his son and was taken into custody by Special Branch detectives. Charged with offences under the Official Secrets Act, Hambleton initially pleaded not guilty, but under cross-examination his case collapsed. He admitted to having fabricated the reference to his war record in *Who's Who in Canada*, in which he had claimed falsely to have worked behind enemy lines with the French resistance in 1943. Half-way through his trial, and confronted by his own contradic-tions, Hambleton changed his plea to guilty and was sentenced to ten years' imprisonment.

Hambleton's arrest brought Zemenek's usefulness to a close, but also served to contaminate Ralph Sigler, who had not been so lucky. He had fallen under the FBI's suspicion as having deliberately compromised himself with the Soviets, and perhaps as having held meetings with the KGB in San Francisco that he had not disclosed to his American handlers. Whatever his motives, or the relationship with the KGB, he was found electrocuted in a motel bedroom near Fort Meade, Maryland, in April 1976, apparently having committed suicide. To the embarrassment of his army and FBI handlers, Sigler's death had occurred between a series of interrogations to which he had submitted, having failed a routine polygraph examination. He had first taken the tests in December 1966, as a standard precaution, and they had been conducted again in August 1971, just before his departure to Korea. However, when he underwent the tests in April his performance had indicated deception. The questions put to Sigler had been designed to determine whether he had sold out to the KGB and had betrayed his role as a double agent, but the issue was to remain unresolved, exacerbating the already strained relations between the FBI and the army over the way Sigler had been handled. Instead, the GRAPHIC IMAGE file was closed, consigned to the archives as the longest-running double-agent case ever mounted against the Soviets and the single most successful operation ever conducted against Soviet illegals, resulting in the turning of Ludek Zemenek and the identification of Hugh Hambleton, a high-level, long-term Soviet asset.

Despite what GRAPHIC IMAGE accomplished, the inter-agency recriminations continued. If Sigler had switched sides, had the change been a gradual metamorphosis or a sudden decision? What had prompted his decision? One possibility considered by the counter-intelligence analysts who conducted the internal inquest was the possibility that Sigler had been affected rather more than he had pretended by the news that his mother in Czechoslovakia had received visits and money from the KGB. Sigler's original selection by the FBI had been influenced by the fact that some of his family had remained in the Soviet Bloc, as ostensibly this had made him a more credible candidate for recruitment by the KGB. However, Sigler had been estranged from his mother from the time his father, an economic migrant, had returned home to his unfaithful wife to bring his son and daughter to a new life in a Pennsylvania mining community. Thereafter, Ralph had rejected his mother, but his sister Anne had received guarded notes from her, confirming that she had met various Russians, unmistakably KGB personnel, who had given her financial assistance. The FBI had counted on his family connections behind the Iron Curtain as just another component in the overall dangle, but had there been a miscalculation?

The West's determination to root out illegals was not without its casualties. Sigler's suicide was an embarrassingly high price to pay for Zemenek and Hambleton, but it was not the only example of a double-agent operation being carried too far in the hope of entrapping an illegal. Nikolai Artamonov, the defector who had been found in Arlington by Zemenek, was also to be a victim of the same operation. The naval officer had originally been run as a double agent in an attempt to build up the reputation of Igor Kozlov (KITTY HAWK), the ambitious middle-ranking KGB officer who, in June 1966, had been tasked to lure Artamonov back into the fold. Kozlov's offer from the KGB had been rehabilitation and reconciliation with his wife Elena and their son, in return for American secrets from the Defence Intelligence Agency. Both the FBI and CIA had supported the scheme, but it had not achieved its original objective. Apart from a couple of 'brush contacts' with CIA personnel in Moscow, at which nothing of any significance had been achieved, KITTY HAWK had dropped from sight, leaving Artamonov as a conduit for classified material to his Soviet handlers in Washington. Gradually it began to look from the FBI's perspective that the KGB had turned the tables. The CIA's star source had proved unforthcoming, but Artamonov, who had been persuaded to become a double agent under American control, was still haemorrhaging secrets.

As the need to support KITTY HAWK had receded, the FBI's main motivation had been concern about Artamonov's first wife and their son. Only by pretending to collaborate could Artamonov be sure of their safety. The fact that he had been contacted by Mrs Zemenek, the wife of the KGB's illegal *rezident*, had breathed new life into the case, as had the promise of a special communications device, a satellite transmitter. This equipment, codenamed SERENA, was highly prized by the FBI as its signals were virtually impossible to detect and therefore made it ideal for use by illegals. To send a message to Moscow an agent simply recorded a message on to a tape which was replayed at high speed in a 'burst' transmission synchronised to the time a Soviet satellite was scheduled to pass overhead. The directional transmission lasted only a few seconds and was virtually undetectable, even by monitors located nearby, because the equipment gave off almost no lateral radiation. When Artamonov started to receive components of the burst transmitter at clandestine drop sites, the FBI had taken a new interest in his case as his potential had increased. As he was within easy reach of legals operating from Washington DC, the suspicion was that the former Red Banner naval officer had been selected as an intermediary and, once the device had been assembled, he would receive instructions on how to pass it on to an illegal. After years of minimal progress, Artamonov was summoned to a rendezvous in Austria with Igor Kozlov in December 1975. The FBI anticipated a breakthrough, with Artamonov perhaps being entrusted with a new role and maybe the identity of an illegal, but although he returned safely to his hotel from his first meeting, held over dinner at a restaurant outside Vienna, Artamonov was not seen again after he met his Soviet contacts for a second time the following day. Both the FBI and the CIA were baffled by his disappearance, at least until August 1985 when Vitali S. Yurchenko defected and described his recollection of the episode. According to the KGB's counter-intelligence expert, Artamonov had been drugged prior to an interrogation and had accidentally suffocated in the back of the car taking him to a safe-house. As for Artamonov's burst transmitter, recovered from the attic of his home in Arlington, it was considered by the FBI to be an inferior, obsolete model.

The loss of KITTY HAWK and the failure to identify a single illegal through Artamonov led to more inter-agency recriminations, of the kind that had emerged after Ralph Sigler's suicide. Whatever the motivation of the two pawns, their handlers and families had paid a terrible price for the FBI's obsession with Soviet illegals.

10 · The End of the Cold War

The absolute cream of the illegals are run personally by the chief of the GRU through his own illegals section. He can use his illegals for the checking of everything and everybody, including illegals under the command of the first deputy.

Vladimir Rezun in *Soviet Military Intelligence*[1]

The paradox at the heart of the West's understanding of illegals is that, despite information from various defectors over a long period, and the capture of the occasional illegal, the security and counter-intelligence authorities responsible for combating the menace knew relatively little about either the modern GRU or the KGB. Tom Polgar, who spent most of his thirty-five-year career in the CIA studying his Soviet opponents, and worked at the coalface in Moscow, remarked that 'our knowledge about the KGB is limited in both substance and specifics'.[2] Harry Rositske, from the Soviet Russia Division, concurs and describes the challenge:

The materials on Moscow were slim in 1946. There was a series of translations into English of German counterintelligence studies based on wartime interrogations of captured Soviet intelligence personnel, as well as a brief analysis of headquarters structure by the British service and a few outdated accounts of prewar Soviet defectors. Out of these sparse items we composed a slim outline that was sent to our field stations. The internal structure of any secret bureaucracy can best be determined from men who have worked inside it. Stalin's death in 1953 and the purge of 'Beria's gang' by his successors sparked several defections from the KGB that enormously enhanced our picture of the inside workings of Soviet intelligence headquarters. Two officers defected in Tokyo, one in Vienna. Several Soviet agents in our employ during the mid-fifties had spent one or more tours at headquarters. Later defectors who had worked in Moscow filled in and updated our knowledge of the organizational components, supplied the names and job titles of department and section heads, traced the shifting of functions, noted policy changes and reported on squabbles among the intelligence services . . . What we now know [in 1982] is infinitely greater than what we knew twenty years ago, but the Moscow picture can never be kept up-to-date without a steady flow of fresh defectors – or an occasional mole in the upper reaches of Soviet intelligence.[3]

In particular, the West lacked a source that could lay bare the secrets of Directorate S, the branch of the First Chief Directorate where the Line N officers dropped out of circulation and no longer mixed with their colleagues from other Directorates. Furthermore, they were even more highly motivated, and less likely to defect, than their FCD colleagues. While several FCD professionals had defected in the post-war era, few had been able to talk authoritatively about the mysteries of Directorate S. Virtually nothing was known about this inner sanctum, not least because its personnel had been selected for their ideological commitment. This had been demonstrated in the case of an illegal living in a flat near Montagu Square in London, who was identified after a tip from an illegal support agent. The CIA in Tokyo had traced the husband-and-wife team, and their apartment had been wired for sound. Their discipline had been so strong that neither was ever recorded speaking Russian at home. Equipped with papers in the name of Donald Arthur Rollins, his photograph had been compared with that of another suspected illegal who had been spotted years earlier in Canada. Both pictures showed the same man, so with permission from Sir Martin Furnival Jones, then the Director-General of the Security Service, the illegal had been visited at his rented apartment soon after midnight and confronted by Alec McDonald from MI5 and an officer from the local CIA station.

Still shocked by his exposure, Rollins had agreed to consider defection and, convinced they had scored a considerable coup, the CIA team withdrew, leaving the flat under MI5's surveillance. However, to the dismay of the watchers, the illegal took a taxi to Heathrow airport early the next morning and caught a plane to Nairobi, where he disappeared. Forty-eight hours later, the illegal's wife vanished from her apartment in Japan. The episode had served not only to highlight the sensitivity with which illegals should be handled but also, more significantly, to prove the effectiveness of Directorate S security. Despite the offer of resettlement in the West, the illegal had chosen flight.

In another unrelated case, in October 1970, the Argentine SIDE arrested an illegal named Vladimir I. Martynov, the owner of a bar in a suburb of Buenos Aires called *Zur Glocke* ('At The Bell') which was popular with expatriate Germans. Martynov had adopted the identity of a German who had returned home as a child with his immigrant parents, and had obtained a valid passport from the Argentine Embassy in a third country under the name Jose Fernandez. Having settled in Argentina Martynov, who had really been born in the Ukraine, had worked initially as a mechanic and later did his required military service in the army. In 1963, he had returned to Europe and then come back to Argentina with his wife, Raisa Vasilyevna. When Martynov resisted SIDE's interrogation, he was handed over to the CIA, together with his wife and child. They were flown to Washington DC in 1971 and installed in a safe-house at Springfield, Virginia, but he still refused the blandishments presented to him. Eventually, his wife walked out of the safe-house and made her way to the Soviet Embassy, and her husband was released, without publicity, into the custody of a Soviet diplomat in February 1972. He returned to Moscow under escort soon afterwards.[4]

The policy of compartmentalisation, the security precautions that prevailed within the entire organisation, was enforced far more rigidly within Directorate S than anywhere else, which meant that the occasional defector from the FCD had little to offer his Western debriefers on the subject of

Line N operations. Indeed, the single officer who, because of his seniority and family connections, did possess some relevant data was actually disbelieved. Yuri Nosenko had first approached the CIA in Geneva in June 1962, when he had volunteered to spy, and had reappeared sixteen months later in February 1964 demanding to be received as a defector. He was promptly flown to the United States and interviewed at a safe-house, where the CIA's questions became increasingly hostile. The explanation for Nosenko's treatment, which was to include incarceration in a specially constructed cell block for three-and-a-half years, was the belief that he had been a 'despatched' agent, a plant deliberately foisted on his hosts with the intention of deceiving them. The wretched defector had been confined in a secret facility sited in a corner of the CIA's training area at Camp Peary, outside Williamsburg, Virginia, and had been questioned on 292 occasions, without any conclusive results. The Machiavellian interpretation of the wretched KGB officer's motives, that he had fabricated his tale to deceive the CIA, had been inspired partly by Nosenko's tendency to exaggerate his own importance and lie about incidents that the CIA could double-check, but mainly by Anatoli Golitsyn's certainty that his own momentous defection from Stockholm in December 1961 would be followed by others assigned to discredit him.

Whereas Golitsyn, who was held in high esteem within the CIA, had spent much of his life in the provinces and knew little about the political atmosphere in Moscow, especially in the higher echelons of the KGB, Nosenko's father had been minister of shipbuilding and his entire career had been in the hothouse environment of the Kremlin. He had served in both the First and Second Chief Directorates and was quite a sophisticate in comparison with Golitsyn. However, as Golitsyn had arrived first and had enabled the CIA's Counterintelligence Staff to initiate promising investigations of authentic Soviet spies around the world, he had beguiled his case officers into accepting his unique analysis of the Communist threat. In retrospect, many of Golitsyn's views were, to say the least, bordering on the eccentric if not the paranoid, and some of his theses now appear ridiculous. He never accepted the Sino-Soviet split and was convinced that Tito's break with Moscow was an elaborate disinformation exercise designed to deceive the West. While Golitsyn gave solid leads to the identities of KGB agents in Britain and France, Nosenko's credibility was constantly undermined by his claims to have enjoyed access to highly sensitive cases, like the dossier of Lee Harvey Oswald, which was of consummate interest to the CIA, but closer examination of his statements invariably revealed flaws. Two hundred and ninety-two days of interrogation failed to determine to the satisfaction of all whether Nosenko was, as Golitsyn insisted, a dangerous spy, or the innocent victim of the CIA's delusions. The controversy that raged over Nosenko's bona fides prevented some of his meal-ticket, which was relevant to illegals, from being taken seriously, so it was to be some years before the CIA could acquire a reliable source on this most perplexing subject.

The irony was that although the CIA remained unconvinced by Nosenko, the FCD was plunged into chaotic recriminations by his defection and nine senior officers were disciplined for breaches of security. When subsequent defectors confirmed the impact of Nosenko's defection on the KGB, they were disbelieved and their assertions served only to undermine their own credibility and standing in the eyes of their sceptical debriefers. Even when the illegal, Ludek Zemenek, admitted to having been tasked to establish Nosenko's current whereabouts in Arlington, Virginia, there were still some hardened counter-intelligence experts who insisted that Nosenko had been a despatched defector.

In the meantime, far from reducing its investment in illegals, the KGB was to make an even greater commitment to Directorate S, considerably enlarging the Directorate's Second Department dedicated to the acquisition of false identities and documentation. The reason was to be the dramatic expulsion from London of more than a hundred Soviet intelligence personnel in September 1971. Whereas in the 1930s the OGPU had leaned too heavily on local Communist Parties for recruits, and on several occasions had compromised Soviet diplomats, the subsequent shift to a greater reliance upon illegals had at least enjoyed the merit of isolating the diplomatic missions from direct complicity in espionage. However, in the 1950s and 1960s, with the growth of the influence of the FCD and the expansion of Soviet representation around the globe, the balance returned once again, not to local Communist Parties, but rather to the legal *rezidenturas* which could operate with very little risk. Whilst the escalation of KGB and GRU activity was easy enough to monitor through routine surveillance on selected target diplomats, the development of Line N was virtually impossible to gauge. Furthermore, towards the end of the 1960s, there was a genuine fear in the West that Soviet espionage was reaching epidemic proportions, with whole embassies and consulates dedicated not to diplomacy but to intelligence-gathering. The size of the Soviet presence in London, in particular, was a cause for concern. It was by far the largest Soviet establishment outside the United States, and the Security Service had neither the budget, the technical resources nor the personnel to keep tabs on its activities. Indeed, the scale of Soviet activity in London was so great, and so obvious, that it seemed likely that the Security Service itself had suffered hostile penetration. Quite apart from the various molehunts that were conducted in the vain hope of identifying a Soviet spy, there was clear evidence of intense Soviet interest in MI5. This was manifested by RAFTER's proof that the KGB intercepted MI5's radio traffic, and the discovery in May 1968 of Yuri A. Dushkin and Vladimir A. Loginov, two Soviet intelligence officers based at the Trade Delegation, keeping a watch outside MI5's garage in Battersea. The solution to the problem of the disproportionate Soviet presence in London of 550, which far outweighed the strength of the British Embassy in Moscow, was the expulsion of the entire KGB and GRU *rezidenturas*.

Positive identification of the membership of both had been made possible by the creation of a highly secret forum within the West's counter-intelligence community known as CAZAB, a name which included the first letters of the participating countries, Canada, Australia, New Zealand, America and Britain.[5] Mutual indoctrination through CAZAB allowed the British to construct an exceptionally accurate order-of-battle of its opponents in the capital. As well as drawing on routine observation and analysis of wireless schedules, the Security Service had collated all the data that had been generated by the joint Movements Analysis project, which had documented the comings and goings of suspected Soviet intelligence personnel across the world as they moved from one post to another. It was not surprising to find a man who had served as a chauffeur in Ottawa turning up as a cultural attaché in Nicosia, and then as third secretary in Singapore. By pooling information MI5 was to capitalise from the identifications made by the CIA sources Oleg Penkovsky and Dmitri Polyakov of their colleagues from inside the GRU, and by Golitsyn, Nosenko and Colonel Evgenny Runge, who defected in Berlin in October 1967. In addition, MI5 had unexpectedly acquired a secret source inside the KGB's London *rezidentura* who could verify the accuracy of each identification.

Prior to the recruitment of Oleg A. Lyalin, MI5 had been obliged to rely upon external, mainly technical sources to distinguish between the genuine diplomats and the contingent of intelligence professionals led since 1967 by the *rezident*, Yuri N. Voronin. Although a relatively junior KGB officer nearing the end of his tour of duty, Lyalin represented the very first recruitment achieved in London, a rare coup accomplished by a joint MI5–SIS team which exploited Lyalin's affair with a Russian secretary, Irina Teplyakova. When offered resettlement and the opportunity to meet his mistress in safety, the thirty-four-year-old Lyalin consented to his recruitment, and this breakthrough effectively postponed the mass expulsions that had been agreed already in principle, albeit reluctantly, by the British Foreign Office. Indeed, the announcement of the expulsions was delayed so that Lyalin could be milked for everything he knew, until the end of August 1971, when he was arrested by the police on a routine drink-driving charge. This unanticipated and inconvenient development forced Lyalin's hand and he accepted MI5's protection for himself and his girlfriend. With Lyalin in custody, the expulsions could go ahead and it was left to the KGB to draw the clear implication that Lyalin had fingered every one

Chart 9 The KGB Reorganisation in 1973

FIRST CHIEF DIRECTORATE	SECOND CHIEF DIRECTORATE	THIRD CHIEF DIRECTORATE	FIFTH CHIEF DIRECTORATE
Foreign Intelligence	Counter-Intelligence	Cheka Joint Commission	Counter-Subversion
	Secret Political Section	Agents	
	Section for Extraordinary Matters	GRU Liaison	
	Records		

SECRETARIAT
PERSONNEL SECTION

Directorate S	Directorate T	Directorate K	Special Service I
Illegals (Line N)	Scientific and Technical (Line X)	Counter-Intelligence (Line KR)	Information Dissemination

DEPARTMENTS

FIRST	Illegal Operations	
SECOND	Documentation	Eastern Section
THIRD	Training	European Section
		Anglophone Section
FOURTH	USA, Canada, Latin America	Latin America
FIFTH	Western Europe	China, Japan
		Infiltration
SIXTH	China, Japan, S.E. Asia	Technical Support
SEVENTH	Arabia, India	
EIGHTH	Direct Action, War Planning	
NINTH	Security	
TENTH	Internal Security	

SEVENTH CHIEF DIRECTORATE	EIGHTH CHIEF DIRECTORATE	BORDER GUARDS	INTERNAL TROOPS	NINTH CHIEF DIRECTORATE
Surveillance	Investigations			Kremlin Security
	Prisons			Provincial Garrisons
	Economic			Registration
	Communications			Training
				Technical

Service A	Service R
Active Measures	Planning and Analysis

OPERATIONAL DEPARTMENTS	SUPPORT DEPARTMENTS
(Line PR)	11 Liaison with satellite services
1 North America	12 Officers under cover
2 Latin America	13 Communications
3 UK, Scandinavia, Australia, New Zealand	14 Documentation
4 West Germany, Austria	15 Records
5 Western Europe	16 Cipher targets
6 China, Vietnam, Korea	17 India
7 Japan, Philippines, Indonesia, Singapore	
8 Near and Middle East	
9 Anglophone Africa	
10 Francophone Africa	

of his colleagues, as well as three low-echelon KGB spies recruited in London. In truth, of course, the operation had been planned for more than seven months, and the fact that news of it had not leaked was a cause of tremendous satisfaction to the two British agencies.[6]

While MI5 congratulated itself on its skilful handling of Lyalin, the CIA also had good reason to join in the celebrations. Vladimir N. Sakharov, a Soviet diplomat co-opted by the KGB, and a source since his recruitment in Moscow in the early 1960s, had defected from the Embassy in Kuwait. In recent years he had served in the Yemen and Egypt, and had compromised several of the KGB and GRU *rezidenturas* in the Middle East. Although no career FCD officer, Sakharov was a member of Moscow's privileged *nomenklatura*, the gilded youth of Communism, and his disappearance in May 1971, three months before Lyalin's, had sent shock waves through the KGB. Lyalin's defection was especially embarrassing to the Soviets because he was a member, albeit a relatively junior one, of an FCD section known as Department V. This highly secret branch had been created in the aftermath of the defections of Nikolai Khokhlov and Bogdan Stashinsky, who had revealed the homicidal purpose of the Thirteenth Department of FCD. The disclosure of the existence of a unit dedicated to assassination within the KGB, confirmed by two of its members, was intensely awkward, so during the KGB's reorganisation in 1968/69 the Thirteenth Department had been abolished and its staff of around fifty officers transferred to Department V, a new section created with a broader role, encompassing sabotage, and placed within Directorate S under the personal authority of the Chairman, Yuri Andropov. Its principal function was to plan disruption in target countries so that in the event of hostilities a fifth column of agents could be mobilised by radio to strike at the heart of government and create chaos.

The West's knowledge of Department V was to be enhanced by a Canadian-born Czech, Anton Sabotka, who had been placed under surveillance by the RCMP several years earlier.[7] Sabotka had returned to Czechoslovakia with his immigrant parents in 1946, aged sixteen, and had subsequently been talent-spotted by the KGB. After lengthy training, he had been sent on an assignment with his wife and child to Canada in 1961 and had remained dormant for four years. He had come equipped with a one-time pad concealed in a toy truck belonging to his son, but he had so enjoyed life in Edmonton that he had failed to respond to any of his signals, until contacted by a Soviet diplomat, Oleg N. Khomenko. Thereafter, the KGB's Thirteenth Department, represented first by Khomenko, then by Viktor M. Myaznikov, and finally by Anatoli P. Shalnev, instructed him to undertake minor missions, but in 1972 the RCMP Security Service had appeared on the scene and had persuaded Sabotka to confess. Under interrogation by the RCMP's Sonny Saunders, Sabotka, who had been abandoned by Department V, identified his contacts from RCMP photographs and recognised Mikhail M. Antipov as the KGB officer who had supervised his training in Moscow. Antipov, who had already served one tour of duty in New York, was attached to the UN Soviet mission between July 1963 and September 1968. Compromised by Sabotka and Lyalin, Antipov was withdrawn from New York in February 1972. As for Sabotka, he was an authentic Canadian citizen and, in view of his cooperation and the absence of any evidence of espionage or sabotage, he and his family were resettled under a new identity.

Lyalin's own contingency plans for war seemed far-fetched, for he had been given responsibility, as the Department V representative in the London *rezidentura*, to draw up lists of leading figures for their assassination and to survey various sensitive military sites in England, including the early-warning radar installations at Fylingdales in North Yorkshire and nuclear bomber dispersal airfields, for sudden attack by Soviet *Spetsnaz* special forces. Lyalin's first-hand confirmation that the KGB still sponsored such activity was to cause acute political embarrassment in the Kremlin, and to prevent any further complications all Department V personnel were withdrawn from the field and Department V was abolished. Created in its place was the Eighth Department of Directorate S, which was henceforth restricted to a planning and training role, with the officers with operational experience dispersed between the Directorate's four geographical departments.

The expulsions announced in September 1971 hit the KGB hard. The *resident*, Yuri Voronin, happened to be at home in Moscow at the time, but as his name was on the list he, like nine others, was banned from ever returning to London. Indeed, MI5's coup was so complete that Leonid A. Rogov, a minor official attached to the Soviet Trade Delegation, was the only person left in London to fulfil the role of acting *resident*. The expulsions caught the KGB unprepared and led to a reassessment of the vulnerability of legal *rezidenturas*. Evidently, MI5 had acquired a far greater knowledge of the London *rezidentura* than Lyalin could ever have known, and the British Foreign Office's decree that the Soviet strength in London should not exceed the existing ceiling of 445 further curtailed the KGB. The scale of Lyalin's impact could be judged by the fact that the KGB subsequently went to extraordinary lengths to obtain a copy of MI5's debriefing report on the defector. In a counter-intelligence sting in Canada, codenamed OBSTACLE COURSE, in which a Security Service officer operated as a double agent, his Soviet contact offered him unlimited cash for the document. The immediate conclusion of the inquest conducted by the FCD was the need to enhance illegal operations as they were immune from interference with the legal *rezidenturas*.

The first sign of the new emphasis on illegals was the appointment in 1974 of Vadim V. Kirpichenko as head of Directorate S with instructions to step up illegal operations in China. Recently the *resident* in Cairo, Kirpichenko enjoyed an impressive reputation and had worked in Egypt once before, a decade earlier, when he had run the head of President Nasser's Mukhabarat, Sami Sharaf, as his key agent. His promotion was disclosed to the CIA in June 1975 by a KGB defector, Konstantin V. Nadirashvili, who switched sides in Vienna, and the news was confirmed by another source, a walk-in to the British in Copenhagen, Oleg A. Gordievsky. Apparently, Kirpichenko's swift promotion had been a consequence of his contradiction of the advice given to the Kremlin by the Soviet Ambassador in Cairo that relations with Anwar Sadat were entirely satisfactory. Within a week all the Soviets had been expelled and the *rezident* had been praised for having provided an accurate warning, albeit one that had been ignored.

Gordievsky's recruitment in Denmark in 1974 was to be a turning-point for Western understanding of illegals.[8] Not only had Gordievsky joined the KGB in 1963 as an illegal, like his elder brother, but his recruitment indicated to SIS, which had been dogged for years by worries of hostile penetration, that its fears had been groundless. Indeed, apart from the wealth of information provided by Gordievsky to the British SIS between 1974 and his eventual defection in August 1985, his continued security was itself eloquent proof that SIS had avoided the attention of moles in the way that it had suffered prior to 1963. Although originally recruited into Directorate S, Gordievsky had been advised by his brother to work in the mainstream political branch, 'Line PR' of the FCD and, having accomplished the transfer and been assigned to the Third Department, dealing with Scandinavia, he had been posted with the rank of third secretary in January 1966 to Copenhagen, where Leonid S. Zaitsev was *rezident*. Zaitsev, of course, was an experienced FCD officer, having served in London between 1953 and 1961, and upon his return to Moscow was to head the FCD's technical intelligence branch, Directorate T. Gordievsky had returned to Moscow at the end of February 1970 and then went back in October 1972 as second secretary. By the time of his departure in July 1978, he had been promoted to press attaché and, as well as having become a regular source for the British, had received good assessment reports of his personal performance from the *rezident*, Alfred F. Mogilevtchek. Although Gordievsky had experienced some problems with his marriage, he claimed to be that most elusive of creatures, a genuine political convert. For SIS, his motivation was largely academic, his worth being rooted in his ease of access to the KGB's current secrets. In a highly classified circular signed by Vladimir A. Kryuchkov, sent to legal *rezidents* dated 6 April 1978 and copied by Gordievsky, the head of the FCD demanded greater co-operation with the illegals:

Side by side with the growing arsenal of counter-intelligence facilities the adversary is making use of mass propaganda on a vast scale to discredit both our intelligence service and also Soviet institutions and citizens abroad. Frequently Soviet intelligence officers are simply seized with a view to forcing them to collaborate with the adversary or be expelled from their country of residence. All this hinders in a very real way the activities of our 'legal' residencies. In the circumstances thus created, illegal espionage assumes great importance. Experience shows that success in illegal espionage depends to a great extent on the level of cooperation with 'legal' residencies, on a skilful combination of the 'legal' and illegal forms of work. Lately, in the light of instructions Nos 3994/N of 28 March 1975 and 7059/N of 17 June 1976, residencies have carried out some work to reinforce the position of illegal espionage in a number of target countries. Illegal espionage carried out in conjunction with 'legal' residencies has enabled us to carry out agent-operational measures resulting in the penetration of some intelligence targets and affording access to secret intelligence of interest to us, including some intelligence of a documentary character, it has provided the way to undertake some cases of 'false flag' recruitment, and it has enabled us successfully to implement combination operations to provide documentation for illegals, as well as for active measures purposes. Nevertheless the results achieved have no room for complacency, in a number of residencies Line N work has only been half-heartedly pursued on the part of the Residents, the deep study of those who could be utilised for illegal espionage, especially as special agents, has not been conducted sufficiently purposefully; work relating to the study of the legalisation problem is proceeding in an unsatisfactory manner, while favourable possibilities for the documentation of illegals are not being exploited. Serious attention must be paid to work to guarantee the security of Line N operations implemented by the residencies, bearing in mind that the adversary's special services, especially in NATO countries with their use of the very latest technical aides, have systematically mounted special search operations to expose illegal espionage on the part of socialist countries. This requires an increase in clandestinity, a raising of the level of responsibility among those connected with the work of Line N – in fact a general tightening of operational security. Of paramount importance is the organisation of work in preparing the ground for increasing illegal espionage in the USA and other NATO countries, the Chinese People's Republic, capitalist countries contiguous with the USSR and also in those countries where espionage from a 'legal' base is difficult or impossible.[9]

With access to material like this, Gordievsky represented the success that SIS had failed so conspicuously to achieve before. Although not of the rank of Dmitri Polyakov, who had been promoted to general when he was sent to Delhi as the GRU *rezident*, Gordievsky was an agent with direct and regular access to Third Department files and communications, the kind of information of specific relevance to Britain and British interests. When Gordievsky was posted to London in June 1982 with the rank of counsellor, there was every expectation that, as a Line PR political specialist, he would prove even more valuable than Lyalin. His performance to date had been exemplary, characterised by his identification of the head of the Norwegian Foreign Ministry's information section, Arne Treholt, as a key Soviet asset run by an FCD Third Department colleague, Gennadi F. Titov. Treholt had been a valuable, ideologically motivated spy and agent of influence for many years, and his arrest had been delayed until January 1984 so that a decent interval could elapse following Gordievsky's departure in order to protect him as the source of the tip. Titov, who had been the KGB's *rezident* in Oslo until his expulsion in 1972, and had arranged to meet his agent in Vienna on the day of his arrest, escaped unscathed, but Treholt's confession compromised Aleksandr Lopatin and Vladimir Zhizhin, the two case officers who had handled him in New York when Treholt had been posted to the United Nations. As well as exposing Treholt, Gordievsky had been responsible for the arrests of two Danes, Bent Weibel and Arne Petersen, and the expulsion of no fewer than seven Soviet diplomats – four KGB and three GRU – from Denmark and a further six from Norway.

As well as exploiting his individual tips, SIS was able to fit Gordievsky's product into the mosaic supplied by two other important defectors: Vladimir B. Rezun, a GRU officer who switched sides while under United Nations cover in Geneva in October 1979,[10] and Vladimir A. Kuzichkin, who walked out of the Soviet Embassy in Tehran for the last time in June 1982, after he had mislaid some classified documents and feared for the consequences. Of the two, Major Kuzichkin, who had been attached to the Soviet Consulate since 1977 and was conspicuously tall, proved the most valuable in terms of revealing the latest Soviet methodology about illegals because he was an authentic Line N illegal support officer with responsibility for handling illegals. Kuzichkin confirmed the change in emphasis in the KGB's policy from legals to illegals, and corroborated Gordievsky's estimate that the strength of Directorate S had doubled to around six hundred personnel, which was regarded as a direct consequence of the expulsions in London.[11] Inspired by the British lead, and the lack of retaliation measures, other countries had taken similar steps, thereby compounding the damage to the First Chief Directorate's operations.

The arrival of Kuzichkin was greeted as a tremendous breakthrough in the West, for he had been a career Directorate S officer and not a 'Viking', the Directorate's term for a KGB officer brought in from the FCD. His debriefing in London gave an unprecedented insight into Line N operations, for Kuzichkin could recall every part of the past decade in what had hitherto been the KGB's innermost sanctum. He had spent five years at Moscow University studying Iran, which had included two lengthy visits as a Farsi interpreter, first in the iron-ore centre of Bafq and then in Tehran. After graduating, he had attended an initial interview with Nikolai A. Korznikov of the KGB, whom Kuzichkin later learned was one of Directorate S's four deputy chiefs, and had undergone the usual two years of training, with a heavy emphasis on languages, at the FCD's Red Banner Institute near Yurlovo, to the north-west of Moscow, where he had been indoctrinated into the secrets of Directorate S by Colonel Pavel K. Revizorov, a retired officer who once had headed the Directorate's First Department, having apparently worked in the field in Canada and the United States. Kuzichkin's English had been perfected by Elena I. Akhmerova, who had taught the ill-fated Yuri Loginov, and he had completed his course at the FCD facility on Festival Street, close to the Moscow River metro station. Having been assigned to Directorate S, which occupied the sixth and seventh floors of the KGB's headquarters in Dzerzhinsky Square, Kuzichkin had joined Colonel Sheyin's Seventh

Department, responsible for Line N operations in Arabia and the Indian subcontinent, headed by Valentin M. Piskunov. After only a short period in the Seventh Department, Kuzichkin had been reassigned to the Eastern sub-section of Colonel Gromushkin's Second Department, headed by Colonel Ismail M. Aliev, in preparation for his first overseas assignment to Iran in June 1977. Following six months of intensive briefing, conducted in part by the Eighth Department of the FCD at Yasnevo, headed by General Polonik and the head of the Iranian desk, Colonel Anatoli M. Lezhnin, Kuzichkin was sent to Tehran under visa officer cover to relieve one of the Directorate S representatives, Sasha Yashchenko, who had completed four years in the Embassy *rezidentura*. The other Line N officer in Tehran was Colonel Sergei P. Kharlshkin, who had operated under cover of an administrator at the Soviet Red Cross hospital, but was fluent in Dutch, not Farsi. Upon his arrival, Kuzichkin had learned from Yashchenko that he only ran four local illegals, one of whom was about to be cut loose. Codenamed TIMUR, he was only a support agent who had been recruited because his brother had seemed a useful target, and now he was judged to be an expensive and unproductive liability. Yashchenko also told him that of the fifty Soviet diplomats at the Embassy, fifteen were KGB personnel and ten were GRU.

The temporary *resident* in Tehran, who had presided over the *referentura* on the fourth floor of the Embassy, was Colonel Lev P. Kostromin, who had recently arrived from his post as deputy head of the FCD's Eighth Department. He had taken over from Leonid Bogdanov earlier in 1977 following a series of operational setbacks, which had been the cause of some dismay in Moscow. In May, a local agent in the Ministry of Education named Rabbani had been arrested by SAVAK, causing the expulsion of Evgenny Venednikov, a Line PR officer. In a second incident soon afterwards, another Line PR officer, actually the TASS correspondent, Boris Checherin, had been compromised and declared *persona non grata*. Kostromin's appointment had been intended to strengthen the *rezidentura*, which had a disproportionate number of new arrivals, including replacements for the heads of the PR and KR Lines. Kostromin's deputy *rezident* was Gennadi Kazankin, a former Directorate S illegal candidate, who had been obliged to join the FCD's Eighth Department because of ill-health and was head of the Line PR in Tehran.

Kuzichkin was to stay in Iran for the next five years, which were to be a period of turmoil in the Middle East, and as his Line N colleague operated independently from his post at the hospital, Kuzichkin enjoyed greater access to Directorate S telegrams than otherwise might have been the case. Furthermore, as the civil war in the Lebanon escalated, Tehran acquired a greater importance in the political and intelligence arenas. Conditions in Beirut deteriorated to such a degree that the regional Line N *rezidentura* was moved to Tehran, bringing Vladimir Golovanov, the senior Directorate S officer who supervised all illegal operations in the area, to the Tehran *referentura*. Meanwhile, Kuzichkin's quota of local agents remained static and consisted of the Afghan Consul, code-named RAM, and KONRAD and EVI, a husband-and-wife team operating on Federal Republic of Germany documentation. In fact, KONRAD was a Latvian, named Karl Kruminsch, and his wife, whom he had pretended to meet and marry in Denmark, was really Katarina Nummerk, an East German. They had been staged through Finland and had intended to settle in Islamabad calling themselves Michel and Ursula Geschwinnt, but, having been rejected by both the Pakistani and Indian authorities, KONRAD had found a job with Pasavant Werke, a West German company in Tehran.

In March 1978, Kostromin had been replaced as *rezident* by Ivan A. Fadeikin, a former wartime partisan in Byelorussia who had headed the notorious Thirteenth Department until 1961, when he had transferred to the Tehran *rezidentura* to supervise the assassination of the Shah by means of a huge car bomb. Even though the plot had been unsuccessful, and the device had failed to detonate in February 1962 as the Shah drove past the vehicle, Fadeikin subsequently was sent as *rezident* to East Berlin and was tipped to become chief of the FCD in 1974. He lasted only fourteen months in Iran before he was replaced by Leonid V. Shebarshin, formerly the head of a section in the FCD's Seventeenth Department, in charge of Line PR work in India. Originally a regular diplomat, Shebarshin had been recruited by the *rezident* in Islamabad, Yakov P. Medyanik, while serving as second secretary in 1958. In 1988, Shebarshin was to be appointed head of the FCD.

Kuzichkin's apparently promising career in Directorate S unexpectedly came to a full stop in June 1982, following what had looked like an improvement in his prospects. In June 1980, Vladimir Golovanov had been arrested in the act of meeting a Swiss agent, codenamed SHAROV, who managed a local transport company. Golovanov had been withdrawn hastily via Damascus, leaving Kuzichkin the senior Line N officer in Tehran. His appointment as head of Line N was confirmed by Yuri I. Drozdov, the new head of Directorate S, and he continued to manage KONRAD, EVI and a new, productive Iranian illegal, VAGIF, who had been infiltrated into the country from Soviet Azerbaijan. However, in mid-1981 KONRAD's performance deteriorated, and Kuzichkin arranged a rendezvous with him in Moscow in June to find out the cause of the problems he had experienced in servicing his dead-letter drops. Kuzichkin flew home in the usual way, ostensibly on leave, but KONRAD neither showed up for the meeting nor left the routine signals in the prearranged sites in Western Europe to indicate that he too was en route for Moscow. Eventually, in September 1981, the Swiss Bundespolizei ended the mystery of KONRAD's fate by announcing his arrest and that of Katarina at Zurich airport on a charge of possession of false German passports. A month later the Swiss Department of Justice declared that the Soviet spies, aged forty and forty-one respectively, had entered Switzerland several times since 1978. Evidently, EVI had renewed her passport at the Federal Republic's Embassy in Tehran, where some discrepancy had been spotted. An alert had been issued by the BND and the result was the loss of Kuzichkin's two best illegals. This incident, followed by the theft in late May 1982 of an undeveloped film containing vitally secret documents in the *referentura*, sealed his fate and caused him to choose defection to the British in favour of confession and harsh punishment.

Although both Gordievsky and Kuzichkin confirmed KGB illegal operations as a new priority, they were not able of course to answer detailed questions relating to the identities or objectives of the individual illegals. Gordievsky, for example, described how he had been sent to the London suburb of Merton to look for a particular person standing at a certain time inside a shop window. He had no direct contact with the agent, who was an illegal, but this arrangement was intended to demonstrate that the agent was still at liberty. By appearing in the appointed place at the right time, the illegal showed that he was operational without making any direct contact with the legal *rezidentura*, which, of course, might be subject to hostile surveillance. The fact that Britain remained a target for illegals was later acknowledged by Boris Bocharov, a Directorate S, Second Department officer who happened to live in the same apartment block as Gordievsky in Moscow. When Gordievsky was recalled for interrogation in May 1985 he chanced upon his neighbour, who clearly had not been told that the SIS spy had come under investigation. 'What happened in London?' he asked. 'I've had to withdraw all our illegals. Our entire organisation has been wrecked.' From this indiscretion Gordievsky realised that the KGB was on his trail and took drastic precautions. As he commented later, 'It is reasonable to conclude that in the summer of 1985 the KGB, for the first time in over sixty years, may not have had a single illegal left in Britain.'[12]

Evidently, the KGB had credited Gordievsky with far greater knowledge of illegal operations in London than had actually been the case. In fact, he had played an occasional role as an illegal support officer, replacing the Line N officer during his temporary absence, the last time to leave a bundle of £8,000 cash in a dead-drop for an illegal passing through the capital. The agent, codenamed DARIO, had experienced difficulty with his radio link and a complicated procedure of signals had been agreed to indicate which dead-letter drop had been selected. The operation had been completed on 18 May 1985, the day before Gordievsky's return to Moscow, and his participation may have suggested to his inquisitors, whom he subsequently eluded, that he had contaminated

DARIO and any other illegals in England. Certainly Gordievsky had compromised every other member of the KGB and GRU *rezidenturas* in London; thirty-one intelligence officers were expelled in September 1985, after the British mole had been exfiltrated from Moscow.

The question of how many agents had been despatched by Directorate S to the West preoccupied the CIA and the Israeli Shin Beth as well as the British Security Service. During his tenure as chief, Vadim Kirpichenko had greatly enhanced the status of the Directorate, just as his predecessor, Anatoli I. Lazarev, had concentrated on the reconstruction of illegal networks. Lazarev's background was entirely FCD, having served in Paris for seven years from 1949, and then having returned in 1959 for a further five years as *rezident* when Hambleton had been the *rezidentura*'s principal source. He later served as *rezident* in Montevideo and finally East Berlin before being recalled to Moscow. A general of considerable influence within the FCD, Lazarev almost certainly increased the number of illegals deployed in the West, and the policy was continued by Yuri Drozdov, the *rezident* in Washington DC, who returned to Moscow in 1979 to succeed Kirpichenko and head Directorate S. However, the exact figure remained elusive, forcing Western experts to resort to vague approximations. Harry Rositske, who spent twenty-five years in the clandestine service and was station chief in New Delhi until 1962, followed by eight years in Washington working on domestic anti-Soviet operations, recalls that 'in the late sixties, estimates ran as high as eight hundred to a thousand in Europe and North America',[13] but these figures were later regarded as exaggerations.

They were based on information supplied by Soviet defectors (who themselves had to guess), by captured illegals who reported the numbers of their 'class-mates', by Soviet agents who participated in their instruction or dispatch, and on estimates of the facilities available in Moscow for training illegals. These estimates were probably much too high. Illegals now in the United States are more likely to be counted by the score and not by the hundreds. Even the professional can only guess, for successful illegals are literally buried in a society like ours, rich in immigrants and ethnic groups.[14]

In the months preceding the collapse of the Soviet Union, there was growing evidence of the KGB's reliance upon Eastern Bloc satellite countries for illegal support. In Britain, where no illegal had been apprehended since the arrest of Konon Molody in 1961, two Cubans, two East Germans and a Czech illegal were taken into custody and convicted of espionage-related offences. Thus, after a period of more than a quarter of a century, Soviet-trained third country nationals were intercepted while preparing illegal operations. But was this indicative of more effective detection systems, or a reflection of a genuine growth in illegal or even surrogate operations? The two Cubans were intercepted at Gatwick airport as they tried to enter the country on forged passports, and the other three were caught before they had been activated to engage in espionage: Reinhard and Sonja Schultze were arrested in January 1986 at their home at Cranford, near Heathrow, Reinhard having adopted the identity of Bryan Waldemar Strunze, the son of a former prisoner of war who had remained in England after the war; and Erich Van Haarlem, a Czech who claimed a Dutch background, was seized while in the act of transmitting at his flat in Hertfordshire in April 1988. Van Haarlem had come to Britain in 1975 and had even been reunited with the Dutch woman who believed him to be her long-lost son. In reality, he was a professional Czech intelligence officer who had adopted the persona of her son, who had died having been adopted as a child. He ruthlessly duped his putative mother and received a ten-year prison sentence prior to his deportation in April 1993.

The potential of these surrogates was best demonstrated by another husband-and-wife team, Karel and Hana Koecher, the Czech 'refugees' who obtained US nationality in 1972 and succeeded in penetrating the CIA. They arrived in New York from Austria in December 1965, and Koecher, who was fluent in Russian, English, French and Czech, took a job as a free-lance translator for Radio Free Europe while his wife worked as a grader in the diamond business. He also took a master's degree at Indiana University and a PhD at Columbia, before accepting an academic appointment as a lecturer in philosophy at Wagner College, Staten Island. In April 1972, Koecher applied for a post as a CIA translator and in February the following year he received a security clearance as an interpreter in an element of the Soviet Division, located in Rosslyn, Virginia. His main function was to translate and analyse tapes of conversations that had been recorded by clandestine means, and among the transcripts he made were several from a source codenamed TRIGON, who was Aleksandr D. Ogorodnik, a Soviet diplomat and CIA asset. Approached in Bogota, where he had been posted to the Soviet Embassy, Ogorodnik had been recruited by the CIA, and when at the end of his tour of duty he was transferred back to Moscow, he continued to photograph classified data and to pass it to his Agency case officer. It was information relating to this material that Koecher gave to Vesek Krelik, his contact at the Czech Embassy in Washington, who in turn handed it over to the KGB. Ogorodnik was caught in the act of copying a secret document and swallowed a deadly poison, hidden in a fountain pen supplied by the CIA, in a bid to escape the KGB's interrogators.[15]

Koecher continued to work full-time for the CIA until February 1975, when he moved to New York and became a contract employee, preparing political analyses of Soviet events and personalities, while also teaching at the State University of New York in Long Island. In 1979, as his work for the CIA diminished, he made an unsuccessful job application to the NSA and soon afterwards came under surveillance by the FBI. He was arrested in November 1984 and charged with passing CIA secrets to the Czechs, but in February 1986 he and his wife were swapped in Berlin in a deal brokered by Wolfgang Vogel, the East German lawyer who had negotiated several such exchanges. In return for the Koechers, the Russian dissident Anatoly Shcharansky was released from a thirteen-year prison sentence, and two agents and a Czech convicted of helping refugees flee to the West were also given their freedom.

Koecher had originally encountered the FBI back in November 1970, apparently in an attempt to ingratiate himself, with a report that without any warning he had been approached at his home by a Czech intelligence officer.

Koecher claimed to the FBI that he had dismissed the incident as a clumsy attempt to recruit him, and he had no doubt calculated that the episode would reflect to his credit. However, the investigation conducted by the FBI in 1983 satisfied them that Koecher and his wife were highly competent illegals.[16]

Such evidence as there is suggests that the 'sleeper' agent, sent abroad to lie low and await activation, is the most popular expedient in the post-Cold War economic and political climate. It is a long-term investment dependent upon loyal patriots who are willing to embrace an alien culture, perhaps for years, before being activated to undertake a specific task. For as long as the new Russian regime seeks financial support from its old adversaries, conventional espionage must be avoided. No administration in Washington DC will contemplate generous credits to Moscow unless hostile intelligence operations are kept to a minimum and the kind of diplomatic incidents which characterised the Cold War are avoided altogether. The only category of intelligence-gathering entirely insulated from the legal establishments, and thereby offering a measure of protection against embarrassing exposure, are the missions conceived by Directorate S. And since the Line N agents require a long period in which to install themselves in their unsuspecting host communities, and develop their legends, the post-Cold War climate is ideal for its activities. Such evidence as there is suggests that the reconstituted First Chief Directorate has recognised the fragility of the new relationship with Washington, and has opted to concentrate on the development of single illegals infiltrated to the West, usually as migrants. In interviews granted by Kryuchkov's successors, the answer is much the same. The illegal is an art form executed best by Russians. To abandon the skills developed by Directorate S would be folly, whatever the political environment.

Certainly the Israeli security authorities are aware of several cases of illegals concealed among the escalating number of Jewish emigrants from the territories of the old Soviet Union. There are also plentiful examples of self-declared illegals within the groups of migrants heading for the United

States, most of whom have volunteered statements to the FBI after having achieved entry into the country. All tell much the same story: their instructions are quite straightforward and take no account of current political considerations or difficulties at home. 'Establish yourself unobtrusively in your host community and await the call. It may be some years, but you may be sure the call will come.'

Postscript

It must not be thought illegals are turned out in their hundreds. Dozens of candidates are selected, but only single individuals succeed in becoming illegals.
Vladimir A. Kuzichkin in *Inside the KGB*[1]

In Choapan, a small town in Oaxaca Province, Mexico, there is a woman whose husband disappeared in 1978. She and their three daughters had left him earlier in the year because the strain of living with him had become too much for them to bear. The friction had begun five years earlier when she had discovered that Morris Broniletto was not the professional photographer from Switzerland he had pretended to be when they had married in 1961. He had reluctantly admitted to her that he was a Soviet agent, an illegal. When she had accompanied him on one of his visits to Moscow, she had been invited by his military intelligence controller to join him in his secret work; she had declined the offer, but had agreed not to denounce him to the Mexican authorities. Later, when he vanished, she and her children were heartbroken, despite a short letter mailed from La Paz, Bolivia, dated December 1978, in which he had assured them that he was safe and well. They never heard from him again.

In April 1992, 'Morris Broniletto' revealed himself in Moscow as Oleg Vasilyevich Skorik, a professional intelligence officer with a wife and family in Russia. In his hands was a photograph, taken in Mexico in 1973, of his first wife and their three children. He had told Lida, whom he had met at university in Odessa and married after his return to Moscow in 1978, nothing of his former life in the West, or of his three daughters still living with their abandoned mother. With tears in his eyes, he described his recruitment by the illegals department of the GRU, and his subsequent double life in the West which lasted twenty-one years, masquerading as a Swiss citizen resident in Mexico, while actually maintaining radio contact with his Soviet case officers, and occasionally undertaking illicit tasks that, to this day, he is unwilling to describe in detail.[2]

Skorik's experience is far from unique. After the collapse of the Soviet Union dozens of intelligence professionals emerged from their hiding-places around the world and sought instructions from 'the Centre'. Some were summoned home and told that their services were no longer required. A few were ordered to remain in place, while a handful of disillusioned agents declared themselves to the local security apparatus and thereby allowed the West a glimpse of an astonishing series of interlocking undercover operations that had become a feature of Soviet espionage.

Not all illegals were as anonymous or as discreet as Skorik. In one celebrated case a Directorate S officer penetrated the Foreign Ministry of Costa Rica and rose to become Ambassador to the Vatican. After his retirement Josef Grigolovich, codenamed LAVRETSKI, returned home to Moscow, where he took up an academic career as a Latin American expert and wrote the biographies of Simón Bolívar, Salvador Allende and Ernesto ('Che') Guevara.

In October 1991, it was announced from Moscow that the KGB was to be wound up, and the organisation's centralised responsibility for security and counter-intelligence would be devolved down to the individual component republics of the old Union. But what of foreign intelligence-gathering? The recently retired deputy chief of the KGB, Leonid V. Shebarshin, was, until March 1989, the head of the FCD, and he is emphatic that the value of illegals is far too great to ever contemplate discarding them. Having been the KGB's legal *rezident* in Delhi and Tehran, he is a KGB officer of considerable personal experience and in a recent interview he confirmed that the break-up of the Soviet Union has created a greater dependency than ever on the use of illegals, principally because the mainstay of most intelligence agencies, the use of diplomatic premises from which professionals could work under protected cover, was no longer an option for the newly created Russian foreign intelligence service, the Sluzhba Vneshney Razvedki (SVR). Whereas, under the *ancien régime*, the KGB and the GRU operated with impunity from Soviet embassies around the world, those organisations can no longer rely on the automatic co-operation of regular diplomats drawn from the eleven different countries within the newly formed Commonwealth of Independent States. Accordingly, the RFIS, the direct successor of the KGB's FCD, the external intelligence arm of the mammoth Soviet security apparatus, not only continues to develop and place illegals in the West, but also openly admits the necessity to do so. Its military intelligence counterpart, the GRU, is rather more reticent and its head, Colonel-General Vladlen Mikhailov, insists that his organisation's old ways have been abandoned for ever, asserting, 'We are interested in all new development, as is the West . . . but the methods that were used in the past, stealing things and bringing them over, are never used now.' But is he to be believed?

Evidence that both the RFIS and the GRU have inherited a legacy of networks in the West, and continue to deploy illegals, is compelling. In March 1991, Anvar Kadyrov was arrested in New Zealand with a forged British passport attempting to obtain a genuine one with a birth certificate in the name of a New Zealander, who had been born in 1960, but had died as a child.[3] He was deported to Moscow via London, where he declined the opportunity to defect. In May 1992, two espionage suspects were arrested in Finland carrying British passports in the names of James Peatfield and Anna Marie Nemeth. Both were really Russians, identified as Igor and Natalia Ljuskova, apparently undertaking a preliminary training assignment, the essential and characteristic feature of illegal operations known as *stazhirovka* or staging. The real Peatfield and Nemeth, living in England, were astonished and mystified by the use of their names by the RFIS. As for the spy rings operated by the GRU, the probability is that they are as active as ever. In June 1992, Colonel Viktor Sherdev was arrested in Magdeburg on a charge of having attempted to recruit a senior local police officer, and other similar espionage cases in the Federal Republic indicate that agents formerly run by the HVA, the foreign branch of the East German Stasi, are still active, apparently financed by the RFIS. According to Peter Frisch of the Federal Office for the Protection of the Constitution (BfV) in Cologne, an estimated three to four hundred Stasi agents have transferred their allegiance to the RFIS.

The unpalatable fact is that although Stella Rimington, the Director-General of Britain's Security Service, and Robert Gates, the recently retired Director of the CIA, have both been to Moscow to discuss co-operation to combat the mutual problems of organised crime, international terrorism and drug trafficking with Academician Evgenny M. Primakov, who now heads a supposedly reformed RFIS, little common ground was established in the field of espionage. Indeed, in a rare television interview in October 1992 he reassured his Russian audience that 'the work with the agent network [abroad] will continue'. This is hardly surprising considering Primakov's background. In 1980, as a loyal Party apparatchik, he was responsible for writing the CPSU's official policy justifying the invasion of Afghanistan. Later, as President Mikhail S. Gorbachev's principal foreign policy adviser, he went to Baghdad to parley with Saddam Hussein.

Superficially, it would appear that the excesses of the domestic KGB, headed by Vladimir A. Kryuchkov until the attempted coup he led in August 1991, have been tamed by Vadim S. Bakatin. Until recently, Kryuchkov has been held in Matrosskaya Tishina prison, facing a death sentence for treachery, and the relatively youthful Bakatin, a leader of the democracy movement and once Gorbachev's Minister of the Interior, has begun a programme of dismantling seven of the organisation's thirteen Directorates, the departments that made the KGB and its headquarters in the Lubyanka bywords for oppression. But the RFIS was excluded from the process and in September 1991 the RFIS, still based at Yasnevo, just off Moscow's ring road, was separated from the rest of the old, discredited KGB by presidential decree and placed in the temporary control of a career FCD professional, Vyacheslav I. Gurgenev. With the appointment of Evgenny Primakov, there is every reason to suppose that the hardliners succeeded in retaining control over one of the Soviet Union's most valuable assets.

Information about the new slimmer RFIS, which remains at the modern, Finnish-built compound of high-rise offices at Yasnevo, has been provided by a series of defectors anxious to exploit the West's thirst for knowledge, not just of past operations, but of future intentions. It is upon their testimony that American, French, German and British security agencies have relied upon to update dossiers on suspects, close ancient files and initiate new investigations. The rot started in the late 1980s with well-publicised defections like that of Colonel Viktor P. Gundarev of the KGB from Athens in February 1986, but there were others that went unreported, including those of Lomov in Tel Aviv, Kutergin in Germany and Shitikov in Holland. In addition, there were at least two clandestine exfiltrations from the Soviet Union, those of Major V. Sheymov and Oleg Gordievsky.[4]

Since the collapse of the Soviet Union several important defectors have taken the opportunity to trade their meal-tickets for a comfortable retirement. In 1990, Igor Cherpinsky defected in Brussels and exposed a KGB network in Belgium, and his disappearance coincided with that of Oleg Spirine, the KGB's *rezident* in Kuwait, who had previously come to public attention in September 1985 when he had been held hostage briefly in the Lebanon. A year later Aleksandr Krapiva, a senior GRU officer under cover at the Soviet Permanent Representation at International Organisations in Vienna, defected to the CIA. In June 1991, Mikhail Butkov, a KGB officer under journalistic cover, defected to the British in Oslo and in April 1992 Lieutenant-Colonel Vladimir Konoplev, based in Brussels, switched sides and identified five members of a KGB ring that had operated undetected since 1967. In August, Viktor Oshchenko, together with his wife and teenage daughter, disappeared in Paris, where he had been posted in 1985, and surfaced in London to receive political asylum in return for the name of an electronics engineer who had kept him supplied with British defence secrets, and for details of an industrial espionage ring in France. Together, these defectors have ensured that the transformed RFIS poses only a minimal threat through its legal representatives in the West. There remains, however, much doubt about the illegals in whom the GRU and the First Chief Directorate invested so much.

Source Notes

Introduction

1 William R. Corson and Robert T. Crowley, *The New KGB* (Morrow, 1985), p. 439.

2 *Falkland Islands Review, Report of a Committee of Privy Councillors*, Cmmd 8787 (HMSO, London, 1983).

3 See *Intelligence and Strategic Surprises* by Ariel Levite (Columbia University Press, 1987).

4 See J. C. Masterman's original assertion that Popov's warning went unheeded in *The Double Cross System in the War of 1939 to 1945* (Yale University Press, 1974).

5 For an account of Lai Teck's activities see *Malaya: The Communist Insurgent War, 1948–1960* by Edgar O'Ballance (Faber & Faber, 1966).

6 See *The Phoenix Program* by Douglas Valentine (Avon Books, 1990); *Ashes to Ashes* by Dale Andrade (Lexington Books, 1990); and *Facing the Phoenix* by Zalin Grant (W. W. Norton, 1991).

7 See *The Fish Is Red* by Warren Hinckle and William Turner (Harper & Row, 1981), p. 114.

8 See *Air America* by Christopher Robbins (Avon Books, 1979).

9 Anthony Cavendish, *Inside Intelligence* (Collins, 1990).

10 See *The Champagne Spy* by Wolfgang Lotz (St Martin's Press, 1972).

11 See *The Spy from Israel* by Ben Dan (Vallentine, Mitchell, 1969) and *Our Man in Damascus* by Eli Ben-Hanan (Crown, 1969).

12 Alexander Orlov, *Handbook of Intelligence and Guerrilla Warfare* (University of Michigan Press, 1963), p. 41.

13 Elwell's account was published under his covername, 'Charles Elton' in the *Police Journal* (Vol. XLIV, No. 2, April–June 1971), pp. 111–16.

14 Robert T. Crowley in *The New KGB*, p. 417.

15 *School for Spies* (Neville
Spearman, 1961). Hutton's
fanciful account may be the
provenance of a similar
statement in Corson and
Crowley's *The New KGB*,
p. 191. The closest the KGB
came to an establishment
approximating to Bykovo,
alleged to occupy a site forty
miles north of Moscow, is the
First Chief Directorate's Red
Banner Institute, also known as
School 101, located just outside
north-west Moscow, fifteen
kilometres beyond Yurlovo
(see Vladimir Kuzichkin's
description, *Inside the KGB:
Myth and Reality* [André
Deutsch, 1990], p. 46).
Although Corson and Crowley
source their extensive
description of Bykovo to Hutton
(whose true name was Joseph
Heissler), the relevant pages in
School for Spies make no
mention of Bykovo but instead
describe a spy school at
Gaczyna, 100 miles south-east
of Kuibyshev, covering an area
of 425 square miles, which
'does not appear on any map'
(p. 52).

Considering that at least two
of the case histories of illegals in
School for Spies (those of Dr
Geoffrey Noble, who is alleged
to have committed suicide in
Gerald Road police station in
1953, and Reginald K.
Osborne, who fled London in
the same year) are wholly
fictitious, it is likely that the
rest of the book is equally
unreliable.

1 *Conspiratsia*: The Pre-War Network

1 William Hood, *Mole* (W. W.
Norton, 1982), p. 210.
2 For a description of
Macartney's documents, see
HO 144/8403 509413/1
'Description of and Instructions
for Wireless Telegraph'
classified as 'Confidential'. Two
Air Ministry papers recovered
in the raid are described in HO
144/8403 509413/17 in a
memorandum dated 14 May
1927.
3 Roger Faligot and Remi
Kauffer, *Histoire Mondiale du
Renseignement* (Roger Laffont,
Paris, 1993), p. 194.
4 The Moness family is
discussed in correspondence
between Hugh Miller and Guy
Liddell of MI5 and Herschel V.
Johnson, Boylston Beal and Ray
Atherton of the US Embassy in
London between July 1928 and
November 1931, US National
Archives 800B 21 July 1928
RG6 84.
5 For details of the Old Bailey
trial of Ethel Chiles see *The
Times*, 3 May 1927.
6 US Congressional Record.
7 Georges Agabekov, *OGPU:
The Russian Secret Terror*
(Brentano's, 1931), p. 196.
8 For Isabel Streater's account
see *The Storm Petrels* by
Gordon Brook-Shepherd

(Collins, 1977), pp. 111–24.
9 Agabekov, *op. cit.*, p. 272.
10 *Ibid.*, p. 196.
11 Delgass quoted in the *New York Herald Tribune*, 11 April 1953.
12 For an analysis of the Switz case see *Soviet Espionage* by David J. Dallin (Yale University Press, 1955), pp. 62–8.
13 Louis Waldman, *Labor Lawyer* (E. P. Dutton, 1944), p. 221.
14 For Olga Gray's account see *The Man Who Was M* by Anthony Masters (Basil Blackwell, 1984), p. 54.
15 The Brandes investigation may be followed in the correspondence between Sir Vernon Kell, the Director-General of MI5, and N. D. Borum of the US Embassy in London, February–October 1938, US National Archives 800 B 'Brandes' RG 84 NA.
16 See *I Was Stalin's Agent* by W. G. Krivitsky (Right Book Club, 1940).
17 Oldham was identified as 'Scott' by Corson and Crowley in *The New KGB*, p. 141.
18 Alexander Orlov, *The Secret History of Stalin's Crimes* (Random House, 1953), p. 230.
19 Elisabeth K. Poretsky, *Our Own People* (OUP, 1969), p. 58.
20 *Ibid.*, p. 73.
21 Orlov, *Handbook of Intelligence and Guerrilla Warfare*, p. 91.
22 Krivitsky, *op. cit.*, p. 157.

23 *Ibid.*, p. 296.
24 The Robinson investigation can be traced through the correspondence in the US National Archives between Guy Liddell of MI5 and N. D. Borum of the US Embassy in London for the period January to August 1938.
25 See *This Deception* by Hede Massing (Duell, Sloan & Pearce, 1951).
26 For the FBI's treatment of Okavimian see *The FBI–KGB War: A Special Agent's Story* by Robert Lamphere (Random House, 1986).

2 *Der Rote Kapelle*

1 Leopold Trepper, *The Great Game* (Michael Joseph, 1977), p. 409.
2 Details of Weiss from Jim Skardon and from Donovan Pratt's *Rote Kapelle: The CIA's History of Soviet Intelligence and Espionage Networks in Western Europe, 1936–1945* (University Publications of America, 1979), pp. 381–3.
3 Guryevitch has collaborated in the preparation of a film treatment of his experiences, *Resident in the Red Orchestra* (1992).
4 Trepper, *op. cit.*, p. 161.
5 *The Rote Kapelle*, p. 371.
6 Trepper, *op. cit.*, p. 249.
7 *The Rote Kapelle*, p. 169.
8 Trepper, *op. cit.*, p. 202.
9 MI5 report cited in *The Rote Kapelle*, p. 96.

10 Copy of the Serpell/Hemblys-Scales report in the possession of the author. Additional data from the MI5 *Personalities Index of the Rote Kapelle* compiled by (Sir) Michael Hanley in author's possession.

3 Sorge's Contacts

1 Whittaker Chambers, *Witness* (Random House, 1952), p. 221.
2 Charles Willoughby, *The Shanghai Conspiracy* (Dutton, 1952).
3 F. W. Deakin and G. R. Storry, *The Case of Richard Sorge* (Chatto & Windus, 1966).
4 Orlov, *Handbook of Intelligence and Guerrilla Warfare*, p. 48.
5 *Ibid.*, p. 49.
6 Ursula Kuczynski published her memoirs under the name of Ruth Werner, *Sonya's Report* (Chatto & Windus, 1991), p. 41.
7 *Ibid.*, p. 37.
8 For more detailed accounts of the Japanese network see *Spies, Dupes & Diplomats* by Ralph de Toledano (Arlington House, 1967); *The Man with Three Faces* by Hans-Otto Meissner (Rinehart & Co., 1955); and *An Instance of Treason* by Chalmers Johnson (Heinemann, 1965).
9 Poretsky, *Our Own People*, p. 64.
10 *Ibid.*
11 Trepper, *The Great Game*, p. 75.
12 Krivitsky, *I Was Stalin's Agent*, p. 113.
13 Massing, *This Deception*, p. 174.
14 Chambers, *op. cit.*, p. 27.
15 *Ibid.*, p. 355.
16 Elizabeth Bentley, *Out of Bondage* (Ivy Books, 1988), p. 110.
17 *Ibid.*
18 For Morros's account see *My Ten Years as a Counterspy* (Viking Press, 1959).
19 Pavel S. Kuznetsov, then Second Secretary at the Soviet Embassy in London, was expelled in July 1952 following his arrest with William M. Marshall, who was subsequently sentenced to five years' imprisonment for selling classified material he had taken from the Diplomatic Wireless Service headquarters at Hanslope Park.
20 Agabekov, *OGPU*, p. 202.
21 Orlov, *The Secret History of Stalin's Crimes* (Random House, 1953), p. 193.
22 Massing, *op. cit.*, p. 259.
23 Poretsky, *op. cit.*, p. 146.
24 Ilya Dzirkvelov, *Secret Servant* (Collins, 1987), p. 62.
25 *Ibid.*, p. 64.
26 Morros, *op. cit.*, p. 28.
27 Dzirkvelov, *op. cit.*, p. 107.
28 Vladimir and Evdokia Petrov, *Empire of Fear* (Frederick Praeger, 1956).
29 See Robert Lamphere's

account in *The FBI–KGB War*,
p. 106.

4 The Swiss Networks

1 Sandor Rado, *Codename
Dora* (Abelard, 1976), p. 11.
2 Foote's autobiography,
Handbook for Spies (Museum
Press, 1949), was written
largely by his MI5 debriefer,
Courtney Young.
3 Ustinov's biography, *Klop
and the Ustinov Family*
(Sidgwick & Jackson, 1973), by
his widow, Nadia Benois, says
only that 'Klop's job was a
"hush-hush one"' and that he
was employed until 1957
(p. 191).
4 Elliott's memoirs, *Never
Judge a Man by his Umbrella*
(Michael Russell, 1991),
mentions Klop and his frequent
visits to Berne, but not the
subject of their collaboration.
5 Ursula Kuczynski has
granted two interviews to the
author.
6 Foote, *op. cit.*, p. 191.
7 Rado, *op. cit.*, p. 33.
8 Rado's list of sub-agents
does not conform to the
CIA's analysis in *The Rote
Kapelle*.
9 Rado, *op. cit.*, p. 137.
10 Apart from the participants,
other authors have contributed
to the story of the *Rote Drei*.
Among their books are:
Codeword: Direktor by Heinz
Hohne (Coward McCann,
1971); *The Red Orchestra* by

'Gilles Perrault', the
pseudonym of Jacques
Peyrolles (Simon & Schuster,
1967); *A Man Called Lucy* by
Pierre Accoce and Pierre Quet
(Coward McCann, 1966); and
Operation Lucy by Anthony
Read and David Fisher (Hodder
& Stoughton, 1980).
11 For a more detailed
discussion of the identities of the
Soviet sources see *Unreliable
Witness* by Nigel West
(Weidenfeld & Nicolson, 1985).
12 Hans Bernd Gisevius, *To
the Bitter End* (Jonathan Cape,
1948), p. 150.
13 Frantisek Moravec, *Master
of Spies* (Bodley Head, 1975),
p. 186.

5 Atomic Secrets

1 Harry Rositske, *KGB: The
Eyes of Russia* (Doubleday,
1981), p. 53.
2 *The Rote Kapelle*, p. 292.
3 *The Report of the Royal
Commission*, p. 565.
4 See *Emma* by June Callwood
(Beaufort Books, 1984).
5 For further details of
Gouzenko see *The Gouzenko
Transcripts* edited by Robert
Bothwell and J. L. Granatstein
(Deneau, Toronto, 1989); *The
Red Spider Web* by Bernard
Newman (Latimer House,
1947); and *Gouzenko: The
Untold Story* by John Sawatsky
(Macmillan, 1984).
6 The identification of H. I.
Sorensen as the Soviet source

identified as SURENSEN remains uncertain. See *The Report of the Royal Commission*, p. 530.

7 *The Report of the Royal Commission*, p. 109.

8 See Lamphere, *The FBI–KGB War*, p. 34.

9 Rupert Sigl, *In the Claws of the KGB* (Dorrance, 1978), p. 31.

10 Orlov, *Handbook of Intelligence and Guerrilla Warfare*, p. 39.

11 In the recollection of one senior FBI officer, Morris and Lona Cohen were not connected with the Rosenberg ring until their photos were discovered among Rudolph Abel's belongings.

12 See *International Herald Tribune*, 5 October 1992.

13 For two accounts of Orlov's last days see 'Escape into Obscurity', by Oleg Tsarev in *Trud*, 20 December 1990; and *Deadly Illusions* by John Costello and Oleg Tsarev (Random Century, 1993).

14 Orlov, *Handbook of Intelligence and Guerrilla Warfare*, p. 46.

15 Poretsky, *Our Own People*, p. 258.

16 Krivitsky, *I Was Stalin's Agent*, p. 101.

17 Edith Tudor Hart made no admission to MI5, but her brother, Wolf Suschitzky, edited a book of her photographs in 1987 entitled *The Eye of Conscience* (Photo Pocket Books 1, Dan Nishen), which gives an insight into her life and motives.

18 Peter Wright, *Spycatcher* (Viking, 1987), p. 227.

6 Squad 34 v. the Line N Illegal Support Officers

1 Allen Dulles in *The Craft of Intelligence*, p. 275.

2 For an account of the GIDEON case see *For Services Rendered* by John Sawatsky (Doubleday, Canada, 1982), p. 34.

3 For Abel's incomplete biographies see *Abel* by Louise Bernikow (Trident Press, 1970) and *Strangers on a Bridge* by James B. Donovan (Atheneum, 1964). Neither author suspected his British origins.

4 Donovan, *ibid.*, p. 185.

5 *Ibid.*, p. 213.

6 *Ibid.*, p. 217.

7 *Ibid.*, p. 216.

8 *Ibid.*, p. 218.

9 *Ibid.*, p. 219.

10 *Ibid.*, p. 221.

11 *Ibid.*, p. 214.

12 *Ibid.*, p. 180.

13 See *North-East Labour History*, No. 22, 1988, pp. 29–33, translated by John Slatter of Durham University. See also Dr David Saunders in *Northern History*, Vol. XXI, 1985, and his account of Genrykh Fisher. Unquestionably, Rudolph Abel was born William Fisher at 140 Clara Street, Benwell,

Newcastle. According to Henkine's *L'Espionnage Soviétique*, Abel had undertaken a mission to London in 1930 to communicate with the nuclear physicist Piotr Kapista. Henken's version is denied by Abel's daughter Evelyn Fisher.

14 J. Bernard Hutton, *School for Spies* (Neville Spearman, 1961), p. 52.

15 *Ibid.*, p. 54.

16 Kulak was first identified publicly as FEDORA in *Molehunt* by David Wise (Random House, 1992), p. 149.

17 For an account of Tuomi's case see *KGB: The Secret Work of Soviet Secret Agents* by John Barron (Hodder & Stoughton, 1974), p. 258.

18 Information from Michael Sokolov and Lise-Lotte Sokolova. Other sources include *Red Spies at the UN* by Pierre J. Huss and George Carpozi (Coward McCann, 1965) and *The Espionage Establishment* by David Wise and Thomas B. Ross (Jonathan Cape, 1968). Peter Wright gives a slightly inaccurate version of Michael Sokolov's involvement in *Spycatcher*, p. 170.

19 Allen Dulles (ed.), *Great True Spy Stories* (Harper & Row, 1968).

20 David Kahn, *The Codebreakers* (Weidenfeld & Nicolson, 1966), p. 696.

21 Now living in Berlin, Thompson alleges that he is Russian in origin, and trained as an illegal. Although the FBI seems satisfied that he was never an illegal, and that his identity of Thompson is genuine, he was exchanged in 1978 after he had served thirteen years of his sentence. This makes him the only known American citizen to be swapped to the Eastern Bloc.

22 See *Loginov: Spy in the Sun* by Barbara Carr (Howard Timmins, 1969). For a more comprehensive account see *Cold Warrior* by Tom Mangold (Simon & Schuster, 1991).

7 The Illegals from Germany

1 Sigl, *In the Claws of the KGB*, p. 116.

2 Petrov, *Empire of Fear*, p. 265.

3 Nikolai Khokhlov, *In the Name of Conscience* (McKay, 1959), p. 249.

4 Michael Burke, *Outrageous Good Fortune* (Little, Brown, 1984), p. 164.

5 Khokhlov, *op. cit.*, p. 261.

6 *Ibid.*, p. 158.

7 *Ibid.*, p. 201.

8 For further details of Khokhlov see *The Executioners* by Ronald Seth (Hawthorn, 1967) and *Spy!* by Richard Deacon with Nigel West (BBC Publications, 1980).

9 See *Mole* by William J. Hood.

10 Prikhodko's lecture, *Characteristics of Agent*

Communications, has been published by Interservice Publishing Co., San Francisco, 1981.

11 *Ibid.*, p. 35.

12 For a more detailed account of RAFTER see Peter Wright's *Spycatcher*.

13 FUZZY and APPLE CIDER are described in John Sawatsky's *For Services Rendered*.

14 Dr Alfred E. Laurence is referred to by Rupert Sigl in *In the Claws of the KGB*, p. 213. Laurence himself has included some biographical data in his *In Praise of St Lawrence: A Song at Twilight* (Privately printed, 1984).

8 LAST ACT and SHAH

1 Prikhodko, *Characteristics of Agent Communications*, p. 28.

2 David J. Dallin, *Soviet Espionage* (Yale University Press, 1955).

3 VENONA was the product of a highly classified inter-Allied cryptographic operation to read Soviet wireless traffic. For a detailed account see Peter Wright's *Spycatcher*, p. 178.

4 The NSA defectors were Bernon Mitchell and William Martin. On 25 June 1960, they flew to Cuba from Mexico and sought political asylum in Moscow.

5 Peter Wright's assertion (*Spycatcher*, p. 134) that RAFTER was installed next to Lonsdale's flat is disputed by another MI5

officer who participated in the operation. He alleges that only a microphone was inserted through the party wall.

6 For an account of his business connections see *Rare Books and Rarer People* by O. E. Snelling (Werner Shaw, 1982).

7 See Professor D. P. Costello's obituary, *The Times*, 25 February 1964.

8 Arthur Tietjen, *Soviet Spy Ring* (Coward McCann, 1961), p. 115.

9 Elwell quoted by Lonsdale in *Spy* (Neville Spearman, 1965), p. 186.

10 John Bulloch and Henry Miller, *Spy Ring* (Secker & Warburg, 1961), p. 110.

11 *Ibid.*

12 *Ibid.*

13 Elwell wrote his account under the cover name 'Elton' in the *Police Journal*, Vol. XLIV, No. 2, April–June 1971.

14 Most Soviet accounts of the Molody case are highly unreliable. In particular, two of his own Russian-language memoirs, *Profession Foreigner* (1989) and *My Profession Is Intelligence: Memoirs of an Intelligence Officer of the KGB* (Orbit, Moscow, 1990), and the version published in *Komsolovskaya Pravda* in which it was claimed that Lonsdale became a millionaire and received a knighthood.

15 Lonsdale, *Spy*, p. 45.

16 Kuzichkin, *Inside the KGB*, p. 117.

17 Lonsdale, *Spy*, p. 112.

18 *Ibid*.

19 Norman Lucas with George G. Smith, *Spycatcher* (W. H. Allen, 1973) and an article entitled 'Soviet Spy Ring' in the *Police College Magazine*, Autumn 1962.

20 Harry Houghton, *Operation Portland: The Autobiography of a Spy* (Rupert Hart-Davis, 1972).

21 Lonsdale, *Spy*, p. 123.

22 *Ibid*., p. 117.

23 *Ibid*., p. 48.

24 *Ibid*., p. 65.

25 Lonsdale arrived in London in March 1955, a month before the Berlin Tunnel, which had been betrayed by George Blake, became operational. Codenamed PRINCE, it remained productive until it was closed by the KGB in April 1956. The coincidence of dates and locations is circumstantial evidence of what may have been part of Lonsdale's mission.

26 Despite the certainty that penetration of GCHQ must have been a high Soviet priority, the only spy to be detected within the organisation is Geoffrey Prime, who in November 1982 confessed to having worked for the KGB since his recruitment in Berlin in 1966.

27 A passage in Gordon Brook-Shepherd's *The Storm Birds* (Weidenfeld & Nicolson, 1988) which gave an account of this suspect prompted a libel action and the withdrawal of the book in 1988.

9 Double Agents and Dangles

1 William R. Corson, Susan B. Trento and Joseph J. Trento, *Widows* (Crown, 1989), p. 221.

2 Peter Wright refers to Lulakov in *Spycatcher*, p. 95.

3 For references to the Skripov case, but not the identity of the MI5 officer, see *Tale of the Scorpion* by Harvey Barnett (Allen & Unwin, 1988); *Anatomy of a Coup* by Stephen Foley and Marshall Wilson (Canterbury Press, 1990); *The Secret State* by Richard Hall (Cassell, Australia, 1978); also, *Daily Telegraph*, 24 September 1971.

4 For further details about Vassall see *Vassall: The Autobiography of a Spy* (Sidgwick & Jackson, 1975).

5 Sigler's case is described in detail in Corson, Trento and Trento, *op. cit*.

6 LI/COZY's role as a double agent is disclosed by Philip Agee in *Inside the Company: CIA Diary* (Stonehill, 1975), p. 529.

7 Zemenek's case is described in detail by John Barron in *KGB Today: The Hidden Hand* (Reader's Digest, 1983).

8 The controversy surrounding Artamonov has

been described by David C. Martin in *Wilderness of Mirrors* (Harper & Row, 1981) and by Henry Hurt in *Shadrin* (McGraw Hill, 1981).

9 Hambleton's biography has been written by Leo Heaps in *Thirty Years with the KGB* (Methuen, 1984).

10 The End of the Cold War

1 Vladimir Rezun in *Inside Soviet Military Intelligence* by Victor Suvorov (Hamish Hamilton, 1984), p. 57. Rezun has adopted the pseudonym of Victor Suvorov for his books on Soviet military intelligence.

2 Tom Polgar, *The KGB: An Instrument of Soviet Power* (The Intelligence Profession Series, No. 2, AF10 Monograph, 1986), p. 15.

3 Rositske, *The KGB: The Eyes of Russia*, p. 114.

4 The Martynov case was disclosed by *Trud* on 9 January 1991, apparently with the intention of blaming Oleg Gordievsky for their betrayal; see *New Counterpoint*, Vol. 6, No. 12, May 1991. During much of the period Gordievsky was supplying the FCD's secrets to the British, Vladimir I. Vetrov was giving data from the Eighth Chief Directorate to the French. Vetrov was imprisoned on another charge in October 1982. He was executed in 1984 after he had confessed to espionage.

5 CAZAB's secret existence was first disclosed by Peter Wright in *Spycatcher*, p. 276.

6 For a detailed account of Lyalin's defection see *The Wilson Plot* by David Leigh (Heinemann, 1988), p. 185.

7 Sabotka is not his true name. For an account of the case see *KGB* by John Barron, p. 321.

8 Since his defection Gordievsky has co-authored, with Christopher Andrew, *KGB: The Inside Story* (Hodder & Stoughton, 1990); *Instructions from the Centre* (Hodder & Stoughton, 1991); and *More Instructions from the Centre* (*Intelligence & National Security*, Vol. 7, No. 1, January 1992).

9 Gordievsky and Andrew, *Instructions from the Centre*, p. 54.

10 Suvorov (Rezun), *op. cit.*

11 Vladimir Kuzichkin's memoirs are contained in his *Inside the KGB*.

12 Boris Bocharov quoted in Gordievsky and Andrew, *Instructions from the Centre*, p. 64.

13 Rositske, *op. cit.*, p. 57.

14 *Ibid.*, p. 205.

15 For details of Ogorodnik see *Inside the CIA* by Ronald Kessler (Simon & Schuster, 1992).

16 Koecher's activities have been documented by Ronald

Kessler in *Escape from the CIA*
(Simon & Schuster, 1991).

Postscript

1 Kuzichkin, *Inside the KGB*,
p. 82.
2 *Izvestia*, 27 and 28 April
1992.
3 *The Times*, 21 March 1991.
4 Viktor I. Sheymov,
reportedly of the KGB's Eighth
Chief Directorate, was
exfiltrated in 1980. According
to the *Literary Gazette*,
29 May 1991, other
unreported defectors
include Koyergin from West
Germany, Lomov from Israel,
Firin from Kuwait, Shitikov
from Holland, and a KGB
officer named Ponamarsev
about which no details have
been released.

Select Bibliography

Accoce, Pierre, and Quet, Pierre, *A Man Called Lucy* (Coward McCann, 1966)

Agabekov, Georges, *OGPU: The Russian Secret Terror* (Brentano's, 1931)

Agee, Philip, *Inside the Company: CIA Diary* (Stonehill, 1975)

Akhmedov, Ismail, *In and Out of Stalin's GRU* (Arms & Armour, 1984)

Andrew, Christopher, and Gordievsky, Oleg, *KGB: The Inside Story* (Hodder & Stoughton, 1990)

Andrew, Christopher, and Gordievsky, Oleg, *Instructions from the Centre* (Hodder & Stoughton, 1991)

Andrew, Christopher, and Gordievsky, Oleg, *More Instructions from the Centre* (*Intelligence & National Security*, Vol. 7, No. 1, January 1992)

Bailey, Geoffrey, *The Conspirators* (Harper Bros, 1960)

Barron, John, *KGB: The Secret Work of Soviet Secret Agents* (Hodder & Stoughton, 1974)

Barron, John, *KGB Today: The Hidden Hand* (Reader's Digest, 1983)

Belfrage, Cedric, and Aronson, James, *Something to Guard* (Columbia University Press, 1988)

Bentley, Elizabeth, *Out of Bondage* (Ivy Books, 1988)

Bernikow, Louise, *Abel* (Trident Press, 1970)

Brook-Shepherd, Gordon, *The Storm Petrels* (Collins, 1977)

Brook-Shepherd, Gordon, *The Storm Birds* (Weidenfeld & Nicolson, 1988)

Bulloch, John, and Miller, Henry, *Spy Ring* (Secker & Warburg, 1961)

Burke, Michael, *Outrageous Good Fortune* (Little, Brown, 1984)

Carpozi, George, *Red Spies in Washington* (Trident Press, 1968)

Carr, Barbara, *Loginov: Spy in the Sun* (Howard Timmins, 1969)

Cavendish, Anthony, *Inside Intelligence* (Collins, 1990)

Chambers, Whittaker, *Witness* (Random House, 1952)

CIA, *The Rote Kapelle: The CIA's History of Soviet Intelligence and Espionage Networks in Western Europe, 1936–1945* (University Publications of America, 1979)

Corson, William R., and Crowley, Robert T., *The New KGB* (Morrow, 1985)

Corson, William R., and Trento, Susan B., and Trento, Joseph J., *Widows* (Crown, 1989)

Costello, John, *Mask of Treachery* (Morrow, 1988)

Dallin, David, *Soviet Espionage* (Yale University Press, 1955)

Deriabin, Peter, and Gibney, Frank, *The Secret World* (Doubleday, 1959)

Deriabin, Peter, and Bagley, T. H., *The KGB: Masters of the Soviet Union* (Hippocrene, 1990)

Donovan, James, *Strangers on a Bridge* (Atheneum, 1964)

Dulles, Allen, *The Craft of Intelligence* (Harper & Row, 1968)

Dulles, Allen (ed.), *Great True Spy Stories* (Harper & Row, 1968)

Dzhirkvelov, Ilya, *Secret Servant* (Collins, 1987)

Dziak, John, *Chekisty* (Lexington Books, 1988)

Elwell, Charles, 'A Russian Intelligence Officer Exposed' (*Police Journal*, Vol. XLIV, No. 2, April–June 1971)

Epstein, Edward Jay, *Deception* (Simon & Schuster, 1989)

Foote, Alexander, *Handbook for Spies* (Museum Press, 1949)

Golitsyn, Anatoli, *New Lies for Old* (Bodley Head, 1984)

Gouzenko, Igor, *The Iron Curtain* (Dutton, 1948)

Gramont, Sanche de, *The Secret War* (Putnam's, 1962)

Hagan, Louis, *The Secret War for Europe* (Macdonald, 1968)

Heaps, Leo, *Thirty Years with the KGB* (Methuen, 1984)

Heilbrun, Otto, *The Soviet Secret Services* (Frederick Praeger, 1956)

Hirsch, Richard, *The Soviet Spies* (Nicholas Kaye, 1947)

Hohne, Heinz, *Codeword: Direktor* (Coward McCann, 1971)

Hood, William, *Mole* (W. W. Norton, 1982)

Houghton, Harry, *Operation Portland* (Rupert Hart-Davis, 1972)

Hurt, Henry, *Shadrin: The Spy Who Never Came Back* (McGraw Hill, 1981)

Huss, Pierre J., and Carpozi, George, *Red Spies at the UN* (Coward McCann, 1965)

Hutton, J. Bernard, *Danger from Moscow* (Neville Spearman, 1961)

Hutton, J. Bernard, *School for*

Spies (Neville Spearman, 1960)

Hutton, J. Bernard, *The Traitor Trade* (Neville Spearman, 1963)

Hutton, J. Bernard, *Struggle in the Dark* (Harrap, 1969)

Kessler, Ronald, *Spy vs Spy* (Scribner's, 1988)

Khokhlov, Nikolai, *In the Name of Conscience* (McKay, 1959)

Kimche, Jon, *Spying for Peace* (Weidenfeld & Nicolson, 1961)

Knight, Amy, *The KGB* (Unwin Hyman, 1990)

Krivitsky, Walter G., *I Was Stalin's Agent* (Right Book Club, 1940)

Kuzichkin, Vladimir, *Inside the KGB* (André Deutsch, 1990)

Lamphere, Robert J., *The FBI –KGB War: A Special Agent's Story* (Random House, 1986)

Leggett, George, *The Cheka: Lenin's Political Police* (OUP, 1981)

Levchenko, Stanislav, *On the Wrong Side* (Pergamon-Brassey, 1988)

Levine, Isaac Don, *The Mind of an Assassin* (Farrar, Strauss & Cudahy, 1959)

Lewis, Flora, *Red Pawn* (Doubleday, 1966)

Lonsdale, Gordon, *Spy* (Neville Spearman, 1965)

Lucas, Norman, *Spycatcher* (W. H. Allen, 1973)

MacKinnon, Janice, and MacKinnon, Stephen, *Agnes Smedley* (University of California Press, 1988)

Mangold, Tom, *Cold Warrior* (Simon & Schuster, 1991)

Manne, Robert, *The Petrov Affair* (Pergamon, 1987)

Martin, David C., *Wilderness of Mirrors* (Harper & Row, 1981)

Massing, Hede, *This Deception* (Duell, Sloan & Pearce, 1951)

Masters, Anthony, *The Man Who Was M* (Basil Blackwell, 1984)

Morros, Boris, *My Ten Years as a Counterspy* (Viking Press, 1959)

Orlov, Alexander, *The Secret History of Stalin's Crimes* (Random House, 1953)

Orlov, Alexander, *Handbook of Intelligence and Guerrilla Warfare* (University of Michigan Press, 1963)

Penkovsky, Oleg, *The Penkovsky Papers* (Doubleday, 1965)

Penrose, Barrie, and Freeman, Simon, *Conspiracy of Silence* (Grafton Books, 1986)

Perrault, Gilles, *The Red Orchestra* (Simon & Schuster, 1967)

Petrov, Vladimir and Evdokia, *Empire of Fear* (Frederick Praeger, 1956)

Philby, Kim, *My Silent War* (McGibbon & Kee, 1968)

Pincher, Chapman, *Their Trade is Treachery* (Sidgwick & Jackson, 1981)

Pincher, Chapman, *Too Secret*

Too Long (Sidgwick &
Jackson, 1984)

Polgar, Tom, *The KGB: An
Instrument of Soviet Power*
(The Intelligence Profession
Series, No.2, AFIO
Monograph, 1986)

Poretsky, Elisabeth, *Our Own
People* (OUP, 1969)

Prikhodko, Ivan E.,
*Characteristics of Agent
Communications*
(Interservice, 1981)

Rado, Sandor, *Codename Dora*
(Abelard, 1976)

Read, Anthony, and Fisher,
David, *Operation Lucy*
(Hodder & Stoughton,
1980)

Richards, Guy, *Imperial Agent*
(Devin-Adair, 1966)

Richelson, Jeffrey T., *Sword
and Shield* (Ballinger, 1986)

Richelson, Jeffrey T., *Foreign
Intelligence Organizations*
(Ballinger, 1988)

Romerstein, Herbert, and
Levchenko, Stanislav, *The
KGB against the 'Main
Enemy'* (Lexington, 1989)

Rositske, Harry, *The KGB:
The Eyes of Russia*
(Doubleday, 1981)

Sakharov, Vladimir, *High
Treason* (Putnam's, 1980)

Sawatsky, John, *Men in the
Shadows* (Doubleday, 1980)

Sawatsky, John, *For Services
Rendered* (Doubleday,
Canada, 1982)

Schecter, Jerrold, and Deriabin,

Peter, *The Spy who Saved the
World* (Macmillan, 1992)

Shipley, Peter, *Hostile Action*
(Pinter, 1989)

Sigl, Rupert, *In the Claws of the
KGB* (Dorrance, 1978)

Smith, George G., 'Soviet Spy
Ring' (*Police College
Magazine*, Autumn 1962)

Snelling, O. E., *Rare Books and
Rarer People* (Werner Shaw,
1982)

Suvorov, Victor, *Inside Soviet
Military Intelligence* (Hamish
Hamilton, 1984)

Taschereau, Robert, and
Kellock, R. L., *The Report
of the Royal Commission*
(Ottawa, 1948)

Tietjen, Arthur, *Soviet Spy Ring*
(Coward McCann, 1961)

Trepper, Leopold, *The Great
Game* (Michael Joseph, 1977)

Tsarev, Oleg, and Costello,
John, *Deadly Illusions*
(Random Century, 1993)

Vassall, John, *Vassall: The
Autobiography of a Spy*
(Sidgwick & Jackson, 1975)

Waldman, Louis, *Labor Lawyer*
(E. P. Dutton, 1944)

Werner, Ruth, *Sonya's Report*
(Chatto & Windus, 1991)

Wise, David, and Ross,
Thomas B., *The Espionage
Establishment* (Jonathan
Cape, 1968)

Wise, David, *Molehunt*
(Random House, 1992)

Wright, Peter, *Spycatcher*
(Viking, 1987)

Index

Abakumov, Viktor S. 63
Abel, Colonel Rudolph xvii, 9, 144, 147–56, 160, 176, 191, 194, 197, 214, 225, 226, 238
Aberdeen Proving Ground 80
Abraham Lincoln Battalion 83, 214
Abramov, Leonid 142
Abramson, Alexander 97, 112–13
Abwehr 3, 48, 50, 51, 52, 54, 57, 59, 62, 66, 92, 104, 107, 225
  Head of see Canaris, Admiral Wilhelm
Adams, Eric 114, 115, 116, 118
Admiralty Underwater Weapons Establishment 204
AE/GUSTO see Loginov, Yuri N.
Aenis-Haenslin, Maurice 65, 97
AFOSI see Air Force Office of Special Investigation
AFSA see Armed Forces Security Agency
Agabekov, Georges 19–21, 30, 84, 85
Agayants, General Ivan 245
AGNES 108
Air America 6
Air Force Office of Special Investigation (AFOSI) 169
Akhmerova, Elena Ivanovna 173, 268
Akmedov, Ismail G. 38, 100
Akmerov, Ishak A. 173

Alamo, Carlos see Makarov, Lieutenant Mikhail
Albam, Jacob 83
ALEK see May, Allen Nunn
Aliev, Ismail M. 269
All Russian Co-operative Society (ARCOS) 14, 16, 19, 35
Altman, Israel see Cohen, Morris
Alvarado, General Velasco 246
American-Romanian Film Corporation 33
Amerikanskaia Torgovoia 18
Amtorg 18, 21, 37, 87–8, 127, 141, 159
ANDRE see Robinson, Henri
Andropov, Yuri A. 196, 247, 262
Angelov, Lieutenant Pavel 114, 118
Anglo-Soviet Trade Treaty 13
ANNA 106
Antipov, Mikhail M. 263
APPLE CIDER 193–5
Archer, Jane 76
ARCOS see All Russian Cooperative Society
Argentine Security Service (SIDE) 255
Arma Engineering Corporation 22
Armed Forces Security Agency (AFSA) 87, 122
Arnould, Rita 48, 50
Artamonov, Nikolai F. 242, 243, 250–1
Artusov, Artur 70–1

Asaturov, Vladimir 21
ASIO see Australian Security and
    Intelligence Organisation
ASKO 153
Aspler, Rabbi J. 27, 28
Austen, Captain Nigel 203
Australian Security Intelligence
    Organisation (ASIO) 177,
    230–1
  Head of see Barnett, Harvey
Automatic Merchandising Company
    Limited 223
Avalov, Ivan I. see Agayants,
    General Ivan
Avro Arrow 142
Ayres, Peter 223

BACK see Lunan, Captain David
BACON see Halperin, Professor
    Israel
BADEAU see Smith, Philip Durnford
Baestlein, Bernhard 55, 58
BAGLEY see Mazerall, Edward
Bakatin, Vadim S. 282
Baltch, Robert K. 161–4
Bandera, Stephan 184,
    185, 186
Bank of Canada 115
BARBAROSSA 109
Barcza, Margarete 46, 56, 60
Barkovsky, Vladimir B. 130
Barnes, Tracy 180
Barnett, Harvey 293
Barr, Joel 129
BARRAS 96
Barron, John 166
Bartok, Josef 33
Bates, Charles 214
BAXTER see Angelov, Lieutenant
    Pavel
Bay of Pigs 6
BEAR 137
Beaulieu, Therese 244
Becker, Annie 97
Behrens, Karl 58
Belfrage, Cedric 82
Bell & Howell 33

Benning, J. Scott 113, 114,
    116–17, 118
Bentley, Elizabeth 36–7, 38, 77,
    80, 81, 82, 88, 117, 125, 127,
    128, 177
Berg, Wilhelm 62, 66
Berger, Helen 97
Beria, Lavrenti 155, 180
Bernstein, Abraham see
    Uzdansk-Yelenski, Colonel
Bernstein, Dr 36
Berzin, General Jan 75, 178
Beurton, Leon 94, 95, 96, 102
Beurton, Ursula see Kuczynski, Ursula
Bianchi, Dr Mario 96
Bircher, Dr Eugen 102
Black, Helen 78, 79
Blake, George 143, 203, 216
Blaser, Edith see Gussfeldt, Kathe
Bloch, Rita 49
Blun, Georges 96, 101, 107
Blunkmine (Blumkin), Jacob
    84–5, 86
Blunt, Anthony 30, 31, 137, 138
BND see Bundesnachrichtendienst
BOB 57, 65
Bocharov, Boris 272
Bodesko 31
Boeckenhaupt, Sergeant Herbert
    W. 170–1, 233
Boemelburg, Karl 60, 62
Boerger, Ruth see Rubens, Ruth
Boettcher, Paul 97, 98, 104
Boetzel, Colonel Fritz 107
Bogdanov, Leonid 269
Bolli, Margaret 96, 103
Borodin, Vladimir 142, 243–5
Bourdine, Vladimir 193
Bourgeois, Henriette 97
Bousu, Alga 217
Boyer, Dr Raymond 113, 115, 118
Brajt, Marza 28
Brandes, Schulem 26–7
Brandes, William 24, 25–6, 29, 31,
    45, 135
BRENT see Rogov, Major
Bressac, Colonel 60

Brett, Marcia *see* Brajt, Marza
British Security Service (MI5) 9,
    13–16, 18, 19–20, 24–25,
    66–7, 76, 91–5, 114, 122,
    125–39, 171, 192, 193,
    201–11, 215–18, 219, 220,
    223, 224, 228, 230, 247,
    254–5, 258, 259, 264, 273
Director-General of *see* Furnival
    Jones, Martin; Hollis, Sir
    Roger; Kell, Sir Vernon;
    Rimington, Stella
Broniletto, Morris 279
Bronstein *see* Trotsky, Leon
Brooke, Gerald 225
Brothman, Abraham 89, 125, 127
Browder, Earl 80–1, 173
Buch, Eva 53
Buchenwald 60
BULL 130
Bundesnachrichtendienst (BND)
    63, 226, 271
Bundespolizei 92, 93, 95, 103, 104,
    108, 193, 271
Bureau of Standards 80
Burgess, Guy 132, 135, 138, 143
Burke, Michael 180
Burman, Major Samuel 116, 118
Butenko, John W. 233
Butkov, Mikhail 283
Bykov, Colonel Boris 34, 79
Bykovo, Illegals school at 10, 286

Cairncross, John 138
Camp King 180
Camp Peary 256
Canadian Affairs 115
Canadian Broadcasting Corporation
    241
Canadian International
    Development Agency (CIDA)
    246
Canaris, Admiral Wilhelm 107
Capre, Marcelle 65
Carlson, Olaf 153
Carr, Barbara 176
Carr, Sam 115, 117, 118, 120, 121

Case of Richard Sorge 70
Caswell, John F. 203
CAT 130
Cavendish, Anthony 7
CAZAB 258, 294
Central Intelligence Agency (CIA)
    1, 4, 5, 62, 63, 66, 106, 107,
    132, 134, 143, 144, 156–8,
    172–6, 179–98, 203, 204, 210,
    211, 227, 235, 236, 242, 250,
    251, 253, 254–5, 256–7, 262,
    273, 274–5
    Clandestine Service 6
    Counterintelligence Staff 157,
        174, 176, 189, 256
    Director of *see* Dulles, Allen W.;
        Gates, Robert
    Soviet Russia Division 156, 253
Chalk River 114, 116, 129
Chambers, Whittaker 69, 79–80
Chapman, Agatha 116, 118
*Characteristics of Agent
    Communications and of
    Agent Handling in the United
    States of America* 189
Charak, Walter 26, 28
Checherin, Boris 269
Cherpinsky, Igor 283
CHESTER *see* Gorshkov, Captain
Chiles, Ethel 16–17, 18
Chistov, Alexei 156
Churchill, Clementine 164
Clandestine Service *see* Central
    Intelligence Agency
Clarac, Louise 14, 15
Clarion 115
CLEMENT 64
Codename Dora 91
Cohen, Eli 8
Cohen, Lona (Helen Kroger) 129,
    152, 207–27, 232
Cohen, Morris (Peter Kroger) 129,
    152, 207–27, 232
Collins, Mark *see* Abel, Rudolph
Comintern 24, 72–4, 93, 101, 137
Committee for State Security
    (KGB) 5, 61, 84, 86, 87, 122,

123–4, 128–32, 138–9, 142–4, 154, 155–9, 166, 169, 170, 172–91, 196–202, 207, 210–13, 221, 223, 224, 227, 230–43, 245–75, 280–4
Chairman of see Andropov, Yuri A.; Kryuchkov, Vladimir A.; Shelepin, Aleksandr N.
Department V 262, 263
Directorate S 147, 254, 255, 257, 262, 263, 268, 271, 276
Head of see Drozdov, Yuri I.; Korotkov, Alexsandr M.; Lazarev, Anatoli I. Kirpichenko, Vadim V.
Directorate T 265
Head of see Zaitsev, Leonid S.
First Chief Directorate of (FCD) 147, 172, 183, 237, 242, 244, 254, 255–6, 257, 258, 264, 265, 268–73, 276, 281
Head of see Kryuchkov, Vladimir A.; Panyushkin, Aleksandr S.
Illegals Directorate see Directorate S
Line KR 159, 270
Line N 159, 254, 256, 258, 266, 268, 269, 270, 271, 276
Line PR 160, 265, 267, 269, 270, 271
Line X 159
reorganisation chart 261–2
Second Chief Directorate 235, 256
Thirteenth Department 262, 263, 270
Communist Party of Great Britain (CPGB) 24, 43, 78, 102, 138
National Organiser of see Glading, Percy
Communist Party of the United States of America (CPUSA) 36, 37, 78–81
General-Secretary of see Browder, Earl; Foster, William Z.
Communist Youth International 44

Communist Youth League 18
Control Commission for Germany 164
Coplon, Judith 87, 88
Coppi, Hans 53, 58
Corbin, Alfred 49, 54
CORBY see Gouzenko, Igor S.
Corson, William R. 1, 229
Costello, Paddy 210
Counterintelligence Corps 233
Counterintelligence Staff see Central Intelligence Agency
CPUSA see Communist Party of the United States of America
Cram, Cleveland 203
Cremet, Jean 14, 18
Crowley, Robert 1, 10

D Branch see British Security Service
D-Day 2
Dachau 197, 198
Dallant, Nicholas 34
Dallin, David 201
Danilov, Anton 48, 49, 50, 61, 62
DARIO 272–3
DAVIE 113
De Laar, Jan 64
De Voukelitch, Branko 75
De Winter, Georgie 47
Deakin, Sir William 70
Dean, Robert W. 173
DEBOUZ see Rose, Fred
Defence Intelligence Agency (DIA) 242, 250
Delgass, Basil W. 21

Department of External Affairs 114
Department of Justice 19, 38, 87
Department 13 see Committee for State Security
Department V see Committee for State Security
Depelsenaire, Elizabeth 64
Deriabin, Piotr S. 173, 183, 184
Deutsch, Arnold 89, 135–6, 137, 139

Deutsch, Josefine 137
Deuxième Bureau 23
DGSE *see* Direction Générale de Sécurité Extérieure
Diffley, Joe 160
Diplomatic Wireless Serive 202
Direction de la Surveillance du Territoire (DST) 132, 163, 245
    Director of *see* Rochet, Jean
Direction Générale de Sécurité Extérieure (DGSE) 7
Directorate of Operations *see* Central Intelligence Agency
Directorate S *see* Committee for State Security
Directorate T *see* Committee for State Security
Dirksen, Herbert von 75
Disch, William 22, 35
Donovan, James B. 176
Donovan, William J. 82
DORA *see* Rado, Sandor
Dozenberg, Nicholas 24, 33–4
Dozhdalev, Vassilli A. 216, 228, 235
Drager, Siegfried *see* Stashinsky, Bogdan
Drailly, Nazarin A. 49
Drama Travel League 36
Dreadnought, HMS 212, 235
Droubaix, Marcel 60
Drozdov, Yuri I. 271, 273
Drummond, Sergeant Nelson C. 167, 233
DST *see* Direction de la Surveillance du Territoire
Ducroux 72
Duebendorfer, Henri 98
Duebendorfer, Rachel 65, 95, 97, 98, 100, 102, 103, 104, 105, 111–12, 113
Duff, Shiela Grant 164
Dulles, Allen W. 107, 141, 144, 168
Dunlap, Sergeant Jack F. 167–8, 234
Duryea, Harry *see* Switz, Robert

Dushkin, Yuri A. 258
Dzhirkvelov, Ilya G. 86, 147
Dzhugashvili *see* Stalin, Josef
Dzumaga, Michael 41–2

Edenski, Colonel Sergei A. 170
Effremov, Konstantin 53, 54, 57, 59–60, 64
Egerov, Alexandra 164
Egerov, Evan D. 160, 161, 164
EIFFEL 56, 59
Eifler, Erna 55
Eisler, Gerhardt 72, 73, 77, 79, 80
ELLEN 65
ELLI 129
    see also Willsher, Kathleen
Elliott, Nicholas 92, 93
Elwell, Charles 9, 10, 217–18, 221, 224
Engelsing, Dr Herbery 53
Erdberg, Alexander 52, 53, 58, 68, 112
ERIC *see* Adams, Eric
Espionage Establishment, The 166–7
EVI 270, 271
Excellent Raincoat Company 42, 46, 47, 67, 126

Fadeikin, Ivan A. 270
Falklands War 1, 2
FBI *see* Federal Bureau of Investigation
FCD *see* Committee for State Security, First Chief Directorate
Federal Bureau of Investigation 16, 18–19, 21, 37, 78, 81, 82, 83, 84, 87, 88, 121, 124–32, 134, 135–6, 138, 139, 144, 145–8, 149, 152–3, 156, 157–63, 187, 188, 214, 215, 217, 224, 232–3, 234–43, 249–51, 275, 277
    Director of *see* Hoover, J. Edgar
    Squad 34 159–76
Federov, Mikhail A. 156

FEDORA see Kulak, Alexei I.
Fedorov, Feodor 187
Fedotov, Pyotr V. 86
Feklisov, Aleksandre S. 126
Feldbin, Leiba L. see Orlov,
    General Alexander M.
Feldbin, Maria see Orlov, Vera
Feldman, Abraham 28
Feldman, Armand Labis 28,
    37, 38
Fellendorf 55
Feoktistov, Georgi 132
Field, Herta 78, 81
Field, Noel 78, 81
Fieldhouse, Jack 174
Firin 295
First Chief Directorate see
    Committee for State Security
Fish, Hamilton 21
Fisher, Evelyn 149, 150, 152
Fisher, Genrykh M. 155
Fisher, William see Abel, Rudolph
Flicke, Wilhelm F. 92, 95
Fomin, Aleksandre see Feklisov,
    Aleksandre S.
Foote, Allan 67, 91–5, 96, 98, 99,
    102, 104
Footman, David 70
Foreman, John H. D. 171
Fort Bliss 236
Fort Bragg 2, 190
Fort Huachuca 154
Fort Leavenworth 154
Fort Meade 248
Fort Monmouth 154
FOSTER see Benning, J. Scott
Foster, Jane 83
Foster, William Z. 36
Fradkine, Boris M. 14
FRANK see Carr, Sam
Franks Committee Report 2
French Communist Party 16, 56, 59
Friberg, Frank 172
Friedmann, Litzi 138
Frisch, Peter 282
Froehlich, Gustav 53
Frolov, Nikolai A. 173

Frost, Inspector Charles 17
Fuchs, Emil Klaus 68, 95,
    124–6, 202
Fuchs, Kristel 127
Furnival Jones, Martin 201, 254
FUZZY see Kneschke, Rudolph
Fylingdales, Yorkshire 263

GABEL 101
Gaczyna 157
Galan, Yaroslav 184–5
Galeva, Lili 247
Galkin, Alexei I. 160, 164–5
Galleon Press 35
Galtieri, General 1
GALYA 117, 118
GAMMA 146
Garber, Joy A. 161–4
Garber, Ossip 36, 163
Garsov, Rachel 16
Gateley, Dr Gerald 18
Gates, Robert 282
GCHQ see Government
    Communications Headquarters
Gee, Ethel (Bunny) 205–6, 209,
    211–12, 213–14, 215–16, 228
Gehlen, Reinhard 226
Geopress 98
German Communist Party (KDP)
    70, 78, 125, 198
Gerson, Harold 114
Geschwinnt, Michel 270
Geschwinnt, Ursula 270
Gessner-Buehrer, Selma 96
Gestapo 51, 62, 66, 69, 122, 198
GIDEON see Soboloff, David
Giering, Karl 62, 63
GINI 117, 118, 129
Ginsberg, Samuel see Krivitsky,
    Walter
Gisevius, Hans Berndt 107
Glading, Percy 24–5, 135
Glass, Ann 217–18
Goebbels, Joseph 74
Goerdeler, Karl 107
Gold, Harry 67, 125–8, 177
Goldfus, Emil see Abel, Rudolph

Goldin, William *see* Orlov, Alexander

Goleniewski, Michal 204, 211

GOLIA 117, 118, 129

Golitsyn, Anatoli M. 173, 174, 235, 245, 256–7, 259

Gollnow, Herbert 52, 53, 58

Golos, Jacob 81, 127

Golovanov, Vladimir 270, 271

Gorbachev, Mikhail xviii, 282

Gordievsky, Oleg A. 223, 264–5, 267, 268, 272, 272–3, 283

Gorin, Mikhail 37

Gorshkov, Captain 116, 118

Gorskaia, Lisa *see* Zubilin, Elizaveta

Gorsky, Anatoli B. 81, 130

Gottheil, Captain Jack 116, 118

Goussarov 117

Gouwlooze, Daniel 64

Gouzenko, Igor S. 67, 82, 111–14, 117, 120, 122, 123, 124, 141, 177, 202

Government Communications Headquarters (GCHQ) 2, 3–4, 192, 207–9, 227, 293

GR/ALLSPICE *see* Popov, Piotr S.

GRANT *see* Zabotin, Colonel Nikolai

Grant Duff, Shiela 164

GRAPHIC IMAGE *see* Sigler, Ralph

Gray, Olga 24

Great Game, The 41, 61

Great True Spy Stories 168

GREEN 117, 118

Greenglass, David 128

Greenglass, Ruth 128

Grey, Charles 143–4

Grigolovich, Josef 280

Grigoriev, Vasili V. 174

Grimme, Dr Adolf 58

Griotto, Medarno 65

Grodnicki, Stephan 14

Gromov, Anatoli B. *see* Gorsky, Anatoli B.

Gromushkin, Colonel 269

Grossvogel, Jeanne 46

Grossvogel, Leon 42–3, 46, 47, 49, 61

GRU *see* Soviet Military Intelligence

Gruber, Malvina 49, 68

Gubitchev, Valentin A. 87, 88

Guddorf, Wilhelm 58

Guehrle, Emil 102

Gundarev, Colonel Viktor P. 283

Gurgenev, Vyacheslav I. 283

Guryevitch, Viktor 46–7, 48, 49, 52, 53, 55, 56, 58, 59, 60, 61, 62, 63, 105

Gussfeldt, Kathe 17–18

Habijanic, Max 65, 96

Hale, Helen *see* Cohen, Lona

Halperin, Professor Israel 113, 115, 116, 118, 124

Halperin, Maurice 82

Hamberger, Rudi 72

Hambleton, Bessie 244

Hambleton, Professor Hugh 242–9, 273

Hamel, Edmund 103, 104

Hamel, Olga 96, 103, 104

Hanako, Mikaya 75

Handbook of Intelligence and Guerrilla Warfare 132

Handbook for Spies 93

Handelsvertretung 16, 32

Hansen, Georg 19–20

Harnack, Arvid von 51–2, 58

Harris, Dr Henry 118, 120

HARRY I 43, 44

HARRY II 43, 44

Hart 78

Harwell 129

Hausamann, Hans 108

Havemann, Leutnant Wolfgang 52, 58

Hayhanen, Reino 8, 143–7, 153, 154, 233

Heilmann, Horst 52

Heinemann, Kristel 124

Heinz, Leonore 196

Heissler, Joseph 10, 286

Helbein, William 97, 112

Helfrich, Dr Karl 55

Hemblys-Scales, Robert V. 66, 94, 122
Hendler, Mikhail 21
Herbert, Edward J. *see* Zubilin, Vassilli
Hermann, Inga 240–1
Hermann, Peter 240, 241
Hermann, Rudolf 240–1
Herrnstadt, Rudolf 51
Heydrich, Reinhard 63
HILDA 57
Hiss, Alger 36, 78, 79
Hitler, Adolf 3, 107, 109
Ho Chi Minh 74
Hoessler, Albert 53
Hofmaier, Karl 97
Hollis, Sir Roger 228
Hood, William J. 13
Hoover, J. Edgar 18–19, 131, 227
Houghton, Harry 203–16, 224, 235
Hozumi, Ozaki 72, 74, 75
Huha, Andrew 230, 231
Humbert-Droz, Jules F. 96
Humphreys, Leslie 179
Hunt, Jim 143
HURON 130
Hussein, Saddam 1, 282
Hutton, J. Bernard 157

Illegal Support Officers *see* Committee for State Security, Directorate S
In the Claws of the KGB 177
In Russia and England: Observations and Recollections of a Petersburg Worker 1891–1821 155
INGE 96
Inside Intelligence 7
Inside the KGB 279
International Brigades 19, 76, 93, 119
International Labour Organisation 98, 112, 113
International Publishers 35
International Settlement Police 72

International Workers Relief Committee 17
Iran, Shah of 4, 270
Iranian Security Service (SAVAK) 269
Isbutsky, Herman 49, 57
Ivanov, Igor A. 233
Izvestia 35, 159, 190

Jackson, Bertha R. 161–2
Jackson, Harry L. 162
Jackson, James D. 161–2
Japanese Communist Party 75
Jaspar, Jules 42, 49
JEAN 65
JENNY 65
Jernstroem *see* Effremov, Konstantin
JEROME *see* Prenant, Professor Marcel
JIM *see* Foote, Allan
Jodl, Field Marshal Alfred 101
Johnson, Sergeant Robert L. 234
Jones, Martin Furnival 201, 254
Joseph, Bella 81
Joseph, J. Julius 81–2

Kadyrov, Anvar 281
Kahn, David 168
Kallmann, Dr Heinz 45
Kantor, Emma 35
Kantor, Solomon 22, 35
Kapelowitz, Louis 42, 67
Kapelowitz, Maurice 126
Kapitsa, Piotr 291
Karin, Aleksandr 70, 71
KAROT *see* Tuomi, Kaarlo
Karpekov, Nikolai P. 202–3, 224, 236
Karpovich, Boris V. 169
Karry, Frema 22
Katz, Hillel 49, 60–1
Kayotis, Andrew *see* Abel, Rudolph
Kazankin, Gennadi 270
KDP *see* German Communist Party
Kedrov, Nikolai G. 174
Kell, Sir Vernon 287

KELLY 130
Kempei'tai 69, 71, 75
KENT see Guryevitch, Viktor
KEYSTONE 143
KGB see Committee for State
     Security
KGB: The Eyes of Russia 111
*KGB: The Secret Work of Soviet
     Secret Agents* 166
Kharlshkin, Colonel Sergei P. 269
Khokhlov, Nikolai E. 174, 178–86,
     189, 197, 262
Khomenko, Oleg N. 263
Khorunsky, Nikita V. 180, 182
King, Captain John 29–30, 31, 45,
     76, 135, 138
KINGSTON see Gottheil, Captain Jack
Kirpichenko, Vadim V. 264, 273
Kisevalter, George 156, 187
KITTY HAWK see Kozlov, Igor R.
Klausen, Max 75
Klimov, Anatoli see Golitsyn,
     Anatoli M.
Kneschke, Rudolph 194–5
Knochel, Alfred 64
Koecher, Hanna 274, 276
Koecher, Karel 274–6
Koenen, Heinrich 52, 55
Kogen, Schmil see Carr, Sam
Kolomyakov, Boris P. 237
Konoplev, Vladimir 283
KONRAD see Kruminsch, Karl
Kopkow, Horst 62
Korotkov, Aleksandr M. 86,
     147, 187
Korovin, Nikolai 202–3, 216, 223
Korznikov, Nikolai A. 268
KOS see Yugoslav Intelligence
     Service
Kostromin, Colonel Lev P. 269,
     270
Kousnetzov 64
Kovich, Richard 156, 173
Kovshuk, Viktor M. 235
Koyergin 295
Kozlov, Igor R. 242, 250, 251
Kozlov, Oleg A. 242–3

Kramer, Liza see Deutsch, Josefine
Krapiva, Aleksandr 283
Krelik, Vesek 275
Kremer, Simon D. 45, 125
Kriatov, Colonel Alexei 187
Krivitsky, Walter 29–34, 36,
     76–9, 131, 133–4
Kroger, Helen see Cohen, Lona
Kroger, Peter see Cohen, Morris
Krotov, Boris M. 130, 138
Krotov, Ivan 117
Kruglov 199
Kruminsch, Karl (KONRAD)
     270, 271
Kruyt, John W. 64
Kryuchkov, Vladimir A. 265, 276,
     282
Kube, Wilhelm 179
Kuchino, KGB school at 182, 184
Kuckhoff, Adam 51, 58
Kuczynski, Jurgen 95, 125
Kuczynski, Ursula 68, 72, 74,
     89, 94–5, 96, 98, 99, 102,
     125, 202
Kudashkin, Fedor D. 168–9
Kudriavtsev, Sergei M. 68,
     112, 113
Kulak, Alexei I. 159, 170–2, 175
Kurikka, Hanna 144, 145
Kurkovich, Hans 180, 181–2
Kurlinsky see Karpovich, Boris V.
Kutepov, General Aleksandr P. 178
Kutergin, General 283
Kuzichkin, Vladimir A. xv–xiii,
     267–9, 270, 271–2, 279
Kuznetsov, Pavel S. 84, 202
Kvasnikov, Leonid R. 130

Labarthe, André 45
Labis, Armand 28
Labis, Marcu 28
Lai Teck 4
LAMBDA 1 see Blake, George
LAMBDA 2 see Houghton, Harry
LAMBERT 96
LAMONT see Motinov, Major
LAST ACT see Molody, Konon

Laurence (Lomnitz), Dr Alfred 197–8
LAVINIA see Goleniewski, Michal
LAVRETSKI see Grigolovich, Josef
Lazarev, Anatoli I. 273
LEADER see Nightingale, Squadron-Leader Matt
Lecap Rainwear Company 127
Lee, Duncan C. 82
Legendre, Paul 60
Lemmer, Ernst 107–8
Lenin Institute 115
Lenin, Vladimir I. xv, 98, 155
Lenz, Dr Friedrich 58
Levakov, Herman 169
Levine, Isaac Don 29
Lewis, Birgette 93, 94
Lezhnin, Colonel Anatoli M. 269
LI/COZY 237
Life 131
LILY AUS VATIKAN 96
Line KR see Committee for State Security
Line N see Committee for State Security
Line T see Committee for State Security
Line X see Committee for State Security
Linton, Freda 115, 116, 118
Lipchitz, Fritzie see Linton, Freda
Litvin, Bunia 119
Litvin, Zalamon 119–20, 121
Ljuskov, Igor 281
Ljuskova, Natalia 281
Lock, Walter see Weiss, Ernest D.
Lockie, Agnes see Syme, Agnes
Loginov, Vladimir A. 258
Loginov, Yuri N. 173–6, 268
Loginov: Spy in the Sun 176
Lomnitz, Dr Alfred see Laurence, Dr Alfred
Lomov 283, 295
LONG see Blun, Georges
Lonsdale, Gordon see Molody, Konon
Lonsdale, Jack E. 217

Lopatin, Aleksandr 267
Lothian, Lord 29
Lotz, Wolfgang 7–8
LOUIS 96
Lubszynski, Hans 45, 67
Lukyanov, Pavel L. 244, 245, 246, 248
Lulakov, Captain Nikolai 229–30, 232
Lunan, Captain David 113, 115, 116, 118
Luschinsky, Rosa (JENNY) 65
LUX 65
Lyalin, Oleg A. 259, 262, 263, 264, 267
Lysov, Yuri 169

Mabey, John 158
MacArthur, General Douglas 69
Macartney, Wilfred 13–14, 19–20
McDonald, Alec 254
Mackenzie Papineau Battalion 119
Maclean, Donald D. 45, 68, 130, 132, 135, 138, 143
Maclean, Melinda 67
MAGIC 2
Makarov, Lieutenant Mikhail 46, 47, 48, 49, 53
Maki, Eugen 144–5
Malaya Special Branch 4
Malinin, Aleksei R. 171, 233
Malmstrom Air Force Base 169
Maly, Theodore 30–1, 45, 89, 134, 135, 137, 138
Manhattan Project 124, 130
MANOLO 96
March Air Force Base 170, 233
Marcovitch, Aaron 27, 28
Markin, Valentin 37, 77, 78, 79
MARS 56, 60
Marshall, William M. 202
Martins, Charles E. 96
Martynov, Vladimir I. 255
Maslennikov, Ivan I. 14, 161, 164–5
Massing, Hede 30, 36, 37, 77–9, 81, 85

Master Switch Company Limited
223
Mathieu, Inspector Charles 54, 66
MAUR 130
Maximowitch, Anna P. 49
May, Allen Nunn 114, 116,
118, 202
Mazerall, Edward 113, 115,
116, 118
Medyanik, Yakov P. 271
Menshikov, Pavel P. see Mikhailov,
Pavel P.
Meredith, Frederick 43–4, 65, 135
Metropolitan Police 13, 17, 71, 248
MI5 see British Security Service
Mikhailov, Pavel P. 112, 113
Mikhailov, Colonel-General
Vladlen 281
Mikler, Adam 41
Miller, Anton 16
Miller, General Eugene 178
Miller, Captain Hugh 18
Milsky see Milstein, Ilya
Milstein, Ilya 120
Milton see Abel, Rudolph
Ministry of State Security (MSS) 7
Minnesota Mining Company 198
Mins, Leonard 81
Minster, Leon 35
Minster, Robert 35
Mirbach, Count de 84
Mitchell, Abe 26
Mitchell, Dr W. E. 217
MITHRIDATE 60
Mitkenbaugh, James A. 233,
234, 238
MITRE 159–60, 171, 172, 175
Mitsusada, Yoshikawa 75
Modin, Yuri 202
Moellendorf, Fritz 197
Moerke, Ingalore 241
Mogilevtchek, Alfred F. 265
Mole 13
Molodaya, Evdokia 221, 222
Molody, Konon (Gordon Lonsdale)
9, 205–28, 235, 274
Moloday, Trofim 221–2

Molotov, Vyacheslav 3, 46
Molotov-Ribbentrop Pact 3
Moness, Jacob 16–17, 18, 35
Moness, Pauline 16, 35
Moness Chemical Company 16
Moravec, Frantisec 108
Morrison, James 143
Morros, Boris 82–3, 84, 86,
87, 147
Moskowitz, Miriam 89, 127
Mossad 8
Motinov, Lieutenant-Colonel 111,
112, 113, 114, 116, 118
Mourier, Louis 65
MOUSNAT 159
Moutet, Marius 96
Mueller, Albert see Foote, Allan
Mueller, Anna B. 65, 96
Mueller, Hans 96
Mukhabarat 264
Mulvena, Cecil W. 171
Munsenberg, Willi 18
MVD see Ministry of State Security
My Silent War 136
Myaznikov, Viktor M. 263

Nadirashvili, Konstantin V. 264
Nagel, Adam 64
Narkomintorg 20
Nasser, President Gamel 264
National Research Council 113
National Security Agency (NSA) 4,
167, 171–2, 239, 240, 292
NATO 204, 234, 244, 245, 266
Needleman, Isadore G. 88
Nemeth, Anna Marie 281–2
New China News Agency 7
New KGB, The 1
Nguen Ai Quac 74
Nicole, Leon 97
Nicole, Pierro 97
Nightingale, Squadron-Leader Matt
114, 118
Nikolaiev, Lev N. 133–4
NKVD 30, 36, 37, 38, 70, 75, 86,
89, 93, 117, 131, 134, 135,
136–9, 215

Nosenko, Yuri I. 174, 235, 236, 242, 256, 257, 259
Noulens, Hilaire 72–4
Novikov, Colonel 61, 93–4
Novikov, Yuri V. 196–7, 198
NSA see National Security Agency
NTS 179–83
Nummerk, Katarina 270, 271

Obermanns, Franz 96
O'Bryan, Terence Tear 143
OBSTACLE COURSE 264
Office of Strategic Services (OSS) 66, 81–2, 83, 106, 107
  Head of see Donovan, William J.
Ogorodnik, Aleksandr D. 275, 294
OGPU 18, 20–3, 32, 37, 76, 77, 84, 257
OGPU: The Russian Secret Terror 20
Okolovich, Georgi S. 179, 180
Okun, Lieutenant-Colonel Oleg 182–3
OLD MAN 130
Oldham, Ernest 30
OLGA 106
OMEGA 142
Oppenheimer, Robert E. 130
Orlov, Alexander M. 8, 30, 31, 33, 42, 70, 85, 123, 131–8
Orlov, Vera 31
Oshchenko, Viktor 283–4
Osman, Robert 22–3
Osprey, HMS 213
OSS see Office of Strategic Services
OSS-SIS Counter-Intelligence War Room 66
Oster, General Hans 106–7
Ostrovsky, Nikolai 142
Oswald, Lee Harvey 257
O'Toole, Jack 160
Ott, Colonel Eugen 75
OTTO see Deutsch, Arnold
OUN 184
Our Own People 33
Ovakimian, Gaik 37–8, 81

Ovakimian, Vera 38
Ozols, General Waldemar 45, 60, 135

Pago Originals Inc 126
PAKBO see Puenter, Otto
Palivoda, Aaron 96
Panfilowska, Halina 219–20, 224
Panyushkin, Aleksandr S. 183–4
Pappin, W. M. 121
Paques, Georges 245
Paramount Studios 82
PASCAL 57, 60
Passklecq, Jean C. 49
Passport Control Officers 25
Patzerney, Captain 117
PAUL (Berlin) 53
PAUL (Zurich) 96
Paulsen, Heinz 59, 62–3
Pavlov, Gleb A. 233
Pavlov, Vitali G. 117, 146–7, 173
Payot, Marc 92, 103, 104
Pearl Harbor 3
Peatfield, James 281–2
Penkovsky, Colonel Oleg V. 169, 188–90, 259
Peper, Maurice 57
Perlo, Victor 88
PERSEUS 130, 215
Pesant, Jeanne 43
Petchenko 171
PETER 102–3
Petersen, Arne 267
Petitpas, Renée 65
Petka, Leontina see Cohen, Lona
Petlura, General Simon 178
Petrov, Evdokia 87, 184, 202, 230
Petrov, Vladimir 87, 147, 177, 184, 202, 230
Phantome Red Cosmetics Company 26, 27
Philaja, Hjalmar 217
Philby, Harold (Kim) 30, 31, 45, 132, 135–9, 143, 224
Pieck, Henri 32, 45, 135
Piepe, Captain Henry 62
Piskunov, Valentin M. 269

Plurenden, Lord 198
Pohl, Inge 184, 186
POISSON 103
Poland, Squadron-Leader Fred 113, 118
Polgar, Tom 253
Poliakova, Maria 100
Police Journal 224
Polish Intelligence Service (UB) 204, 211
Polonik, General 269
Polyakov, Dmitri F. (TOP HAT) 157-61, 165-71, 175, 229, 233, 259, 267
Ponomarsev 295
Pontecorvo, Bruno 129
Popov, Dusko 3
Popov, Piotr S. 156, 157, 158, 186-9
Poretsky, Elisabeth 31-3, 73, 85, 133
Posnanska, Sofia 48-50
Powers, F. Gary 154
Pravda 190
Prenant, Professor Marcel (JEROME) 45, 65
Prikhodko, Ivan E. 188-9, 191, 201
Primakov, Evgenny M. 282, 283
Prime, Geoffrey 293
Pritt, Denis N. 44
PROFESSOR (Canada) *see* Boyer, Dr Raymond
PROFESSOR (UK) 65, 137
Prokhorov, Evgenni M. 167
PROMETHEUS *see* Shugar, David
Provincial Reconnaissance Units 4
Provost, Pierre 14
Puenter, Otto 96, 100-2, 104
Putna, Vitovt 36
QUEBEC *see* Rhodes, Sergeant Roy

Rabbani 269
Rabinowitch, Hermina 97, 111-12, 113, 118
Rado, Sandor (Alexander) 91, 92, 94, 96-106
RAFTER 192-5, 209, 231, 258
Raichmann, Abraham 49, 66, 68

RAM 270
Rasin, Jacob 81
Rastvorov, Yuri A. 184
Ravitch, Helen 36
Reader's Digest 166
Rebet, Lev 186
Red Banner Institute 268, 286
Reich Security Agency (RHSA) 52
Reif, Ignaty 138-9
Reiser, Heinrich 62
Reiss, Ignace 31, 32, 73, 74, 78, 134, 135
Remington, William J. 88
Revizorov, Pavel K. 268
Rezun, Vladimir B. 253, 267, 294
RFIS *see* Russian Foreign Intelligence Service
RHINE 183
Rhodes, Sergeant Roy A. 144, 146, 153-4, 235
RHSA *see* Reich Security Agency
Ribbentrop, Joachim von 3
Rimington, Stella 282
Ritsu, Ito 75
Roberts, John 144
Robinson, Donald *see* Rubens, Adolph
Robinson, Henri 44, 45, 54, 56, 61, 64, 65, 66, 67, 135
Rochet, Jean 61
Roessler, Rudolf 68, 97, 99, 102-8
Rogov, Leonid A. 264
Rogov, Major 118, 120
Rogov, Mikhail S. *see* Tsymbal, Mikhail S.
Rohrer, Sergeant Glen R. 233
Rollins, Donald A. 254-5
Roman, Howard 203
Romashin, Yuri A. 233
Rose, Fred 82, 114-15, 117, 118, 123
Rosenberg, Ethel 128, 129, 130
Rosenberg, Julius 128-9, 130
Rosenberg, Liza *see* Zubilin, Elizaveta
Rositske, Harry 111, 253, 273
Ross, Colonel Franz H. 190

ROT 97
Rote Drei 99–109, 191
Rote Kapelle 41–68, 91, 95, 112, 127, 191
Roussel, Arthur 15, 66
Royal Air Force 93
Royal Aircraft Establishment 43
Royal Canadian Mounted Police (RCMP) 27, 28, 38, 39, 111, 112, 114, 115, 121, 141, 142, 193–5, 202, 216, 243, 244, 248, 262, 263
Royal Commission 113, 116, 177
Rubens, Adolph 34–5, 36, 77
Rubens, Ruth 34–5, 36
Rudewitz *see* Rubens, Adolph
Ruegg, Paul 73
Runge, Colonel Evgenny E. 195–6, 259
RUPEE 188
Russian Foreign Intelligence Service (RFIS) 281–4
  Head of *see* Gurgenev, Vyacheslav I.

Sabotka, Anton 262–3
Sachsenhausen 197
Sadat, Anwar 265
Sakharov, Vladimir N. 262
Sale, Tony 192
Salich, Hafis 37
Salten, Felix 96
SALTER *see* Suss, Louis
Santa Lucia Corporation 7
Sarant, Alfred 129–30
Saunders, F. F. (Sonny) 263
SAVAK *see* Iranian Security Service
Schabbel, Klara 65
Schabbel, V. 55
Schildbach, Gertrude 32
Schloesinger, Rose 58
Schneider, Christian 97, 103, 104
Schneiders 64, 65
Schneiper, Xavier 68, 103
School for Spies 10
Schottmueller, Oda 53

Schultze, Reinhard 274
Schultze, Sonja 274
Schulze, Kurt 53, 55
Schulze-Boysen, Harro 51–3
Schulze-Boysen, Libertas 52
Schumacher, Otto 53, 61
Schuster, Anton V. 45
Scott, Dr Winton M. 237
Second Chief Directorate *see* Committee for State Security
Secret History of Stalin's Crimes, The 131
Secret Intelligence Service (SIS) 4, 5, 66, 92, 106, 107, 136, 137, 142, 179, 188, 221, 222, 227, 259, 265, 267, 272
Sedlacek, Colonel Karel 108
Semmelmann, Georg 32
Senkin, Anatoli B. 160, 165
SERENA 250–1
Serpell, Michael 66, 94, 122
SHAH *see* Houghton, Harry
Shalnev, Anatoli P. 263
Shanghai Conspiracy, The 69
Sharaf, Sami 264
Sharfin, Arthur 36
SHAROV 271
Shcharansky, Anatoly 275
Shebarshin, Leonid V. 270–1, 280
SHEILLA 65
Shelepin, Aleksandr N. 186
Sherdev, Colonel Viktor 282
Sheyin, Colonel 268
Sheymov, Major Viktor 283, 295
Shin Beth 247, 273
Shitikov 283, 295
Shmelyov 183
SHOT 130
Shugar, David 113, 118
Shumaev, Mikhail M. 170
Sicherheitsdienst (SD) 54, 62, 63, 95
SIDE *see* Argentine Security Service
Sieg, Johannes 58
Sierra, Vincente *see* Guryevitch, Viktor

Sigl, Rupert 123, 177, 196–9
Sigler, Sergeant Ralph 236–40, 248–50
Sily 31
Simexco/Simex 46, 47, 52–4, 56, 61
Singre 14
SISSY see Duebendorfer, Rachel
Skardon, William J. 44, 95
Skoridov, Boris A. 173
Skorik, Oleg S. 279–80
Skripov, Ivan F. 230–2
Skrzypczynski, Leo 58
Sloboda, Vladimir 190
Sluzhba Vneshney Razvedki (SVR) 281
Smedley, Agnes 72, 73, 74, 89
Smersh 63
    Head of see Abakumov, Viktor S.
Smirnov, D. 133
Smith, Detective Chief Inspector Ferguson 212
Smith, Superintendent George 212, 224
Smith, Philip Durnford 113, 115, 116, 118
SNIPER see Goleniewski, Michal
Sobelivicius see Soble, Jack
Sobell, Morton 128, 144, 146
Soble, Jack 83–4, 87, 131
Soblen, Dr Robert A. 83, 84
Soboloff, David (GIDEON) 141–3, 193, 244
Soboloff, Dr John 121
Soja, Walter A. see Tairov, Igor A.
Sokol, Dr Hersog 56–7
Sokolov, Alexandre V. 163–7
Sokolov, Major 113
Sokolov, Michael (Misha) 163–4
Sokolov, Vincent 163
Sokolova, Lise-Lotte 164–7
Sokolova, Moura 164
Solokov, Aleksandr 242
SONIA see Kuczynski, Ursula
Sorensen, Henning I. 117, 118
Sorge, Christiana 70
Sorge, Richard xvi, 3, 68, 69–89, 98, 102, 109, 135

Sorge Spy Ring, The 69
Sorokin, Vadim V. 168
Sosnovski, Lev B. 160, 165
SOSUS 204
Soustelle, Jacques 45
Soviet Espionage 201
Soviet Military Intelligence 253
Soviet Military Intelligence (GRU) 5, 18, 38, 42–8, 51–60, 63, 68, 72, 74, 82, 91–105, 109, 112, 113, 117, 120–5, 156–71, 186–90, 201, 202, 229, 239, 253, 258, 259, 262, 267, 280–4
    Head of see Mikhailov, Colonel-General Vladlen
Soviet Russia Division see Central Intelligence Agency
Soviet Trade Delegation 68, 133, 171, 258, 264
Special Operations Executive 136–7
Spencer, Arthur 208–9
Spetsnaz 263
Spirine, Oleg 283
Springer, Isadore 48, 49, 56, 61
Spy 224
Spycatcher 224
Squad 34 see Federal Bureau of Investigation
Stahl, Lydia 23–4, 77
Stalin, Josef xv, 29, 33, 36, 41, 61, 77, 85, 86, 124, 136, 178
Staros, Filipp 129
Stashinsky, Bogdan 178, 184–6, 197, 262
Stasi 282
State Department 34, 38, 77, 79, 80, 165
Steinbruck 30–1
Stephens see Brandes, William
Sterling Group 198
Stern, Alfred 83, 84
Stern, Leah 27
Stern, Martha 84
Stern, Mary 27
Stern, Michael 27

Stern, Moishe 22, 23
Sternberg, Rudi (Lord Plurenden) 198
Stoebe, Ilse 51–2, 55
STONE *see* Sobell, Morton
Strangers on a Bridge 176
Strategic Air Command 233
Streater, Isabel 20, 21
stutzstaffel see Goleniewski, Michal
SUCCESSOR 137
Sudoplatov, Pavel A. 180, 181
Sukolov, Viktor *see* Guryevictch, Viktor
SURENSEN *see* Sorensen, Henning I.
Suschitzky, Edith 138
Susloparov, General 47
Suss, Louis 92, 102, 103
Sutterlin, Heinz 196
Sutterlin, Leonore 196
Sviatsky 97
Svirin, Mikhail N. 145
SVR *see* Russian Foreign Intelligence Service
Sweeny, Charles 142
Sweetosh, Philip 27–8
Switz, Marjorie 23, 43
Switz, Robert Gordon 18, 22, 23, 43, 77
Syme, Agnes 42

Tairov, Igor A. 187–8
Tairova, Margarita 158, 187–8
TANNE 57
TASS 7, 117, 159, 269
TAYLOR *see* Schneider, Christian
Tear O'Bryan, Terence 143
TEDDY 106
Tenney, Helen 82
Teplyakova, Irina 259
Tet Offensive 3
Thiebault, Charles 97
Thompson, Robert G. 169, 170, 233, 291
TIFF 130
Tikhvinsky, Sergei 202
Tilley, Marjorie *see* Switz, Marjorie
Tilton, Alfred 24, 77

Tilton, Maria 77
Timashkevits, Yania 179, 180
Time 79
Times, The 136, 137
TIMUR 269
TINO *see* Winterink, Anton
Titov, Gennadi F. 267
Todt Organisation 48
Tompkins, Paul 169
TOP HAT *see* Polyakov, Dmitri F.
Tower Commission 6–7
Treasury Department 80
Treholt, Arne 267
Trepper, Leopold 41, 42–50, 54–9, 60–1, 65, 66, 89, 94, 100
TRIGON *see* Ogorodnik, Aleksandr D.
Trinka, Edmund *see* Loginov, Yuri N.
Trotsky, Leon xv, 31, 34, 74, 85
Tschatzky 19
Tsymbal, Mikhail S. 173–4
Tudor Hart, Dr Alex 138
Tudor Hart, Edith 138
Tuomi, Kaarlo 160–1, 165, 166–7, 238

U-2 154
UB *see* Police Intelligence Service
ULTRA 2
Ulyanov *see* Lenin, Vladimir I.
UN/ACUTE *see* Popov, Piotr S.
Underwater Detection Establishment 204
UNESCO 104
United Nations (UN) 8, 87, 158, 159, 161, 164, 168, 169, 170, 189, 198, 233, 267
United Press International 7
University of Miami 6
US Special Forces School 2, 190
Ustinov, Klop 92
Uzdansk-Yelenski, Colonel 14

VAGIF 271
Van den Bergh, General Henryk 175
Van Haarlem, Erwin 274

Van Proosdy, August J. 64
Vandel Heuvel, Count Frederick 92
Vassall, W. John 235–6
Vauck, Dr Wilhelm 50, 51, 59
Veall, Norman 116, 118
Venednikov, Evgenny 269
VENONA 202
VERA see Linton, Freda
Vernon, Major Wilfred 43–4, 65, 135
Viet Cong 4
Vigier, Tamara 97
Vladislavovna, Marya 132
Vlassov, Vassilli 245
Voelkner, Hans 67
Voelkner, Kathe 67
Vogel, Wolfgang 275
Voice of the Mineworkers 70
Von Brockdorf, Gräfin Erika 53
Von Grimm 96
Von Harnack, Arvid 51–2, 58
Von Scheliha, Rudolf 51, 52, 55
Voronin, Yuri N. 259, 264
Vyrodov, Ivan Y. 167

Wald, Lilian 102
Waldman, Louis 22–3
War Production Board 88
Watcher Service see British
    Security Service
Watson, Nigel 16
Webber 27
Weber, Kurt 180, 181–2
Weibel, Bent 267
Weingarten, Seber 72
Weisenborn, Gunther 53
Weiss, Ernest D. 43–4, 45, 65,
    67, 135
Weitz, John see Kneschke, Rudolph
Wenzel, Johann 50, 52, 53,
    54–62, 64
WERTHER 106
WEST WIND 39
Whalen, Captain William H. 170
Wheeler, Donald N. 82
White, Robert B. 160
Widows 229
Willoughby, General Charles 69, 72

Willsher, Kathleen (Kay) 114, 115,
    118
Winterink, Anton 57–9, 64
Wise, David 166
Wisner, Frank 203
Witczak, Ignacy S. 119–20, 121
Witness 69
Woikin, Emma 113–14, 115–16
Wolff, Theodore 51
Wolisch, Max see Reif, Ignaty
Woolwich Arsenal 24
Wright, Peter 138, 187, 192, 224
Wynne, Greville M. 221

Yablin, Nikolai 70
Yakovlev, Anatoli A. see Yatskov,
    Anatoli
Yashchenko, Sasha 269
Yatskov (Yakovlev), Anatoli 117,
    125, 130, 215
Yatskov, Pavel 237
Yezhov, Nikolai I. 29–31
Yom Kippur War 3
YORIK 130
Yotoku, Miyagi 75
Young, Courtney 91, 93
Yu Zenshan 7
Yugoslav Intelligence Service
    (KOS) 247
Yurchenko, Vitali S. 251

Zabotin, Colonel Nikolai 113–20
Zaitsev, Leonid S. 265
Zaporozhet 85
Zarubin, Lisa see Zubilin, Elizaveta
Zarubin, Vassilli see Zubilin, Vassilli
Zemenek, Colonel Ludek 241–2, 243,
    246, 247–8, 249, 250, 257
Zenith Technical Enterprises Inc. 6
Zhenikhov, Colonel 172
Zheveinov 117
Zhiltsov, Boris A. 173
Zhizhin, Vladimir 267
Ziavkin, Feodor 22
Zlatovsky, George 83
Zubilin, Elizaveta 38, 78–9, 84–6
Zubilin, Vassilli 38–9, 79, 82–3, 84, 86